Christian Women at University

Come as a girl.
I will. I am still arriving among you,
looking for a safe place to be born,
a welcome, a home.

(Nicola Slee, *Seeking the Risen Christa* (London: SPCK, 2011), p. 33)

Those who have entered deeply into their hearts and found the intimate home where they encounter their God ... come to the awareness that the intimacy of God's house excludes no-one and includes everyone.

(Henri Nouwen, *Lifesigns: Intimacy, Fecundity, and Ecstasy in Christian Perspective* (Garden City, NY: Doubleday, 1986), p. 43)

Christian Women at University

Faith, Feminism and Feeling at Home

Jenny Morgans

scm press

© Jenny Morgans 2025

Published in 2025 by SCM Press

Editorial office
3rd Floor, Invicta House,
110 Golden Lane,
London EC1Y 0TG, UK

www.scmpress.co.uk

SCM Press is an imprint of Hymns Ancient & Modern Ltd
(a registered charity)

Hymns Ancient & Modern® is a registered trademark of
Hymns Ancient & Modern Ltd
13A Hellesdon Park Road, Norwich,
Norfolk NR6 5DR, UK

All rights reserved. No part of this publication may be reproduced,
stored in a retrieval system, or transmitted,
in any form or by any means, electronic, mechanical,
photocopying or otherwise, without the prior permission of
the publisher, SCM Press.

Jenny Morgans has asserted her right under the Copyright, Designs and
Patents Act 1988 to be identified as the Author of this Work

Scripture references, unless otherwise marked, are from the New Revised Standard Version Bible: Anglicized Edition, copyright © 1989, 1995 National Council of the Churches of Christ in the United States of America. Used by permission. All rights reserved worldwide.

Scripture quotations marked NIVUK taken from The Holy Bible, New International Version (Anglicised edition) copyright © 1979, 1984, 2011 by Biblica (formerly International Bible Society). Used by permission of Hodder & Stoughton Publishers, an Hachette UK company. All rights reserved.

Scripture references marked TJB taken from The Jerusalem Bible, published and copyright © 1966, 1967 and 1968 by Darton, Longman and Todd Ltd and Doubleday, a division of Random House, Inc. and used by permission.

British Library Cataloguing in Publication data

A catalogue record for this book is available
from the British Library

ISBN: 978-0-334-06196-0

EU GPSR Authorised Representative
LOGOS EUROPE, 9 rue Nicolas Poussin, 17000, LA ROCHELLE, France
E-mail: Contact@logoseurope.eu

No part of this book may be used or reproduced in any manner for the
purpose of training artificial intelligence technologies or systems.

Typeset by Regent Typesetting

Contents

Acknowledgements   vii

1   Introduction   1

Part I: From Home to Home   15

2   Arriving   17
3   Crafting Home   47

Part II: Faith at University

4   Faith Change and Development   71
5   Christian Spaces and Activities   98

Part III: Identities at University

6   Being Women   131
7   Intersectionality and Faith   155

Part IV: Crafting Home and Looking Forward

8   A Model of Homing   211
9   Conclusion   231

Bibliography   243
Index of Names and Subjects   257

Acknowledgements

This book has been many years in the making, beginning with the first drafts of my PhD proposal back in 2012. It has taken a community of people to generously support, sustain and love me in that time, without whom this book would be nothing more than an unspoken passion of mine stuck, unformulated, inside my head.

Mostly, I want to thank the 26 brave and inspiring women who kindly gave me their time, and whose words are the heart of this book. It was a privilege to hear your stories, reflections and wonderings, and to be entrusted to handle them with care. I hope I have done them justice. Whenever my motivation was flagging or the busyness of life crept in, it was the desire to share your important experiences that kept me writing, because they need to be heard. I hope that your words will comfort, encourage and resource many more women at university as they try to feel at home.

In finding women to interview, thanks to the two university chaplains who took an interest in my work and supported me in recruiting students.

I'm grateful to my colleagues at King's College London Chaplaincy for resourcing and affirming me in this work, particularly with the gift of time. Permission to read and write is not always so forthcoming in church contexts, and I thank you for believing in my research enough to be generous. As a priest in the Church of England, I have promised with God's help to 'be diligent ... in all studies that will deepen my faith and fit me to bear witness to the truth of the gospel'.[1] This book is part of my commitment to this promise. My research is an area of sustenance and nurturing for my life and my ministry, and I'm grateful to be in a pastoral and academic context at King's that affirms that.

My PhD supervisor and now dear friend Professor Nicola Slee has been instrumental on this journey from the very beginning, and continues to encourage me to find my academic voice and to be the best woman that I can. As well as reading early drafts of some sections of this book, she continues to remind me, with Julian of Norwich, that 'all manner of things shall be well', and I believe her. At The Queen's Foundation for Ecumenical Theological Education, Nicola convenes (now with a fabulous team) the Symposium on the Faith Lives of Women and Girls which has consistently been a fellowship of support, encouragement and creativity, for which I'm heartily thankful. It was also at Queen's that my cell group, Cookies and Candles, began, with four wonderful women. To each one of you, thank you for listening to me and always hearing me; I'm so glad that we have each other.

In writing this book, I've perhaps unexpectedly found myself thinking about the amazing women who supervised my work and mentored me academically, from being a bewildered undergraduate through to my doctorate. You have not only shaped my academic journey, you helped me feel at home and, in turn, contributed to who I am. You are: Professor Elaine Fulton, Dr Deryn Guest, Dr Cecelia Clegg, Revd Canon Dr Margaret Whipp and Professor Gerdien Bertram-Troost – as well as Nicola, of course. You are an inspiring company and I gratefully work in your shadow.

Several people have commented on drafts of various sections of this book. Thanks to Angela, Rosie and Ruth for taking the time to read this work and offer your honest and thoughtful insights. Your areas of expertise exceed mine, and this book is much richer for your kind involvement. I'd also like to thank David Shervington and Rachel Edge at SCM Press for believing in the potential of my PhD thesis and challenging me to continue the research. You have been patient and reassuring throughout. In developing my model of Homing presented in this book, I must thank Christopher Todd, 'Toddy', for its amazing visual representation.[2] It is perfect.

I'm glad to thank both my family of origin and my chosen-fam. Mam and Dad, I make more sense to people once they've met you. Thanks for believing in me and for giving me the space to become who I'm becoming. Brawd Bach, I'm so proud of you, you're one of my favourite people; and Rachel, Gethin and Sara, you bring me so much joy. Grandma and Auntie Marilyn, thank you for being strong women of God. To paraphrase 2 Timothy 1.5, I'm reminded of your sincere faith, a faith that dwelt first in Grandma and then in my aunt and now, I gladly hope, dwells in me as well.

I'm amazed at how blessed I am by my chosen-fam. In fact, I'm not sure where the cut-off is. First, and most sadly, my feline familiar Satine died while I've been writing this book, but she will remain constantly in my heart (and inscribed in ink on my forearm). My household fam at the moment consists of my beloved Stephen, Jasper and kittens Cosmic Creepers and Madam Mim. You are all my home and I love you dearly. Jasper, thanks for generously sharing your wisdom and insight, and for

ACKNOWLEDGEMENTS

patiently answering my questions when Gen Z bewilders me! You are brilliant. Stephen, thank you for encouraging me all the way through this book, celebrating its milestones with me and making me laugh throughout. Being married to you is an adventure full of surprises. I don't know who I would be without your persistent, loving support.

Notes

1 The Archbishops' Council, *Common Worship: Ordination Services* (London: Church House Publishing, 2007). Quote changed to first person.

2 You can see more of Christopher's art and contact him yourself on Instagram: @cjtoddillustrated.

I

Introduction

What is it like, being a young Christian woman studying at university at the moment? The student years are often summarized by older generations with phrases such as 'having the time of your life', 'making your forever-friends' and 'taking every opportunity'. Yet being a student in the current post-Brexit, post-Covid and neoliberal climate in the UK can result in bewilderment, loneliness and overwhelm, while the current mental ill-health epidemic is going largely untreated. Such phrases contribute to the unnecessary pressure that students feel to fit in and enjoy themselves. The intersections of age, gender, faith, race, class and sexuality further complicate young Christian women's experiences as they try to find their place in the world and in the life of God's people. Despite the complexity of this intense transitional time, young adults are often ignored or politicized. Anthony Reddie identifies 'being young' as a new category for liberation theology, a 'category of marginalization ... because of how they have traditionally been treated by the Church and wider society'. Churches, he writes, 'patronize, fetishize and simply ignore young people'.[1] I argue that this is also true for society in general.

This book grew out of my own journey, first as an emerging adult navigating my way within church, then in leadership positions working with young Christian adults, and now working as a university chaplain and a priest in the Church of England. I am both harrowed and awed as I walk alongside women students in particular, as they courageously find strategies for negotiating university life amid complex challenges.

This research speaks from the experiences of 26 Christian women at university over nearly ten years, and I hope that it offers encouragement to many others. Academically, this book is aimed at those trying to understand the faith practices and beliefs of Generations Y and Z (and soon Generation Alpha) as they, as Ruth H. Perrin writes, are 'the most recent of multiple generations of religious decline'.[2] Practically, I hope this book resources ministers and chaplains working alongside young adults. And if any young Christian women (or their allies) find themselves reading this book, I hope you find something of your own stories mirrored here and take comfort in knowing that you are not alone.

This opening chapter introduces significant contexts and cultures impacting upon the women's experiences of faith at university: emerging adulthood and religious engagement, transition, post-feminism and feeling at home. I then detail the methods employed in carrying out this research, before describing the structure of this book.

Emerging adults

In the early 2000s, Jeffrey Jensen Arnett identified the period of 'emerging adulthood' as the specific exploration that occurs between the ages of 18 and 30. Arnett recognized that traditional maturity markers – leaving home, securing permanent employment, purchasing a home, marriage and parenthood – were being delayed beyond the twenties or being dismissed altogether.[3] Instead of building stability, emerging adults experience multiple transitions and uncertainty. They are more likely to be unemployed or in unstable work, to be in debt, to change accommodation or return to the family home, to have multiple romantic partners, to be childfree, and to remain in education.

Emerging adults are not adolescents, nor are they 'grown up', and they often resist maturity. This suspension from commitment or responsibility can feel discombobulating or even traumatic. However, they can use it to their advantage, taking the opportunity to explore the world and themselves without adult pressures. This is a liminal threshold whereby normality can be redefined. Emerging identities – including intersecting religious, gender, racial, class and sexual identities – come to be tested, reinvented and perhaps rejected. I use the term 'emerging Christian women' to describe students in my research, demonstrating their intersectional *emerging* both as Christians and as women.

An explanatory note about terminology may be helpful. The term 'millennial' is sometimes wrongly used to describe anyone under the age of 40. In fact, millennials, also known as Generation Y, were born between 1981 and 1995, and those born after 1995 are Generation Z. Generation Alpha were born after 2010 and will be attending university in the next few years. Of course, it is not always useful to group people simply by the year of their birth, but there are clear commonalities between people who experience the same cultural trends. Stereotypes are common, however. Gen Zers are erroneously criticized as 'snowflakes', constantly offended, spending their money on take-away coffee, and unable to work hard because they are too afraid or too lazy.[4] These stereotypes have been debunked,[5] yet they persist in popular discourse.

Since my first interviews in 2014, the last decade has been a time of significant change nationally and globally. The #MeToo movement, after first naming sexual predators in the entertainment industry in 2017, spread to a social media campaign recognizing that a majority of (if not all) women had suffered some kind of harassment. While the impact of the Brexit vote in 2016 was still to be realized, the Covid-19 pandemic profoundly affected daily life from March 2020. Just two months later, the murder of George Floyd in the US boosted the seriousness with which the Black Lives Matter campaign began to be taken. In 2021, the murder of Sarah Everard in London renewed protests about male violence against women.

Meanwhile, attitudes to people identifying as lesbian, gay or bisexual have largely become more accepting, especially among young people. This is perhaps less the case in Christian circles, although many religious young people (both heterosexual and queer) promote LGBTQIA+ rights and equality. I have observed that emerging adults now tend to refer to themselves as *queer* rather than using lesbian, gay or bisexual, to remove what are seen as unnecessary labels. In this book, I switch between the terms 'queer' and 'LGBTQIA+'. While recognizing that 'queer', as Susannah Cornwall writes, has 'an idea of elusiveness, uncertainty, non-fixity, and a resistance to closed definitions', I use it since many of the women identified themselves in this way, perhaps due to its elusive nature. Cornwall also argues that 'queer' is not merely another term for 'gay', but must include the 'specific concerns of lesbians, transgender people and people of colour' and seeks to 'demystify power relations … [and] disturb gay male hegemony'.[6] Narratives about transgender people in particular are far from resolved, with 'the trans issue' shaping political rhetoric and causing deep divisions. While the hatred and harm of anti-trans activism represent one extreme in the so-called TERF wars,[7] Generation Z can, at the other extreme, take a hardline stance against anyone who questions inclusion. Nonetheless, stating one's pronouns in email signatures and on badges is common in spaces populated with emerging adults, including in higher education, in a normalizing of gender fluidity.

Emerging Christians

Changing Shape, Perrin's excellent study of Christian millennials retrospectively reflecting upon their faith, identifies Arnett's theory as limited to the educated middle class. More work is needed to understand the lives of young adults globally, as well as non-privileged young adults in the West. Yet, Perrin continues, emerging adulthood does describe many young British Christians, given that they *are* often educated and middle class.[8] However, it is also significant that Christians are more likely than their peers to follow traditional heteronormative patterns and to marry young,[9] bucking emerging adult trends.

Emerging adults are increasingly turning away from church, with just 2–3 per cent of 18–30-year-olds regularly attending.[10] Large conservative evangelical congregations, often focused on student ministry, are an exception to this rule.[11] Roberta Katz and her colleagues argue that religious decline is partly due to cultural shifts, meaning that young adults do not always understand institutions, 'even when they and their elders have similar values and aspirations because Gen Zers' ways of doing things have been so profoundly shaped by digital technology, leading to new methods of working, connecting with others, [and] activism'.[12] Nonetheless, religion provides an important setting for many emerging adults' identity development; and for religious students, higher education is a significant context in which faith is enacted. Christianity at university has been brought to attention particularly by Mathew Guest and colleagues in their 2013 publication *Christianity and the University Experience*. The authors identify 51 per cent of students in England as belonging to the Christian tradition. A proportion of these are 'hidden Christians', holding a resilient faith despite not attending church or religious activities. However, many are active in their faith and engaged in a breadth of Christian communities.[13] Damon Mayrl and Jeremy E. Uecker show that students frequently maintain their religious beliefs by engaging with multiple 'moral communities', including religious student organizations.[14] For Nick M. Shepherd, such communities act as 'plausibility shelters', validating young Christians' faith.[15] Rather than students leaving their faith behind, university environments are formative in their engagement with Christianity. For example, students are more likely to join a congregation[16] or engage in evangelistic activities[17] than their non-student peers.

University chaplaincies coordinate religion on higher education campuses in the UK, and there has been renewed interest in the theology and practice of chaplaincy in the last decade.[18] Chaplaincies have a responsibility to the institutions they serve to encourage reflection, as Rowan Clare Williams argues, on 'the purpose of human existence, the wider good of society and the transformation of unjust structures'.[19] It is these very questions that often preoccupy emerging adults in their meaning-making attempts.

Religion and faith communities can have a significant influence on a student's identity and their process of individuation.[20] Emerging Christians usually arrive at university with little understanding of the breadth of Christianity and its practices. Those who attend church assume their experience to be normative: they attended a normal church, which had normal beliefs and worshipped in the normal manner. At university, those who actively engage with their faith often realize that no such normality exists. Some students experience a spectrum of the theologies, worship styles and denominations available to them at university. This process can be challenging for those who find themselves disagreeing with practices or beliefs that they encounter. Many feel under-resourced in exploring different Christian communities, or do not actually know what their church believes. Churches do young people a disservice in not helping them understand their specificities or educating them in the diversity of the Christian faith. Upon arriving at university, they can easily feel confused by their choices, and some find themselves unable to critique a community engaging in harmful practices. While most emerging Christians are post-denominational,[21] this is sometimes due to ignorance rather than intentional non-committal.

Transitioning to university life

This book is concerned with emerging Christian women settling into university life after leaving home. This is a unique time of transition: geographically leaving behind everyone they have known, at a young age, to be surrounded by vast numbers of unknown others all going through the same thing. Nancy K. Schlossberg and her colleagues offer a useful model for understanding students' transitions. They define transition as anything 'that results in changed relationships, routines, assumptions and roles ... A transition is not so much a matter of change as of the individual's own perception of change.'[22] Women arrive at university and find themselves having to navigate a new way of life, often needing to live independently for the first time, with varying levels of familial support. Along with the physical and relational changes that happen in the move from home comes psychological reassessment, with women often having to do the necessary 'identity work'.[23] A term coined by Richard Johnson and his colleagues, identity work is the process by which individuals modify aspects of the self to be accepted.

The nature of universities has shifted within the neoliberal culture. Neoliberalization encourages individualism and self-management, influencing policies that govern institutions and attitudes through the twentieth and twenty-first centuries. Neoliberalism is defined as 'a value system in which the economic has replaced the intellectual and political and in which the competitive, rational individual predominates over the collective.'[24]

For higher education, neoliberalism prompted a significant rise in tuition fees in England in 2012, positioning graduate education in transactional terms, for equipping students with the skills for societal economic growth.[25] This is in opposition to John Henry Newman's insistence that universities develop the spiritual and social as well as academic constituents of human beings.[26] Recent decades have seen much theological critique of such a culture, proposing the necessity of universities in forming wisdom and as contexts for human flourishing, demanding transformation of the structures that govern higher education, and asking how a Christian university might differ.[27]

Trevor Gale and Stephen Parker critique neoliberal assumptions about students' transitions which, they argue, ignore their lived realities. The authors understand transitions not as linear or involving sequentially defined periods of adjustment. Instead, they advocate transitions as subjective *becoming*. Being at university, they argue, encompasses every aspect of students' lives, and often involves fluid, short-lived identities. When universities emphasize becoming, they argue, students can themselves define their transitions.[28] Carol A. Taylor and Jean Harris-Evans's complementary article offers a model of becoming that recognizes its fluid and unpredictable nature. Students' transitioning, they write, is 'not based on a conscious, rational evaluation of choices'.[29] Helen Colley argues that such complex transitions are common among women. She demonstrates that women's transitions do not conform to linear growth but rather demonstrate 'life-as-transition' which is 'uncertain and fragmented', where time itself is redefined as flexible and unpredictable.[30]

Post-feminism

Gendered experiences have largely been ignored in research with students, including with Christian students.[31] Yet the emerging women in this book studied and practised their faith in a culture saturated with post-feminist narratives and assumptions. Perrin outlines three tenets of post-feminism: a backlash against feminism as irrelevant; a shift in third wave feminism, focused on individual experience rather than political change; and an ambiguous neoliberal view of equality where 'feminist values are both endorsed and rejected'.[32] Patricia Lewis and her colleagues argue that post-feminism is regarded as 'moderate', contrasted with 'excessive feminism' that focuses unnecessarily on 'mutual struggle, communal relations ... [and] collective solutions'.[33]

The two most entrenched post-feminist principles are gender essentialism and bodily femininity. From the 1970s onwards, feminists have argued that distinct gender roles are social construction rather than biological inevitability, created by sexist structural injustice. However, popular culture consistently reinforces such roles. Catherine Redfern and Kristin Aune argue that while chromosomally women and men are approximately 5 per cent different, popular culture 'encourage[s] viewers to see these differences as "real" and essential'. In reclaiming language of the 'feminine', post-feminism portrays 'gender differences [as] hard-wired into us as a product of evolution'.[34] While all four waves of feminism have fought to equalize the roles and rights of women with men, popular culture has increased polarity between genders, prescribing women a heightened, specifically bodily, femininity.

Rosalind Gill argues that the emergence of femininity as a bodily property involved a shift in the male gaze, from women's presentation in media as 'mute objects' to their portrayal as 'desiring sexual subjects who choose to present themselves in a seemingly objectified manner because it suits their liberated interests.' While previously defined by caring roles, femininity is recast by post-feminism as 'a bodily property'.[35] Women are required to constantly maintain their desirable appearance in media culture, which, as Alison Phipps and Geraldine Smith argue, especially targets emerging women whose 'sexual identities are formed through consumption in the service of fashion and beauty'.[36]

I take feminism to be a crucial opposing force to the structures of patriarchy which limits women's lives because of their gender, from everyday sexism to the socio-cultural factors that influence everyone's lives. Post-feminism, by contrast, is a patriarchal narrative that women are encouraged to internalize and proselytize. The fourth wave of feminism, since the early 2010s, has emphasized women's intersectional identities, taking seriously critiques from womanist scholars who have argued that women's other marginalized identities impact directly upon their gendered experiences. It also combats post-feminist demands that bodily femininity be women's primary concern, arguing instead for bodily positivity and diversity.

Feeling at home

As the women shared their stories with me about their faith, gender and transitions at university, a dominant thread was the experience of feeling at home, and the strategies employed in making that happen.

In the Christian tradition, there are three connected theologies of God's relationship with *home*. The first two are defined by movement or journeying. First, God *sends* God's people away from home on a journey of discovery, and danger is often involved. There are many biblical exemplars, and one could argue that faith is first conceived in the Bible when Sarai and Abram are called to leave their home of Haran. Second, God is the one who draws Christians *towards* home. Just as students are transitioning away from home but awaiting their mature and adult home, so too Christians understand themselves to live in transitional, in-between times, actively waiting for the eternal now-but-not-yet of the Kin-dom, the ultimate Home.[37] This destination is often understood as an afterlife in heaven, as is sung in the classic hymn, 'Amazing Grace': "Tis grace hath brought me safe thus far, and grace will lead me home.'[38] In God's grace, Christians are to make their home safe upon the earth, yet they are invited to a greater homecoming with the divine. Stories of unlikely heroes beginning their salvific yet perilous journeys by first leaving home also populate wider literature and cinema,[39] from Dorothy to Frodo to Harry Potter. While these characters leave home and make new homes elsewhere, all also return home in some form, suggesting the dual sending-and-calling of home.

Third, God is understood *as* humanity's home – all dwell in God and God dwells in them in iterative relationship. As Jesus states in one translation of John's Gospel: 'Make your home in me, as I make mine in you' (John 15.4–5 TJB). Julian of Norwich describes such intimacy and familiarity between God and humanity, believing that 'we shall, in love, be *homely* and near to God'. She describes this mystery, whereby God 'who is highest and mightiest, noblest and worthiest, is the lowest and meekest, *homeliest*.'[40] The first understanding of home, as a place which is left behind, is present throughout this book, yet it is this third and final understanding that resonates most with the women's experiences. In God, making oneself at home involves living in safety, exploring with playfulness, and becoming in joy. However, to refer to God in a homely way is not something that can be applied uncritically. Can all people be safe in one home? If God is home for some, who then are excluded? And if God is home, why have churches excluded and damaged so many for so long?

Home has been explored by many different theological and developmental authors. Writing about emerging adults, Sharon Parks argues: 'To be at home is to have a place in the scheme of life – a place where we are comfortable; know that we belong; can be who we are and can honour, protect and create what we truly love'.[41] Home then is a place where the self can be first understood and tested. It is also the place where initial processes of faith development occur, in relationship with God and significant others. John O'Donohue cites Meister Eckhart, who argued that 'there is no such thing as a spiritual journey'. O'Donohue continues,

> If there was a spiritual journey, it would be only a quarter-inch long, though many miles deep. It would be a swerve into rhythm with your deeper nature and presence ... You do not have to go away outside your self to come into real conversation with your soul and with the mysteries of the spiritual world. The eternal is at home – within you.[42]

The traumatic nature of the women's transitions at university reflects how they were student-orphans far from home, sometimes without the support and resources to craft a new home. To be *unhome* is to be unable to craft a safe home; to be vulnerable and lonely; and to lack the confidence or awareness to interpret one's own experiences. If someone is *unhome* in their life or faith, what can a model of home or a homely God have to offer them?

Feeling at home and crafting home at university are topics that this book returns to repeatedly. To be clear, the women's crafting of home presented in this book is in no way reinforcing traditional stereotypes that determine women's place within the domestic sphere. Rather, home is an iterative process of individuation, in relationship with self, God and others. A detailed model of Homing based upon the women's experiences is presented in Chapter 8.

Method

Practical theology is concerned with the praxis, belief and well-being of ordinary believers, attempting not only to understand but to enable transformation of the unjust or oppressive structures that constrain the marginalized. This book is situated amid a growing body of qualitative research in the field of feminist practical theology.[43] Such theology refutes gender essentialism, yet claims the particularities of women as significant in understanding the nature of God and the world, together with their intersectional and diverse identities. In such research, questions of methodology are central, shaping both the data and any conclusions made, and thus should be made transparent. Reflexively paying attention to my own emotions and experiences as I worked was 'useful, ongoing and hard', as I have detailed elsewhere.[44]

The research for this book took place in three rounds of interviews with 26 Christian cisgendered women, over a period of eight years. Most of these women were interviewed only once, while some were interviewed two or three times. Some also completed an online questionnaire. Three of the 26 were very close friends, and I also interviewed them together in what I have termed a 'facilitated gathering'.[45] All were undergraduate students for their first interview, none of whom were mature students, and two were international students. All had left the family home. Research took place at three different universities, using the categories set by Guest and his colleagues: one traditional elite, one redbrick, and one post-1992. The first two universities were members of the Russell Group.[46] Two women identified as queer, one as bisexual and one as a lesbian. While the other 22 described themselves as heterosexual, one of those thought that she was probably also asexual. The women included five working-class, two working-middle-class and two upper-middle-class women. The remaining women were middle-class. Two women identified as mixed race,[47] two were Black, one Chinese and one Indo-Trinidadian. I did not ask the women if they had any disabilities or were neurodivergent, an omission which I discuss further in the Conclusion. The women came from a plethora of Christian traditions and churches and had identified as Christian for varying lengths of time. The women were studying a broad range of subjects. The women span two generations, with the first interviews conducted with young millennials born in 1995, while the youngest student interviewed is firmly within Generation Z, born in 2003. Pseudonyms are used for all the women.

The shape of this book

This book is divided into four parts, each with two chapters. In Part I, 'From Home to Home', Chapter 2 details the women's arrival at university. It focuses on their challenges in the transition, including their mental ill-health, loneliness, and – for those interviewed most recently – studying during the Covid-19 pandemic. Chapter 3 is then more positive, discussing how the women crafted a sense of home for themselves at university through making new friends, growing in confidence and recognizing their interdependence.

In Part II, 'Faith at University', Chapter 4 explores the women's experiences and understandings as Christian students. It includes the extent to which faith was integrated in daily life, a growth in confidence in faith, and understandings of God. Chapter 5 outlines the different spaces in which the women practised their faith, including churches, student Christian societies, and university chaplaincies. It then details some of the women's faith practices, including evangelizing, engaging with sermons and volunteering.

Following on from experiences of faith, Part III, 'Identities at University', focuses on the students' intersectional identities, and how these

INTRODUCTION

were experienced as Christian women. Chapter 6 explores the impact of post-feminism on the women, emphasizing the importance of gender in their everyday experiences. Chapter 7 concentrates on the intersection of gender, race, class and sexuality in the women's faithing and academic studies.

Finally, in Part IV, 'Crafting Home and Looking Forward', Chapter 8 offers a model of Homing drawn from the experiences of the emerging Christian women in this research. The model of crafting home at university is structured as five rooms in which the women dwell and through which they move. Bringing the book to a close, in Chapter 9 I draw some conclusions based on the women's experiences of faith, feminism and feeling at home. I offer recommendations for pastoral practice before finally suggesting areas for further research.

Notes

1 Anthony Reddie, 'Prologue' in *Young, Woke and Christian: Words from a Missing Generation*, ed. Victoria Turner (London: SCM Press, 2022), p. xi.

2 Ruth H. Perrin, *Changing Shape: The Faith Lives of Millennials* (London: SCM Press, 2020), p. xi.

3 Jeffrey Jensen Arnett, *Emerging Adulthood: The Winding Road from the Late Teens Through the Twenties* (Oxford: Oxford University Press, 2004).

4 For more about the so-called 'snowflake' generation, see Victoria Turner, 'Introduction' in *Young, Woke and Christian: Words from a Missing Generation*, ed. Victoria Turner (London: SCM Press, 2022), pp. 1–16.

5 See Roberta Katz et al., *Gen Z, Explained: The Art of Living in a Digital Age* (Chicago, IL: University of Chicago Press, 2022).

6 Susannah Cornwall, *Controversies in Queer Theology*, Controversies in Contextual Theology Series (London: SCM Press, 2011), pp. 9, 21, 32.

7 The acronym TERF stands for Trans-Exclusionary Radical Feminism, and is a 'gender-critical' feminism arguing against the inclusion and rights of transgender people. For further reading, I would recommend the articles included in this excellent collection: Ben Vincent, Sonja Erikainen and Ruth Pearce, eds, 'TERF Wars: Feminism and the Fight for Transgender Futures', *Sociological Review* 68, no. 4 (2020).

8 Perrin, *Changing Shape*, pp. 5–6.

9 Brian Willoughby and James L. Spencer, *The Marriage Paradox: Why Emerging Adults Love Marriage yet Push It Aside* (Oxford: Oxford University Press, 2017).

10 Perrin, *Changing Shape*, p. x.

11 See Peter Brierley, *Pulling Out of the Nose Dive* (London: Christian Research, 2006).

12 Katz et al., *Gen Z, Explained*, p. 4.

13 Mathew Guest et al., *Christianity and the University Experience: Understanding Student Faith* (London: Bloomsbury, 2013), pp. 33, 208–17. See also Mathew Guest, 'The "Hidden Christians" of the UK University Campus' in *Young*

People and the Diversity of (Non)Religious Identities in International Perspective, ed. Elisabeth Arweck and Heather Shipley (Cham, Switzerland: Springer, 2019), pp. 51–67.

14 Damon Mayrl and Jeremy E. Uecker, 'Higher Education and Religious Liberalisation Among Young Adults', *Social Forces* 90, no. 1 (2011), pp. 181–208. See also Christian Smith and Patricia Snell, *Souls in Transition: The Religious and Spiritual Lives of Emerging Adults* (Oxford: Oxford University Press, 2009), pp. 248–51; and Guest et al., *Christianity and the University Experience*, p. 107.

15 Nick M. Shepherd, *Faith Generation: Retaining Young People and Growing the Church* (London: SPCK, 2016).

16 Jonathan P. Hill, 'Faith and Understanding: Specifying the Impact of Higher Education on Religious Belief', *Journal for the Scientific Study of Religion* 50, no. 3 (2011), pp. 533–51.

17 Mayrl and Uecker, 'Higher Education'.

18 See Chapter 5 for literature about university chaplaincy.

19 Rowan Clare Williams, *A Theology for Chaplaincy: Singing Songs in a Strange Land* (Cambridge: Grove Books, 2018), p. 14.

20 See, for example, Nick M. Shepherd, 'Religious Socialisation and a Reflexive Habitus: Christian Youth Groups as Sites for Identity Work', in *Religion and Youth*, ed. Sylvia Collins-Mayo and Pink Dandelion (Farnham: Ashgate, 2010), pp. 149–55.

21 Phillip Richter, 'Denominational Cultures: The Cinderella of Congregational Studies?' in *Congregational Studies in the UK: Christianity in a Post-Christian Context*, ed. Mathew Guest, Karin Tusting and Linda Woodhead (Aldershot: Ashgate, 2004), pp. 169–84; Perrin, *Changing Shape*, p. 18.

22 Nancy K. Schlossberg, Elinor B. Waters and Jane Goodman, *Counselling Adults in Transition: Linking Practice with Theory*, 2nd ed. (New York: Springer, 1995), p. 27.

23 Richard Johnson et al., *The Practice of Cultural Studies* (London: Sage, 2004), p. 265.

24 Alison Phipps and Isabel Young, 'Neoliberalisation and "Lad Cultures" in Higher Education', *Sociology* 49, no. 2 (2015), p. 306.

25 See, for example, Henry A. Giroux, 'Neoliberalism, Corporate Culture, and the Promise of Higher Education: The University as a Democratic Public Sphere', *Harvard Educational Review* 72, no. 4 (2002), pp. 425–63.

26 John Henry Newman, *The Idea of a University* (London: Baronius Press, 2006); see also Alasdair MacIntyre, 'The Very Idea of a University: Aristotle, Newman and Us', *British Journal of Educational Studies* 57, no. 4 (2009), p. 353.

27 See, for example, David F. Ford, *Christian Wisdom: Desiring God and Learning in Love* (Cambridge: Cambridge University Press, 2007).

28 Trevor Gale and Stephen Parker, 'Navigating Change: A Typology of Student Transition in Higher Education', *Studies in Higher Education* 39, no. 5 (2014), pp. 734–53.

29 Carol A. Taylor and Jean Harris-Evans, 'Reconceptualising Transition to Higher Education with Deleuze and Guattari', *Studies in Higher Education* 43, no. 7 (2018), p. 1261.

30 Helen Colley, 'Understanding Time in Learning Transitions Through the Lifecourse', *International Studies in Sociology of Education* 17, no. 4 (2007), pp. 430, 434.

INTRODUCTION

31 An exception is this excellent article: Kristin Aune and Mathew Guest, 'Christian University Students' Attitudes to Gender: Constructing Everyday Theologies in a Post-Feminist Climate', *Religions* 10, no. 2 (23 February 2019), pp. 1–22.

32 Ruth H. Perrin, *The Bible Reading of Young Evangelicals: An Exploration of the Ordinary Hermeneutics and Faith of Generation Y* (Eugene, OR: Pickwick Publications, 2016), pp. 178–9; see also Stéphanie Genz, 'Third Way/ve: The Politics of Postfeminism', *Feminist Theory* 7, no. 3 (2006), pp. 333–53.

33 Patricia Lewis, Yvonne Benschop and Ruth Simpson, 'Postfeminism, Gender and Organisation', *Gender, Work and Organisation* 24, no. 3 (2017), p. 217.

34 Catherine Redfern and Kristin Aune, *Reclaiming the F Word: Feminism Today* (London: Zed Books, 2013), pp. 181–3.

35 Rosalind Gill, 'Postfeminism Media Culture: Elements of a Sensibility', *European Journal of Cultural Studies* 10, no. 2 (2007), pp. 149, 151.

36 Alison Phipps and Geraldine Smith, 'Violence Against Women Students in the UK: Time to Take Action', *Gender and Education* 24, no. 4 (2012), p. 358.

37 'Kin-dom' is used here as a non-hierarchical variation on the biblical 'Kingdom of God'. The term was first coined here: Ada Maria Isasi-Díaz, 'Solidarity: Love of Neighbour in the 1980s' in *Lift Every Voice: Constructing Christian Theologies from the Underside*, ed. Susan Brooks Thistlethwaite and Mary Potter Engel (San Francisco, CA: Harper, 1990), pp. 31–40.

38 Words by John Newton (1725–1807).

39 This observation was first made most clearly in Joseph Campbell's classic text: Joseph Campbell, *The Hero With a Thousand Faces*, 1st ed. (New York: Pantheon Books, 1949).

40 Julian of Norwich, *Revelations of Divine Love Recorded by Julian, Anchoress at Norwich*, trans. Grace Warrack (London: Methuen and Company, 1901), pp. 17, 182, italics author's own.

41 Sharon Parks, *Big Questions, Worthy Dreams: Mentoring Young Adults in Their Search for Meaning, Purpose, and Faith* (San Francisco, CA: Jossey-Bass, 2000), p. 34.

42 John O'Donohue, *Anam Cara* (London: Bantam Books, 1999), p. 120.

43 Especially since the publication of Nicola Slee, *Women's Faith Development: Patterns and Processes* (Aldershot: Ashgate, 2004).

44 Jenny Morgans, 'Reflexivity, Identity, and the Role of the Researcher' in *Researching Female Faith: Qualitative Research Methods*, ed. Nicola Slee, Fran Porter and Anne Phillips (Abingdon: Routledge, 2018), pp. 189–202.

45 Jenny Morgans, 'Faithing, Friendship and Feeling at Home: Three Women Encounter University Chaplaincy' in *From the Shores of Silence: Conversations in Feminist Practical Theology*, ed. Ashley Cocksworth, Rachel Starr and Stephen Burns (London: SCM Press, 2023), pp. 95–111.

46 Traditional Elite universities are the first universities established in England and Scotland before 1880, including in Oxford, Cambridge, St Andrews, Durham and the umbrella institution the University of London. Redbrick is a term ascribed to universities established from 1880 to 1970. Post-1992 universities are those that were formerly polytechnics before applying for university status after the Further and Higher Education Act. The Russell Group comprises 24 large, research-intensive higher education institutions, awarded significant funding and prestige. See Guest et al., *Christianity and the University Experience*, Chapter 1.

47 While I recognize that 'mixed-race' is not an uncontested term, I continue to use it in this book because it is how the women identified themselves.

PART I

From Home to Home

2

Arriving

This chapter discusses the women's experiences in their first term at university. Almost all the students were away from home for the first time, were aged 18–20, and were adjusting to a new life and new city. These transitions were often traumatic as the women negotiated the challenges of leaving home: loneliness, mental ill-health, navigating the 'drinking culture' and (for those interviewed most recently) the impact of the Covid-19 pandemic. While the following chapter demonstrates the women crafting a new home for themselves at university, this chapter presents the women as feeling home*less* and uprooted.

When students first arrive at university, they must navigate 'Freshers' Week'. This is the first week (or fortnight) at university each September, before academic teaching begins, in which students attend induction events, orientate themselves on their new campus, and participate in social activities. Many universities are actively renaming Freshers' Week as 'Welcome Week', 'Intro Week' or 'Well-being Week' in an attempt to remove its associations with alcohol consumption and sexual promiscuity. However, it is often still referred to as Freshers' Week, including by women in this book. Freshers' Week is a cause of anxiety for many students, and is mentioned repeatedly in this chapter as they felt pressure to be organized during the day and to socialize in the evenings, while familiarizing themselves with a new location far from home.

Traumatic transitions

Schlossberg recognizes the necessity of contextual resourcing in the successful negotiating of transitions. Her '4 S System' enables individuals to 'take stock' and then 'take charge' of their transition. The first three Ss are concerned with the former, while the fourth is necessary for taking charge:

- *Situation*: such as whether individuals feel in control, the duration of the transition, previous experience with transitions, and stress levels.

- *Self*: in particular, demographic characteristics such as socioeconomic status, gender, age, health and class; and psychosocial resources including resilience, spirituality, ego development and value commitment.
- *Support*: including affirming relationships with mentors, family and friends.
- *Strategies*: especially being able to reframe the situation and manage stress levels.[1]

It initially surprised me how much the women's narratives of transition resonated with narratives of trauma. Of course, not all transitions are traumatic.[2] Whether or not a transition is understood as traumatic depends partly upon Schlossberg's 4 Ss: What is the situation? Where is support? What about past experiences? Are new strategies developed? Different personalities, history, or what Pierre Bourdieu calls 'habitus',[3] can influence an individual's experience of a transition as traumatic or otherwise. Moreover, some transitions are more affecting than others; for example, not all transitions overwhelm people's resources, result in a loss of assumptions, or break a person's supportive connections.

There is a growing field of research about trauma. Bessel van der Kolk's popular work, *The Body Keeps the Score*, draws upon experiences of war and abuse, yet his research is valuable here.[4] He defines a person's experience as traumatic when it is: 'overwhelming'; difficult to integrate 'into the ongoing stream of their life'; preventing them from 'spontaneously engaging in their day-to-day lives'; and leading to the 'reorganization of perception'.[5] All these traits are evident for the women in this book. Richard G. Tedeschi and Lawrence G. Calhoun compare 'trauma' with 'crisis', with both 'mean[ing] sets of circumstances that seriously challenge or overwhelm an individual's capacity to cope'.[6] Trauma in transitions involves the person's assessment of and reaction to an event, rather than necessarily the event itself. Erik H. Erikson observes similar crises among young soldiers returning from war, recognizing a loss of continuity resulting in identity confusion. Young adults, he writes, experience 'a war within themselves'.[7] Moreover, David E. Balk's work with students suffering from bereavement suggests they are under-resourced and under-supported in their transitions at university, arguing that 'loss, often unresolved, simply form[s] the story of the students' lives'.[8]

All the women had difficulty transitioning in their new life, and many of the women's transitions were traumatic. Often this trauma had a relational aspect, and adjustments with old and new friends or flatmates were significant. Students experienced this trauma as *normal*, also witnessing it in other students around them. Its normality, combined with the experience of being *unknown*, meant that students did not seek support with coping. As Taylor said, 'If I had a problem, I'd just deal with it ... I don't think I'd go anywhere.'

Clare Holdsworth identifies how students adapt to their new environment and incorporate a student habitus. In these early months at university, some working-class students 'leave behind' parts of their class identity and are then 'in a better position to adapt ... away from the pressure of having to negotiate between two distinct worlds on a daily basis'.[9] This notion of *two distinct worlds* is useful, not merely for students from the working classes, but for all students navigating university life away from the familial home.

Negative terms that women used to describe arriving at university, from most to least common, included: 'nervous', 'hard', 'homesick', 'scary/scared', 'struggle/ing', 'overwhelming/ed', 'panic', 'emotional', 'lonely', 'daunting', 'unsettled', 'terrified', 'shock', 'confused', 'horrible', 'stressful' and 'exhausted'. These words illustrate my understanding of their traumatic transitions and contributed to the women feeling unhome at university. Here are three students using some of these terms:

> I had a bit of, like, a bit of a cry ... I was just like, 'argh', it was really overwhelming ... and I was just sat there on my own, like, 'Oh no, I'm never gonna make any friends' ... so I was having a bit of a panic about that. (Alexis)

> I was homesick ... really bad, I haven't been home all term cos I was thinking ... 'If I'm going home, I'm not coming back' ... it wasn't just necessarily being homesick but, like, 'oldlifesick'. (Kimberly)

> I was quite homesick ... I was quite emotional and ... it was a bit hard ... I'm normally very chatty and I was really quiet ... [My brother] was really worried [because I] seemed really scared. (Sarah)

Kimberly's term 'oldlifesick' echoes Holdsworth's notion of two distinct worlds. These students were processing the end of their old world, while coming to terms with their new world at university.

Leaving home

Leaving the familial home involved loss and confusion, including for those who also expressed some relief. Leaving home was a significant ending, a time of grief requiring considerable negotiation before new connections could be made. This negotiation often felt ambiguous in ways that the women had neither expected nor (been) prepared for. Some students felt embarrassed about missing home, with several like Kimberly making the decision not to return during their first term. The women wrestled with a tension between feeling drawn back home and feeling confused by this pull. Amber thought that if she returned home, 'I'll just miss it even more, I think it's better to just sort of stick it out.' Kat felt that returning home briefly had 'made me feel a bit more unsettled'. Olivia noticed 'a bit of shame [about] going home'. The students wanted a clean break from their familial home while establishing themselves in their new home.

However, some students intensely missed their family, or the emotive symbols of security and home. Stephanie wanted her own bed, while Kimberly missed sharing morning cups of tea with her family. Kat craved home comforts after being unwell, and this intensified rather than diminished during her first few weeks. She described herself as 'a bit more of a home person' than she realized. Similarly, Nicole was struggling, saying, 'I am very much a home girl.' Through leaving, Kat and Nicole had realized the central place of home in their identity. Using Holdsworth's theory, their sense of self was embedded in their home 'world', and they felt adrift when in an unfamiliar 'world'.

In moving away, parental contact and support was significant to the women in different ways. Most students remained in close contact with immediate family. For example, despite Olivia enjoying her new life, being able to ring her parents eased her initial transition. Students sought both practical as well as emotional support from their parents. Mothers were particularly important, and the language used when discussing their mums revealed a closeness. In contrast, fathers were often either emotionally or geographically distant from themselves or their mothers. For example, Tumi said, 'I tell my mum everything, my dad would find out just via my mum ... that's just how I've done life.' Caitlin was distant from her 'abusive father' while Alexandra's father was 'sexist' and 'has the tendency to get violent'.

Practical support sought from mothers and fathers was also different, demonstrating gendered connotations with the everyday – for example, mothers were asked about decisions linked with daily life and identity, such as clothing choices, washing and cooking, whereas fathers were asked practical questions, for example about money and a broken boiler. Whether the students' parents were together or separated did not appear to make a significant impact on the women in leaving home. In cases of separation, students only gave vague details, perhaps because none were recent.

In a project entitled HOME: Harnessing Opportunities for Meaningful Environments, Eszter Hegymegi and colleagues identify four core categories related to feeling at home: 'objects', 'people', 'habits and routines' and 'places'. Stephanie and Kimberly's reflections about their own bed and cups of tea reflect the importance of 'objects' and 'habits and routines'. Other students spoke about missing their mothers, reflecting what Hegymegi calls 'symbolic presence' under the core category of 'people'.[10] When loved ones were not physically present, students found symbolic ways to feel connected to them.

Parks's theorization of emerging adults' faithing takes seriously this transitional time, arguing that they experience 'two great yearnings'[11] between being independent and autonomous, and requiring parental and emotional support. When Taylor's father visited her at university, she described it as 'like two spheres ... colliding', a dramatic, even violent, metaphor reflecting tension between her 'two distinct worlds'. Briana found her parents' visit uncomfortable, forcing her to reflect: 'I felt like my relationship had changed, which I didn't really like ... But I don't think our relationship *has* changed, I think *I've* changed.'

Christian Smith and Patricia Snell undertook extensive research with young adults in the US. They argue that parents often misread their teen's behaviour, believing the 'myth' that they are irrelevant in their children's lives and so step back, when in reality they are the 'most crucial players in teenagers' lives'.[12] Often, emerging adults want to improve and renegotiate relationships with parents, and several women said that since leaving home they 'get on better because of the distance' (Amber). Smith and Snell notice that old habits of conflict can be broken upon emerging adults' departure from home, enabling them to understand their parents better. For those who were not close to their parents, the physical distance created after leaving home was often useful in accepting any hurt in the relationship.[13] This was true for Samantha who, since moving to university, was able to exist primarily in one of her two 'distinct worlds'. She said about her mother: 'We don't really get on ... but it doesn't really matter to me anymore, it doesn't play on my mind as much, because I'm not thinking, "Oh, in so-and-so hours I have to go home and face everything".'

In the move to university, students benefit from the reassurance that they have a secure base available to them, to which they can return if necessary. One study suggests that students with secure attachment styles are better prepared for higher education, finding their transitions less psychologically threatening.[14] Other research finds that students in Canada were aided in their university transitions by a sense of mutual reciprocity with their parents, and by having learned models of coping with transition by witnessing parental behaviour.[15] Abigail's narrative demonstrates the significance of positive parental approaches to (and thus positive previous experience of) transitions. Abigail's transition to university was relatively smooth, without much of the trauma and identity confusion that other women experienced. A white student born in the UK, she spent much of her childhood with her parents in Uganda, returning to school in the UK without them aged 16. Positive experiences of transitions between different homes, and her parents' support in these, equipped Abigail with many of the strategies she needed upon arriving at university. She narrated fewer traumatic challenges, and was rather matter-of-fact about her move to university. In discussing not feeling at home at university, she said,

> I'm so multicultural ... that's sort of OK for me ... I know I'm kind of like a child of the world [laughs] so I can go anywhere, and that's good for me. Like, I'm quite glad to be here for these three years but then who knows where I'll be.

In contrast, for some students the transition to university was more difficult than anticipated. Sarah 'hadn't really thought about it properly before – the fact that I was moving away – and then just, sort of, land[ing] here, was a bit ... of a shock'. She was 'daunted by the challenge of moving away from home, where I felt safe and comfortable, into a new environment where I didn't know anybody.' It seems remarkable that Sarah had not given much thought to leaving home beforehand, suggesting that she could have been better prepared by her family and school. Sarah's own personality was potentially significant in this lack of forethought. Perhaps she often jumped into situations feet-first without advance preparation; perhaps she optimistically assumed that all would be well; or perhaps she lacked the ability to live with ambiguity. Whatever the reasons, Sarah felt surprised at how adrift and alone she was.

In general, students who had felt positive about moving away beforehand and had prepared emotionally were less likely to find the move 'a shock'. Some women who had felt worried or nervous before leaving found the move somewhat easier than expected. Several said that the transition had been 'fine'. For example, Mary explained that she was simply 'getting used to being somewhere else ... it was fine.' At first, such responses might seem glib or unreflective. However, I read them as optimistic, trusting, resilient and determined. Taylor said, 'It's been been been fine, I haven't, haven't missed home as much as I thought I might have done, it's been fine, yeah, I haven't really ... um, yeah, it's been fine, I suppose.'

The repetitions in Taylor's words are noteworthy, however. She may have been giving herself time to think, but perhaps there was more going on than she was articulating, reflected in her tentative 'I suppose'. It is possible that she was putting on a brave face – either for my or her own benefit.

Loneliness and grief

In the first term at university, loneliness was a common experience as the students felt uprooted from their family and previous communities, and even from their previous selves. Contributing factors included moving from large families to quieter accommodation with fewer people (and vice versa); and a perception that other students had already formed social groupings, leaving them feeling isolated. Several felt acute loneliness in Freshers' Week due to the prevalence of activities focused on alcohol consumption, which I explore later in this chapter. Olivia felt 'lonely' despite meeting so many new people:

> I just realized how lonely I was ... to have no one, *no one*, that knows you is just so weird and yet you're surrounded by so many people ... All I've been doing for days is just meeting people for like two minutes at a time ... but yet ... I don't know anyone really and no one knows me.

Being geographically (and sometimes emotionally) distant from old friends and feeling isolated from new flatmates, many students felt unknown at university, and lacked the support and reassurance that close friendships provide. In leaving behind old friends that knew them well, they were leaving the safety of valued and trusted support networks. For Melissa, 'one of the harder things of coming to university' was 'if I was tired and stressed, I couldn't phone one of my friends and say, "Do you want to go for a walk?"' Courtney was concerned that, were something to 'go wrong, I don't really know anyone well enough here to talk to'. Briana, a self-aware introvert, 'hit a wall' a few weeks into her first term, and thought, 'I'm tired, and I've got too many people around me, and I just want to go home.'

As well as being surrounded by unknown faces, many students recognized with confusion or sadness that relationships with old friends were changing. Courtney found that staying in touch with friends at home took 'effort', and some students worried that they 'might lose' old friends that had 'changed' or been 'turned' in their own new environments.

Others recognized that they were themselves changing, and that this contributed to the friends losing touch. At this stage, these relationships were breaking down, as Mary said, 'not on purpose', without intent. Jennifer L. Crissman Ishler and Staci Schreiber refer to 'friendsickness' during the early phase of university life, a form of what Kimberly called 'oldlifesickness' above. They argue that the distance between female students and old friends results in a form of grief, inhibiting their transitions.[16] Samantha discussed friends from school:

> I really, *really* miss them. [Pause] I mean, they weren't the best sort of friends, occasionally they treated me quite badly, I just really wish I was living with them instead of my flatmates cos it's so hard for me to build up a body of people. I really miss them.

Samantha was nostalgic about having *familiar* people around her – even if not necessarily *safe* people – in contrast with her flatmates, from whom she felt isolated and excluded, and with the challenging experience of having to make new friends. Repetition of the word 'really' four times in this short excerpt emphasizes the struggle that Samantha experienced.

Many other students struggled with their new flatmates. Living with compatible friends is central to a positive experience of transition at university, with some studies advocating that universities match flatmates according to pre-entry personality tests.[17] Differing approaches to alcohol consumption were a common cause of tension between flatmates. Because she did not go out drinking, Samantha's flatmates 'don't interact with me in the same way'. Stephanie joked that her flatmates 'all quite like partying, so I think that I'm ... their amusing hermit or something.' Despite the comedic tone, their behaviour was affecting Stephanie's well-being and contributing to her insomnia. She moved into different accommodation later in her first year, where she was much happier.

Samantha was also not alone in finding it difficult to meet new people. Several students talked about taking part in activities outside of their comfort zone to make friends. This attempt to 'fit in' influenced many of the women's decisions, particularly early on at university. Taylor attended a church and Christian student society where she felt she was most likely to make friends, despite disagreeing with the theological approach of both. Melissa attended an event in a bar, despite it being:

> not really my sort of [laughs] thing, I more went cos I needed to meet people and I didn't want to look antisocial ... When you get here you just have to talk to people or you're going to be miserable.

Exerting considerable effort in making new friends was a reasonable risk-avoidant strategy, even when it was difficult or scary. For Ulrich Beck and Elisabeth Beck-Gernsheim, identity is formed through behaviours that avoid and manage risk, especially at a time of vulnerability,[18] such as arrival in a new environment. As Melissa said, she *needed* to create a new support network around her to survive her traumatic transitions.

Ola gave a lot of thought to having to make new friends, and had a tearful conversation with her pastor about it. She said,

> I absolutely hate making friends [laughs] ... I'm just so awkward with people and I hate talking to new people ... because I think so much [about] what people think of me and, like, 'So am I saying the right words, am I asking the right questions' ... so I'd just rather not do that and just sit on my bed all day [laughs].

The word 'hate' is strong here, and it is interesting to see it alongside laughter. Perhaps Ola felt embarrassed by what she was saying, or felt that she should find making new friends easier. The self-monitoring and identity negotiation reflected in her hypervigilance around new people was also displayed in other students' behaviour, and is discussed later in this chapter. Unlike other students who felt able to step out of their comfort zones to make friends, Ola would not 'go to random parties ... just to meet people'. Her plan was to 'try to make friends ... to survive, basically.'

Aside from experiencing loneliness, the students also felt overwhelmed by the pressures of what Tim Clydesdale calls 'daily life management' (DLM), which consumed a significant amount of their time and energy. For first-year students, Clydesdale argues, 'The pressure to successfully manage an increasingly complex daily life leaves little time for anything else.'[19] Examples of DLM included handling money, meeting day-to-day needs and managing relationships. Many students spoke about performing household chores, budgeting or cooking for the first time. Others were relieved to live in catered accommodation, or glad that a gap year had given them many of the skills they needed for DLM. Vicky explained that, 'Coming to uni, there's just been like so many more things to think about ... the practicalities of actually, like, living on my own.' She called this 'basic survival', expressing that DLM was 'stressful' and 'pushed' out time for other priorities. Several women relied on parental support when faced with DLM, finding it an area of conflict between Parks's 'two great yearnings' for independence and support.[20] For example, Olivia rang home: 'I was making soup, I'm like, "Mum, I can't actually remember how to make soup, how do you do it?!"'

Some students reflected on being confronted with too many opportunities or activities, resulting in a fear of missing out or paralysis in the face of choice. Nicole felt pressure to 'have as much fun as possible and get out there and do different things'. Vicky said that being able to 'do like *anything* at uni' with people 'throwing themselves at you' to be involved in different activities, made her feel 'like you've got to make the most of [it]'. These were unhelpful anxieties at a time when learning to cook, manage money or meet new people was at the forefront of their minds.

A devastating example of overwhelm at university was the experience of bereavement, made more intense by being away from family and support structures. Studies suggest that between one-quarter and one-third of all students at any one time have suffered a bereavement in the past year.[21] In this book, a quarter of students shared an experience of losing a loved one, including Alexis who sadly lost two grandmothers in her first year. The impact of bereavement on the students' experience of their transitions was devastating. Nicole found that at university her elderly friend's death 'didn't feel real', prompting her to travel home regularly in search of comfort and support from family and old friends. When grieving, Alexis and Olivia – although they did not visit home as often as Nicole – *wanted* to be with friends and family, feeling homesick, lonely and guilty that they 'should be at home'. The impact of bereavement was exacerbated when the loved one's death was ill-timed, especially at the beginning of the first term or during the examination period. Tapping into close relationships when grieving was important, yet only Olivia discussed confiding in a new friend at university, perhaps enabled by her extrovert personality. She found that the experience both deepened the friendship and helped her feel supported. Balk finds that, more often, students' new friends 'dismiss the intensity and duration of grief'.[22] Cynthia L. Battle and her colleagues report that grieving students experience inadequate support which intensifies their isolation, including from peers who generally have less experience of death and so struggle to provide comfort.[23]

Experiencing a bereavement in the first year at university often obstructed attempts to craft home at university by intensifying the students' bond with the familial home. Connections with family and old friends were strengthened at a time when emotional distance is usually intentionally created. This forced interaction between the two 'worlds' of home and university, hindering the process of individuation that usually signifies moving away. In contrast, Chloe experienced a bereavement later in her time at university. By then she felt that she had more internal resources and external support, reflecting that 'As I've got older ... I've become more open to talking about my feelings', including attending therapy. While the grief was still 'difficult', she 'was more open' and felt that 'the person I am [now] has made it easier'.

Mental ill-health

Half the women discussed struggling with their mental health, seven of them to a striking extent. For some of these, mental illness predated their arrival at university. For example, Lauren felt low, anxious and disengaged in the summer before university, while Caitlin experienced 'severe depression' while at school. However, for many students, being at university came with previously unknown mental health diagnoses, including anxiety, clinical depression and insomnia.

The mental ill-health of students at UK universities has been called a 'crisis'.[24] Even before the Covid-19 pandemic, explored later in the chapter, universities were struggling to cope with high numbers of students needing mental health support, and sometimes came under attack for seemingly failing to put safeguards in place. As Richard Cooke and his colleagues argued in 2006, 'While higher education is expanding, there is concern that the structures currently in place to support students are not developing ... [Yet] students fare worse than the general population on measures of psychological wellbeing.'[25]

For Christian Bröer and Broos Besseling, it is important not to medicalize low mood and 'normal sadness' or emphasize 'patients, pills and professionals', recognizing that the term 'depression' can describe experiences ranging from the effect of bad weather to long-term clinical illness.[26] While some of the women in this book define their mental ill-health as clinical, others are less clear about the nature of their low mood. This could be due to several factors, including: casual usage of terms including 'stress' and 'depression'; not having spoken to a medical professional; self-regulating their negative emotions; or a lack of life/health experience, meaning that these students were figuring out what was 'normal' for them. For example, along with suffering insomnia, in her first term Stephanie experienced 'low points' where she would 'go for very long walks ... and cry', and was not receiving any medical support for this. In contrast, Chloe experienced years of 'clinical depression, anxiety and stuff' due to 'low self-esteem ... from like bullying and family'. She was undergoing trauma therapy and Cognitive Behavioural Therapy (CBT).

Samantha was diagnosed with 'emotionally unstable disorder' while at university, and was trialling different medications and CBT. Over 10 per cent of Samantha's two interviews included reflections on her mental health, and she explained that 'Since I moved [to uni], my mental state has gotten quite a bit worse', including 'depression and anxiety ... and high moods as well'. Her mental health was negatively impacting her study, relationships, self-esteem, faith, general well-being and sense of personhood/womanhood. Her biggest decision upon arriving at university was not about her studies or social activities, but about going to see a doctor. She had 'hurt myself a bit', which I interpreted as self-harm.

Vicky suffered debilitating bouts of depression. She described things 'crashing down' following an unexpected bereavement during an exam period. She found it 'quite difficult to talk to people about it ... I don't wanna burden people with, like, with how I'm feeling', although she realized that distancing herself 'actually made it worse'. When feeling depressed, she described how 'the routine things seem, like, overwhelmingly difficult ... cooking and washing up just become absolutely impossible tasks ... like, "Can I actually get out of bed?", "Will I actually be able to make any toast?"' Vicky feared a relapse in her second year: 'There's just this ... doubt, that it will happen again, but I guess that's part of living with depression.'

The students that I interviewed in their second year or beyond were significantly more likely to discuss their mental health challenges than those in their first year, and I consider two possible reasons for this. For a number of these students, it was not the first time that they had been interviewed, and so perhaps there was an increased rapport and trust between them and me. More likely, the women may have been buoyed either by increased confidence in their second year; or by a recognition of the commonality of mental illness as they had more experience, making the subject less taboo. Just as emerging adults are unprepared to deal with bereavement in their first year at university, so too with mental illness. Into their second year, they were better equipped to share their experiences, and perhaps also better able to respond to their needs, as Chloe noted at the end of the previous section.

According to the World Health Organization, British teenagers report lower levels of happiness and higher existential dread than their peers in other Western nations.[27] While I expected the women to discuss their global concerns, especially climate chaos, war and xenophobia, being amid their own traumatic transitions meant that the women's primary worries were closer to home. The women gave several causes for a decline in their mental health, but all involved their daily living, the most common being academic expectation. Studying was a source of worry and fear in the first few months at university. In research conducted by Amy Poots and Tony Cassidy, academic stress is shown to have a significant negative correlation with well-being, often leading to mental ill-health, especially during exam periods. Positive coping strategies included social support, self-compassion and psychological capital including hope, resilience and optimism.[28] Academic difficulties reported by women I interviewed included feeling stressed, anxious or scared; feeling pressure to do well or meet deadlines; having an unrealistic amount of work; and doubts about being good enough. In the women's second year, the stress of academic work was a significant memory when they thought back to their arrival at university, including a lack of support and suffering anxiety. Negative experiences of academia were felt equally for women across a range of subjects with varying contact hours, including humanities, science and law. At a particularly low point, Lauren 'was having problems with my essay, and I just wanted to be at home and talk it through with my mum.' Melissa worried: 'I've got lots of essays and I don't understand what I'm meant to be writing.' She became visibly upset as she discussed feeling anxious and depressed during her exams.

Megan 'hated' how intense her course was, a strong word to describe her academic work, to which she was deeply committed. Despite prior warning, she said, 'It's a shock, I don't think they can really prepare you for that … there's just so much to do.' While laughing, she added, 'This sounds like some sort of counselling.' Her laughter gave her words a light touch, but it seemed that she was not accessing any support, and I wondered if she had shared the depths of her hatred with anyone else. Many studies uncover students' lack of interest in academic work, with education considered an underwhelming hurdle on the path to adulthood.[29] However, such a perfunctory approach to education was not seen in my research, perhaps due to the top rankings of the Russell Group universities included, alongside high motivation among these mostly middle-class Christian women. Generally, the women I interviewed at the post-1992 university spoke less about their academic work.

The academic pressure that these students were experiencing was often gendered. Some noticed that their women friends were 'more stressed' than men about their studies. That Kat had been '*so* stressed' at school contributed to her not achieving the grades needed for her first choice of university, while 'If I'd been a guy, I probably would have been a bit more relaxed about it.' Demonstrating the gendering of emotions, while men are encouraged to hide anxiety, Kat's stress had not been noticed as requiring attention. Alexandrina Scarbrough and Carolyn Hicks find that female students with mental health disorders are less likely to be referred to counselling services than their male peers, regardless of the nature or severity of the complaint. For women, some degree of internalized psychological disturbance is considered normative.[30] Poots and Cassidy suggest that women are more likely than men to place high expectations upon themselves, to report higher stress levels, and to experience educational pressure from their parents.[31]

Receiving lower A level grades than expected, Kat altered her university plans, leaving her feeling 'really miserable'. Like Kat, three other women struggled to adjust to attending their second preferred choice of university. This intensified homesickness and even isolation from other students, and contributed to their traumatic transitions. Kimberly found attending her second choice 'daunting' and 'was confused … and stressed due to the last-minute rush to find accommodation'. Lauren said, 'I spent about four years deciding I wanted to do medicine and that was going to be my life goal and everything, I had my next sort of 20 years planned out, and then that fell to pieces.' This visceral metaphor of plans and expectations shattering unexpectedly leaves no wonder that these women felt disorientated and unhome. Surprisingly, however, there seems to be no specific support aimed at students whose applications to their first choice of university are unsuccessful.

Discussing mental health – or at least well-being – is now largely normalized at university, and has become less taboo especially for students from Western cultures. Students are better able to discuss their emotions, access support and prioritize their well-being, in keeping with Gen Z's values.[32] Kathleen J. Greider argues for the need to reframe depression as a quality of the human condition, for 'psychic anguish may in some cases be a more appropriate response than the numbness, denial, and adaption that so-called healthy persons manage to maintain in the face of our society's sicknesses.'[33] In this case, a level of mental ill-health might be expected for women at university. They thus need help understanding their own mental health; discerning what is 'normal' sadness, overwhelm or anxiety for them; and finding the necessary strategies and support. Moreover, academic support must be improved for students upon their initial arrival at university. As Kimberly said, 'there was pressure to find your feet quickly as deadlines began to appear'. Handling new daily responsibilities, unexpected changes, social isolation and academic pressures were pressing concerns for the women, resulting in high levels of anxiety and depression. Too often, the women felt under-resourced and unsupported in handling these overwhelming circumstances.

Alcohol and the drinking culture

Alcohol consumption increased in popularity and acceptability towards the end of the twentieth century, becoming a key component in public social lives in the UK. In the 1990s, nightlife was at the heart of strategies to transform cities, and, rather than focusing on older men, diverse communities were being targeted, including young adults and women.[34] Since the late 2000s, however, alcohol consumption has decreased, and Gen Z drink less alcohol than generations of students before them.[35] Nonetheless, universities have a distinctive relationship with alcohol, with many student activities geared towards its consumption. Campuses have a range of discounted drinking venues as well as student societies aimed at enjoying alcoholic beverages. In 2013, Guest and colleagues supposed that extreme drinking may be 'the number one behavioural concern among university students in the United Kingdom'.[36]

Christian students' opinions on alcohol and the student drinking culture are complex. While Guest and colleagues report that twice as many Christian students than those who identify as non-religious say they dislike the drinking culture, over a third of all Christian students say they have no problem with it.[37]

Navigating the culture of excessive alcohol consumption at university was often traumatic for students. They were uncertain about what they thought, while aware of others' assumptions about Christian attitudes to alcohol. Some felt pressured to drink alcohol, in keeping with research pinpointing an intolerance towards abstinence.[38] For example, Nicole was dismayed that, 'People, when they find out that I don't, sort of, get drunk, they're like "Right, a challenge!"' While many students enjoyed alcohol, none expressed this without caveat, explaining either that they did not get drunk or that they were not interested in what Briana called the 'party culture'. Many of these women were involved in a church, reflecting research finding that regular church attendees are most likely to find excessive alcohol consumption problematic.[39] Only Chloe discussed drinking alcohol to excess, and she had since realized that this was a coping strategy where, 'In first year, if I felt really unhappy, I drank too much.' She critiqued the 'UK drinking culture' where people turn to alcohol when feeling both 'happy' and 'upset'.

When I asked students about their Freshers' Week experiences, all but one mentioned alcohol without prompting, and it was often the first thing that came to mind. Several women found that the focus on alcohol hindered opportunities to meet new people. Briana had been 'dreading it' beforehand because she did not want to participate in alcohol-centred activities. Nightclubbing gave Kimberly panic attacks, while Ashley said that the prevalence of alcohol at events made her feel bored and lonely. Thinking back to their Freshers' Week a year later, students remembered feeling 'pressure' 'to go out' and being 'worried' about 'a lot of partying and alcohol' and the need to 'join in ... or risk being left out'. Although Alexandra enjoyed going to pubs, she had thought 'I don't feel like I would belong' because 'I don't like to club.'

Caitlin was teetotal. She became involved with the Christian Union (CU) where she 'formed such quick attachments' at the start of university because 'they don't do the whole clubbing and drinking culture thing, whereas all the other societies ... were based around, "let's go clubbing".' She saw joining the CU 'as my only opportunity to meet people who weren't wanting to go out'. The CU provided not just an alternative way to spend her social time, but the opportunity to meet people with whom she was more likely to share things in common. This was despite being queer and quickly feeling excluded from the society, which I explore in more detail later. Her priority was avoiding alcohol-centred activities, which took precedence over finding spaces accepting of her queer identity.

Navigating the drinking culture, while traumatic, enabled the women to find a student identity that fitted with their self-understandings, and to locate themselves in university life. Resistance to the culture of alcohol consumption gave them an opportunity to assert themselves and their Christian identities amid their traumatic transitions. However, this process did not appear deliberate. The students named their faith alongside many reasons why they did not fully engage in alcohol-focused activities, including: not enjoying losing control; disliking the taste; limited finances; alcohol-dependent family members; not liking noise or crowds; having early morning lectures; not wanting to vomit or have a hangover; family/cultural influence; fear of assault; not enjoying the music in nightclubs; closest friends also not drinking; and fear of doing something they might regret. Moreover, the students were unclear about what it *actually was* about their faith that determined their refraining from alcohol. For example, Taylor admitted, 'I've never thought about it' and Ola reflected, 'I don't know, I've just never gone [to a club].' Megan did not think that her decision to not drink alcohol was 'really faith-driven', adding 'although, you know, you could have these discussions about how much your faith is internalized.' In these interviews, Taylor, Ola and Megan were thinking as they spoke, unsure quite why they did not participate in drinking alcohol. A sense of faith being 'internalized' also arose for Haley and Nicole. Haley's response was particularly muddled as she oscillated between her faith being central to her choice to abstain, and saying that her faith had nothing to do with the decision:

It's nothing to do with my faith ... and I think like based on my faith ... I didn't think that [getting drunk] was really showing people [my faith], and I wanted to show people straight away that I was a Christian ... [It's] nothing to do with my faith, but I don't go out because [my lectures] start at 9am every day.

Other students elaborated on a missional approach to drinking alcohol, as hinted at by Haley, but by engaging with rather than abstaining from the culture. This included: attending pubs and 'pre-drinks' but not nightclubs; drinking but not getting drunk; framing their nights out in terms of evangelism; and volunteering to distribute bottles of water outside nightclubs with other Christian students, aiming to engage clubbers in conversations on faith. Briana played 'drinking games' with water rather than alcoholic drinks, and Olivia thought it was important to demonstrate to non-Christian friends that she could have fun on a night out without alcohol.

Some students suggested that a level of negotiation was required in living out their student Christian identities, to 'make it work'. Assertion of their Christian identity (distinct from praxis) was an important consideration for many women as they negotiated who they were becoming at university. Alcohol acted as a boundary marker between who they were and who they were not – and similarly between who they were like and who they were not like. Drinking alcohol, particularly binge drinking, was very much considered to be a *normal* part of the student experience, despite many students not conforming to this stereotype. Going 'out' was shorthand communication for attending a club night, while alcohol-free events were considered 'alternative'. Expanding upon George H. Mead's theory of a 'generalized other',[40] Holdsworth finds a strong sense of a universal, typical student, whose key characteristics include going 'out' drinking.[41] By defining themselves in opposition to this 'other', the women were able to carve a distinctly separate space for understanding themselves as Christians. For example:

I think this is probably where I'll be really different to most [first-year students]. (Abigail)

[T]he way I'm going to approach certain situations like going out is going to be a lot different to ... other people. (Ashley)

You can't live ... [a] typical student lifestyle and be a Christian at the same time ... like, drinking and ... getting ridiculously drunk. (Courtney)

I don't enjoy it as much as I think most people do. (Lauren)

Given the level of confusion as to whether/how faith impacted students' abstinence from alcohol, these expressions assuming Christian students – in contrast with other students – have a conservative approach to alcohol consumption are surprising. In the words of Guest and colleagues, Christianity seemed to give the students 'an ethic by which to say "no"'.[42] Kimberly recognized this, saying, 'I think my faith ... gives me justification for that viewpoint.' While she did not enjoy going out for other reasons, her Christian identity gave her a framework to explain her decision and an excuse to opt out. The construction of identity in opposition to the mythical student helped the women navigate being Christian in their daily life at university. Refusing to fully participate in the drinking culture was a way of maintaining integrity amid so much change.

Smith and Snell find that for active Christian adolescents, 'cognitive and emotional forces operate to sustain the high importance of faith into the emerging adult years'.[43] In rejecting the drinking culture at university, the women were prioritizing their new faith communities as safe and meaningful spaces for such liminal experimentations, rather than the secular alternative of attending nightclubs and getting drunk, which are arguably more escapist and less rich in value, as Chloe noted above. Instead of drinking alcohol, the women were choosing nourishing experiences elsewhere in their transitions. Yet the role that alcohol played in the experience, identity and approach of Christian students was unclear to the students themselves. In their second year, alcohol was much less of an issue, partly because the women were becoming secure enough in their identities both as Christians and as students who did not get drunk, and no longer needed to navigate asserting their identities to the same extent. However, when reflecting on their arrival at university more than 12 months later, negotiating the prevailing attitudes to alcohol was still a vivid, difficult memory for many of the women.

Identity shifts

Leaving home and arriving at university was a key time for both intentional and accidental identity work. The students underwent varying levels of confusion, distress, uncertainty, insecurity, discovery and re-evaluation. Relationships were vital, so being surrounded by high numbers of new people was particularly influential in navigating shifts in identity. For most students, to refer to an adolescent 'identity crisis', as theorized by Erikson,[44] would be to exaggerate their experiences. Yet identities were certainly being navigated and negotiated by the women in this research, and university was experienced as both a safe and a disturbing place in which to resolve dilemmas in identity.[45]

The students usually understood themselves as having an essential core identity. Some women suggested having previously made decisions in shaping this core, while others assumed it was innate and unchanging. Even students who reflected on their formation at university found this process compatible with having a core unchanging self. This essentialist viewpoint is outdated in identity theory, as well as in a postmodern culture which assumes that everything is changeable, yet it is still common in popular culture.[46] It is also common in the Church, reinforced by images of God as unchanging and knowing 'the real you', as I discuss in Chapter 4. The idea of a core self was comforting for the women – suggesting stability and continuity during their transitions. Yet it was also a source of angst when they felt unable to be themselves in certain situations, or when they noticed themselves changing regardless of the belief that they would stay the same.

In the 1960s and 70s, Generation X prized authenticity, honesty, truth and integrity over doctrines and creeds, a shift which has continued into Generations Y and Z.[47] This change is reflected in Girlguiding's decision in 2013 to remove the phrase 'to love my God' from the Promise that all members make, replacing it with the vow 'to be true to myself and develop my beliefs'. Alison Webster argues that authenticity is a key source of identity confusion and insecurity: 'Which is the real me? ... Am I being "real"? How do I know? Does it matter?'[48] Smith and Snell find that emerging adults are:

> concerned with knowing, confirming, and protecting their own and others' sense of who they *are*, that is, their personal and social identities ... [they] have a strong interest in conserving their senses of self, of sustaining the continuity of their identities.[49]

Vicky articulated this clearly:

> I do feel like myself whereas ... I didn't feel like I was myself at college [pause]. I don't feel like I have to alter myself to go back home [pause]. Yeah, like, if I'd come to university and been a completely different person [from who I was], I would have felt when I went back home to my family or church I'd have to alter myself back to how I was when I left.

Failure to achieve this integration could result in cognitive dissonance, and would contribute to the sense of being in two distinct worlds, as discussed above. This was the case for Lauren, whose words contrast with Vicky's. Lauren felt some emotional distance between herself and her family: 'I feel like the outsider when I go home, I think it's just part of being away.' When she went home, she realized 'I'm glad to be away,' where her identity could continue to shift without reminders of who she once was.

As Gale and Parker argue, integration between different identities and experiences is not linear, and there is no normative pattern. Rather, they describe the process as 'rhizomatic', making zigzags and spiral movements, with space for multiple narratives and fluid identities. Transitions at university, they argue, should thus be framed as a process of *becoming*, 'a perpetual series of fragmented movements involving whole-of-life fluctuations in lived reality or subjective experience.'[50] Taylor and Harris-Evans argue that transition is a 'more spontaneous, connective, happenstance, affective and transversal practice than is normally thought.' They continue: 'becoming is about change as ongoing flux and dynamic flow, as emergence and unfolding in micro-moments and instants.'[51] The students in this book demonstrated this kind of rhizomatic transition, often contradicting themselves or shifting their thoughts as they spoke, and there are many examples of this (see, for example, Haley discussing alcohol in the previous section).

Alongside Vicky, several other women said that they felt able to be themselves at university, and often this was framed as not being negatively influenced by others. Olivia resisted the idea that other people affected or shaped her: 'Whatever's gonna happen's gonna happen, I'm still who I am and I'm not identified by who I spend my time with or anyone else.' Stephanie approached meeting new people with the mantra: 'This is me, this is who I am, if you don't like me now you're never going to.' Sarah agreed: 'There's no point pretending' to be someone different. Kimberly was confident in how she made decisions: 'I feel like I can be myself ... I can say "no" to what I don't wanna do, and do things that I do wanna do.' Courtney realized that 'There's always people who are gonna accept you, because there's just so many people' and so felt able to assert who she was. She continued, 'Sometimes you worry too much about what people will think and that can hold you back, you kind of just have to be, like, "Well it doesn't really matter as long as *I* like who I am".'

Mary had an idea of herself that she created 'ages' ago which helped her feel safe amid her transitions. She thought that by the time of leaving home for university, 'You already like know who you are ... You've got certain morals and beliefs which you just believe ... [and] that stays with you as everything else changes ... You just go with what you want to, be who you want to be.' Shifting to using the first person, she summarized, 'I know who I want to be and who I am, and I'm not gonna change that because of other people.'

However, other students found it more difficult to express who they authentically were, or who they were becoming, in their new environment. Often the process of identity formation took place alongside trying to establish safe relationships, and some students struggled more than others to develop close friendships. These students described how making new friends sometimes came with a willingness to compromise on being themselves or expressing what they thought, perhaps contrary to their desire for authenticity. This was the case with Ola, quoted earlier in the chapter. As Webster argues, people are more likely to be honest about themselves when around others with whom they feel emotionally and psychologically safe, who are most often 'those whom we assume to be like us'; while when with people who are less well known or are considered to be different, it is not unusual to change how meaningful stories are narrated.[52]

The students noticed that they somehow changed around new people, or people they experienced as being different from themselves. These women were living under the 'tyranny of the they'; the perceived assumptions of others about themselves.[53] For example, Olivia would sometimes intentionally 'tailor conversations to what you think people want you to talk about' depending on who she was with and what they might think. Several students described their shyness as a barrier to being themselves in public. Some were only able to relax and be themselves around family or friends from home, and 'restrained' the 'silly', 'playful', 'naughty' or 'insane' parts of themselves at university. Echoing Ola's self-monitoring above, Melissa saw that her behaviour 'depends on who I'm around, I think, whether or not I feel entirely comfortable around that person yet'. Lauren would think, 'No, I shouldn't say something like that, cos how are people going to react when I say that.' Taylor described how 'I kinda analyse what I'm doing and what I'm saying quite often, just to check, like, "Oh, what are they going to think if I say this? I won't say that, I'll say this instead, they'll like that".' These women saw their authentic selves as something to protect until they felt safe, and practised strategic self-disclosure until they felt comfortable enough to share their 'true' self in their new environment.

Despite this, a few women demonstrated a level of awareness that their identities were shifting rather than being kept hidden. They reflected that their authentic self was itself changing and being shaped by their new experiences and relationships, yet this was still difficult to share with others due to its vulnerable newness. For example, contrary to her determination to 'not change' noted above, Mary also said, 'It's sort of hard saying whether I'm myself, because you have to change to be able to live at uni.'

All the women were attempting to create a new sense of normality in which they could safely both be and become themselves around the new people they were encountering. For many of the women, courage to step out of their comfort zones had given them increased confidence in being themselves. Briana said that although this was 'really scary', she had 'become a lot more confident, outgoing potentially, because I've kind of made an effort to meet people and put myself out there.' Danielle was an evangelical Christian who described herself as a lesbian. Undoubtedly, she was navigating these identities in her new environment at university, and was figuring out what she thought as she spoke to me. She talked courageously about being authentic to her identity despite encountering other people's beliefs that being queer was wrong. In doing so, she also demonstrated her vulnerability as she sought safety and protection for herself amid change and challenge. Mirroring Mary's words above, she said that at university, 'I know who I am … I just go somewhere and who I am is who I am, and if you don't like it then fair enough, not, like, I won't change myself just because people want me to or because I think I'll fit in more.'

Danielle was worried that if she allowed fluidity and development in her identity then previous understandings of herself would be lost and her sense of self diminished. Danielle demonstrated a determination and resilience, although her apparent vulnerability suggested some defensiveness to her words. This relationship between courage and vulnerability is a tension that is perhaps unsurprising amid traumatic transitions.

Danielle was not content simply to meet others' expectations of her, but rather demonstrated a strength in her identity choices, albeit rather naively. She had perhaps placed her most valued selves inside Clydesdale's 'identity lockbox',[54] refusing as much as possible to let them be altered by external pressure. For Danielle in particular, this appeared to come from a place of vulnerability as an attempt to keep herself psychologically and emotionally safe from other's judgements and criticism. The intersection between Danielle's sexuality and faith is explored further in Chapter 7.

The impact of the Covid-19 pandemic

While the Covid-19 pandemic affected the global population, the Office for National Statistics (ONS) recognizes that higher education students found themselves in a 'unique situation' due to the experience of living away from home, or being forced to return to living with family unexpectedly. They report that students' mental health worsened due to the pandemic, and they experienced lower levels of life satisfaction. During lockdowns, students went outside less often than the general population, only doing so for essentials and exercise, with 20 per cent of students not having left home at all in a seven-day period. They also found that many students struggled with adapting to studying online: 29 per cent were dissatisfied with their academic experience; 16 per cent of students did not feel equipped to engage with online learning; and 22 per cent considered withdrawing from their course if online teaching continued.[55]

Maria S. Plakhotnik and her colleagues find that the pandemic 'brought suffering, frustration, discomfort, fear, loss, and other negative emotions and experiences' to students across Europe, continuing:

> COVID-19 disrupted the balance point between the students' resource pool relevant to their academic pursuits and [their] numerous challenges ... The more worried students are about the impact of COVID-19 on their studies, the more their levels of wellbeing decrease.[56]

Jennifer A. Appleby and her colleagues report significant gender differences in the experiences of Covid-19 among UK students. They find that women students were more likely to self-isolate and to report higher anxiety about catching or transmitting Covid-19. Women were also significantly more likely than other students to feel that their access to support was negatively affected.[57]

Students' experiences pre-pandemic proved overwhelming and traumatic enough, as my earlier interviews show. Covid-19 exacerbated what were already stressful transitions. Four students were in their first year when the Covid-19 pandemic began in March 2020 (Caitlin, Chloe, Ola and Tumi), Alexandra began university in September 2020, and Taylor was a doctoral student during the pandemic when I interviewed her a second time. For these six students, the confusion of social restrictions and lockdowns threw life into unprecedented uncertainty, with significant consequences for their well-being.

Chloe felt that her university demonstrated 'mediocre organization' during the lockdowns, saying, 'They don't really help you, like, lecturers and stuff, they can get away with not putting lectures up [online] … It's weird because [this] is supposed to be a top uni.' Alexandra, an international student, was forced to stay in the Caribbean for her first year of university, 'Studying in a different time zone … [with] classes at 4am … [so] I missed a few.'

As discussed above, student mental ill-health in the UK was already concerning prior to the pandemic, with undergraduates reporting lower well-being than the general population.[58] Unsurprisingly, the experience of Covid-19 had an adverse impact upon several women's mental health. Caitlin 'struggled' to motivate herself in her studies. Her physical health also took a downturn, first being hospitalized with Covid, then suffering from long Covid, which proved debilitating. She said, 'It's just been a very stressful and difficult year, where I've wanted to give up so many times.' Tumi remembered her sense of hopelessness during the initial months of the pandemic. She fell out with her flatmates, and was snubbed by friends for dating someone who was not a Christian. Tumi felt lonely and anxious, and she 'had zero expectations of anything happening in my life'.

The ONS describes 50 per cent of students as feeling lonely at least weekly, compared to 39 per cent pre-pandemic.[59] Several women vividly remembered feeling isolated and being unable to make new friends. During lockdowns, Caitlin remained in her student accommodation because going back home 'wasn't even an option on the table', effectively meaning that she lived alone. Fortunately, she 'quite enjoyed it', saying, 'I'm an only child, so I think I'm quite used to being, sort of, on my own.' Taylor found herself living with just one other person, finding it 'hard to meet people' as a postgraduate student, made even harder by the pandemic, resulting in her feeling lonely much of the time.

Chloe, who moved back to her family home, was affected by being 'alone all the time and I had a fear of missing out'. During the pandemic, her grandmother sadly died in her parents' home country in East Asia. Restrictions meant that she could not attend the funeral, and so felt that she had not been able to say goodbye. Being 'stuck at home', she could not see friends or spend time with her supportive aunt who was 'extremely vulnerable'. Chloe felt anxious about members of the public not adhering to social distancing rules, and worried that the government was relaxing restrictions prematurely. She was attempting 'to detach myself from worrying' about things that she could not 'control', such as 'what the government does' and people not wearing face masks. However, she did worry, and carefully restricted her own behaviour.

Students reflected upon how the pandemic impacted their sense of belonging at university. Mirroring the ONS's findings that 50 per cent of students did not feel part of a university community during the pandemic,[60] Chloe and her friends 'didn't feel like we were at [this uni] ... like, they didn't go [here] anymore.' Alexandra said that although she had made new friends, 'We only met through video call' and so 'I wouldn't say I feel like I belong.'

Arguably, Covid-19 had the biggest impact upon Ola. Ola arrived in the UK from Nigeria in March 2020 for a foundation course, aged just 16, days before the first lockdown was announced. She found herself isolating with another student:

> Lectures were online anyway, so I was always in my room, I'd come out to the kitchen when I needed to get food, maybe say 'hi' to my housemate ... oh, it was so horrible! ... Like, 'I literally have no one, I'm in my room' ... I just felt so isolated from the world, and ... it was a nasty time.

Ola was adjusting to a new country as well as university, including registering with a doctor and using British supermarkets. Lectures remained entirely online for 2020 and 2021, and so she was at university for almost two years before experiencing lectures in person. She only had a few friends, and wondered, 'What was the point in doing all of this and putting in so much effort when I can't even meet people?' When restrictions started to ease, she thought, 'I've been in my room this whole time, so I know absolutely nothing, I have to start everything all over again.' The experience had a huge impact on her confidence and well-being. She concluded, 'There's a bit of trauma from that, I don't know if I have recovered from it.'

Amid such adverse experiences, however, several women reported positive change during the pandemic. Interestingly, the ONS reports that 14 per cent of undergraduates felt their mental health improve, with similar results reported elsewhere.[61] Tumi met her boyfriend while experimenting with dating websites during lockdown, which had 'changed my life completely'. Alexandra's closest friendships developed through weekly video calls. The friends realized how important they were to one another, to the point of making plans to live together. She was 'sceptical' when her original plans to move to the UK were cancelled. However, her 'roots ... at home grew a lot'. She began to feel more settled in her community, and began volunteering in her church, recognizing 'how integrated [I am] and how much work I see needs to be done' at home. Although she had not had the university experience that she hoped for, her actual experience was interesting and fulfilling, including studying online which inspired her to 'do research projects and papers [here] a bit more than I probably would have if I was away ... which helped me to gain a more nuanced understanding ... from an academic standpoint.'

Chloe recognized that the pandemic had given her 'more time to think about how I want to live my life and what my values are'. Due to not having to 'be in contact with so many people [laughs]', she felt free to 'develop my thoughts and be a bit more understanding to myself', including 'not feeling the pressure to go out all the time and do all this-and-that.' Chloe was able to look after herself and grow in confidence. These positive experiences are perhaps not unsurprising given Generation Z's emphasis on prioritizing well-being and forging community both in person and online.

Further retrospective research is needed to understand more fully the long-term impact that Covid-19 has had upon the lives of emerging adults. In Chapter 5, I discuss how the pandemic impacted upon the women's faith.

Conclusion

This chapter has discussed many of the challenges that women students faced as they arrived at university, impacting negatively upon their attempts to feel at home in their new environment. Many students described traumatic transitions in this time as they navigated: leaving home, loneliness, mental illness, the 'drinking culture', a global pandemic, and their individual identity work.

Several students in these initial months at university reflected directly upon not feeling at home. Kat was surprised that she did not feel at home, because, 'I thought I'd be like fine with it, cos I'm quite independent.' Nicole discussed 'slowly ... not quite yet' being able to 'confide things in other people', which she considered an important aspect of making home. Samantha's response was ambiguous, and reflected Hegymegi and colleagues' conclusions about 'objects' and 'places' as necessary to homeliness.[62] She had thought that university would feel 'really good ... because I don't get on very well with my family', yet she 'miss[ed] the house, not necessarily the people but just the house'. If making home is largely an internalized process that is transposed to a new setting, since Samantha did not feel at home among her family, she probably brought those conflicts with her to university. Her prior experiences informed the processes of negotiating these transitions,[63] so Samantha would have to navigate her conflicts in her new environment before she could feel at home there.

Tumi was finishing her second year at university when I interviewed her. She recognized many factors contributing to her traumatic transitions, including difficulties in her friendships and studying during the pandemic. She said, 'I don't think uni is meant to feel like home ... I'm just here to get a degree.' She continued, 'Too much has happened, I think, for me ... to feel truly settled here, it's been quite traumatic ... like, there's always *something* and it feels very tiring ... it still feels disjointed.'

The pull between the students' two distinct worlds proved challenging. They were negotiating their 'old' and 'new' identities and homes in multiple transitions that were iterative and tentative. Students missed home, responding to difficult experiences with the desire either to be home or to speak to their mum or an old friend. Accepting being away from sources of support and comfort took energy and resilience. The emotional pull of home continued throughout the first term of traumatic transitions, and often beyond.

Nevertheless, the next chapter considers how the students were able to craft home for themselves in their new university environment.

Notes

1 Nancy K. Schlossberg, 'The Challenge of Change: The Transition Model and Its Implications', *Journal of Employment Counseling* 48 (2011), pp. 160–1.

2 This work is distinct from the important area of trauma theology, although there are of course some intersections. See Karen O'Donnell and Katie Cross, eds, *Bearing Witness: Intersectional Approaches to Trauma Theology* (London: SCM Press, 2022).

3 Pierre Bourdieu, *The Logic of Practice* (London: Polity Press, 1992).

4 There are allegations of employee mistreatment against van der Kolk. I want to acknowledge this here, while recognizing the value of his important research.

5 Bessel van der Kolk, *The Body Keeps the Score: Mind, Brain and Body in the Transformation of Trauma* (London: Penguin Books, 2014), see especially pp. 3, 12, 15, 40, 47.

6 Richard G. Tedeschi and Lawrence G. Calhoun, *Trauma and Transformation: Growing in the Aftermath of Suffering* (London: Sage, 1995), p. 13.

7 Erik H. Erikson, *Identity: Youth and Crisis* (London: Faber, 1968), p. 17.

8 David E. Balk, 'Grieving: 22 to 30 Percent of All College Students', *New Directions for Student Services* 121 (2008), p. 6.

9 Clare Holdsworth, 'Don't You Think You're Missing Out, Living at Home? Student Experiences and Residential Transitions', *Sociological Review* 54, no. 3 (2006), p. 510.

10 Eszter Hegymegi et al., 'Developing a Tool to Empower the Disempowered: The Components of the Feeling of Home', 2024.

11 Sharon Parks, *The Critical Years: The Young Adult Search for a Faith to Live By* (New York: Harper & Row, 1986), p. 63; see also Sharon Parks, *Big*

Questions, Worthy Dreams: Mentoring Young Adults in Their Search for Meaning, Purpose, and Faith (San Francisco, CA: Jossey-Bass, 2000).

12 Christian Smith and Patricia Snell, *Souls in Transition: The Religious and Spiritual Lives of Emerging Adults* (Oxford: Oxford University Press, 2009), p. 284.

13 Smith and Snell, *Souls in Transition*, pp. 43–5, 78.

14 Robert M. Kurland and Harold I. Siegel, 'Attachment and Student Success During the Transition to College', *NACADA Journal* 33, no. 2 (2013), pp. 16–28.

15 Maxine Gallander Wintre and Mordechai Yaffe, 'First Year Students' Adjustment to University Life as a Function of Relationships with Parents', *Journal of Adolescent Research* 15, no. 1 (2000), pp. 9–37.

16 Jennifer L. Crissman-Ishler and Staci Schreiber, 'First-Year Female Students: Perceptions of Friendship', *Journal of Higher Education* 63 (2002), pp. 441–62.

17 See, for example, Paula Wilcox, Sandra Winn and Marylynn Fyvie-Gauld, 'It Was Nothing to Do with the University, It Was Just the People: The Role of Social Support in the First-Year Experience of Higher Education', *Studies in Higher Education* 30, no. 6 (2005), pp. 707–22.

18 Ulrich Beck and Elisabeth Beck-Gernsheim, *Individualization: Institutionalized Individualism and Its Social and Political Consequences* (London: Sage, 2001).

19 Tim Clydesdale, *The First Year Out: Understanding American Teens after High School* (Chicago, IL: University of Chicago Press, 2007), p. 27.

20 Parks, *The Critical Years*, p. 63.

21 See, for example, Balk, 'Grieving'; Cynthia L. Battle et al., 'Developing and Implementing a Bereavement Support Program for College Students', *Death Studies* 37, no. 4 (2013), pp. 362–82.

22 Balk, 'Grieving', p. 9.

23 Battle et al., 'Developing and Implementing', pp. 364, 373.

24 See, for example, Fiona Campbell et al., 'Factors that Influence Mental Health of University and College Students in the UK: A Systematic Review', *BMC Public Health* 22, no. 1 (20 September 2022), art. 1778; National Union of Students, 'Mental Health Policy', 2021, https://www.nus.org.uk/mental_health#2021, accessed 5.07.2024.

25 Richard Cooke et al., 'Measuring, Monitoring and Managing the Psychological Well-Being of First Year University Students', *British Journal of Guidance and Counselling* 34, no. 4 (2006), p. 506.

26 Christian Bröer and Broos Besseling, 'Sadness or Depression: Making Sense of Low Mood and the Medicalization of Everyday Life', *Social Science and Medicine* 183 (2017), pp. 28–36.

27 World Health Organization, *Growing Up Unequal: Gender and Socioeconomic Differences in Young People's Health and Well-Being* (Copenhagen: World Health Organization, 2016).

28 Amy Poots and Tony Cassidy, 'Academic Expectation, Self-Compassion, Psychological Capital, Social Support and Student Wellbeing', *International Journal of Educational Research* 99, no. 101506 (2020), p. 7.

29 Clydesdale, *The First Year Out*, p. 153.

30 Alexandrina Scarbrough and Carolyn Hicks, 'Student Gender and the Probability of Referral for Counselling in a College of Further Education', *British Journal of Guidance and Counselling* 26, no. 2 (2007), p. 235; see also Riet Bons-

Storm, *The Incredible Woman: Listening to Women's Silences in Pastoral Care and Counselling* (Nashville, TN: Abingdon Press, 1996).

31 Poots and Cassidy, 'Academic Expectation', p. 1.

32 Roberta Katz et al., *Gen Z, Explained: The Art of Living in a Digital Age* (Chicago, IL: University of Chicago Press, 2022), p. 5.

33 Kathleen J. Greider, *Much Madness Is Divinest Sense: Wisdom in Memoirs of Soul-Suffering* (Cleveland, OH: Pilgrim Press, 2007), p. 95.

34 Gill Valentine, Sarah L. Holloway and Mark Jayne, 'Contemporary Cultures of Abstinence and the Night-Time Economy: Muslim Attitudes Towards Alcohol and the Implications for Social Cohesion', *Environment and Planning A* 42, no. 1 (2010), p. 8.

35 In 2019, 26 per cent of 16- to 25-year-olds were teetotal: https://www.drinkaware.co.uk/research/alcohol-facts-and-data/alcohol-consumption-uk#howmanypeopledonotdrinkalcohol, accessed 1.06.2023.

36 Mathew Guest et al., *Christianity and the University Experience: Understanding Student Faith* (London: Bloomsbury, 2013), p. 122.

37 Guest et al., *Christianity and the University Experience*.

38 Johan Andersson, Joanna Sadgrove and Gill Valentine, 'Consuming Campus: Geographies of Encounter at a British University', *Social and Cultural Geography* 13, no. 5 (2012), p. 506.

39 Guest et al., *Christianity and the University Experience*, p. 124.

40 George H. Mead, *Mind, Self and Society* (Chicago, IL: University of Chicago Press, 1934).

41 Holdsworth, 'Don't You Think You're Missing Out', p. 511.

42 Guest et al., *Christianity and the University Experience*, p. 126.

43 Smith and Snell, *Souls in Transition*, p. 236.

44 Erikson, *Identity: Youth and Crisis*.

45 See James E. Côté, 'Emerging Adulthood as an Institutionalized Moratorium: Risks and Benefits to Identity Formation' in *Emerging Adults in America*, ed. Jeffrey Jensen Arnett and Jennifer L. Tanner (Washington, DC: American Psychological Association, 2006), pp. 85–116.

46 Norbert Elias, *The Civilising Process*, ed. Edmund Jephcott (Oxford: Blackwell, 1994).

47 Ruth H. Perrin, *Changing Shape: The Faith Lives of Millennials* (London: SCM Press, 2020).

48 Alison Webster, *You Are Mine: Reflections on Who We Are* (London: SPCK, 2009), p. 36.

49 Smith and Snell, *Souls in Transition*, p. 236, italics authors' own.

50 Trevor Gale and Stephen Parker, 'Navigating Change: A Typology of Student Transition in Higher Education', *Studies in Higher Education* 39, no. 5 (2014), p. 737.

51 Carol A. Taylor and Jean Harris-Evans, 'Reconceptualising Transition to Higher Education with Deleuze and Guattari', *Studies in Higher Education* 43, no. 7 (2018), pp. 1255, 1262.

52 Webster, *You Are Mine*, pp. 21–22, 25.

53 Parks, *The Critical Years*; Parks, *Big Questions, Worthy Dreams*, p. 63; James W. Fowler, *Stages of Faith: The Psychology of Human Development and the Quest for Meaning* (New York: Harper Collins, 1981), p. 179.

54 Clydesdale, *The First Year Out*.

55 Office for National Statistics, 'Coronavirus and the Impact on Students in Higher Education in England: September to December 2020: A Summary of Research into How the Coronavirus (COVID-19) Pandemic Has Affected Students in Higher Education in England During the Autumn Term of 2020' (December 2020), pp. 1, 3, 5–6.

56 Maria S. Plakhotnik et al., 'The Perceived Impact of COVID-19 on Student Well-Being and the Mediating Role of the University Support: Evidence from France, Germany, Russia, and the UK', *Frontiers in Psychology* 12, no. 642689 (July 2021), pp. 2, 9.

57 Jennifer A. Appleby et al., 'Impact of the COVID-19 Pandemic on the Experience and Mental Health of University Students Studying in Canada and the UK: A Cross-Sectional Study', *BMJ Open* (January 2022), pp. 1, 3–4, 10.

58 Plakhotnik et al., 'The Perceived Impact of COVID-19', p. 2.

59 Office for National Statistics, 'Coronavirus and the Impact on Students', p. 8.

60 Office for National Statistics, 'Coronavirus and the Impact on Students'.

61 Office for National Statistics, 'Coronavirus and the Impact on Students', p. 9.

62 Hegymegi et al., 'Developing a Tool'.

63 Wintre and Yaffe, 'First Year Students' Adjustment'; Schlossberg, 'The Challenge of Change'.

3

Crafting Home

In negotiating the ambivalent and traumatic transitions of leaving home, presented in the previous chapter, the women needed to feel secure and comfortable in their new environment, and adopted the common strategy of crafting home. Whether explicitly or subconsciously (and often a mixture of both), they wanted to craft home to survive and thrive at university. The first step was to feel safe, enabling a sense of well-being and belonging, which in turn firmed the foundations of the women's lives. This chapter demonstrates that crafting home created safety and ensured survival, but also became the foundation from which student life could be explored and enjoyed. This was an iterative process of fragmentation and formation, tentative although sometimes confident. For some students, patterns of becoming were relatively straightforward, while others wrestled with them as they were more complicated or perhaps took longer. This becoming involved the whole of the women's lives, identities and relationships; was influenced by their multiple spaces; and happened day-by-day, in times of both joy and crisis.

William Bridges recognizes the necessity of transitions for development, highlighting them as commonalities in people's lived experiences. He describes transition as the 'disorientation and reorientation that marks the turning points in the path of growth'. As such a turning point, university enabled the women 'to loosen the bonds of who we think we are so that we can go through a transition toward a new identity'.[1]

Briana recognized that making her physical surroundings feel like home was important to her, and achieved this relatively quickly. She described making her bedroom in student accommodation 'quite homely': 'I love my room … I've got my photos, and I've got my books there … so it feels quite like home from home.' For most students, however, making home was a tentative and creative *process*, neither automatic nor immediate, and sometimes feeling at home happened almost while they were busy getting on with life. Alexis found that travelling home to see family had unexpectedly felt 'weird', yet when arriving back at university she realized, 'Oh, I'm home now!' Courtney thought it was 'weird' that she was 'beginning to call [university] "home"'. Stephanie expected calling university 'home' to be 'weird', but was 'surprised by how quickly I've felt at home here'. Melissa at first 'didn't feel comfortable referring to [university] as "home"', but then she 'noticed a few times ... [when] I've started saying, "Oh, I'll go home now."' Vicky felt at home 'more than I was expecting to' even though it had initially felt 'weird'. For these women, crafting home was an unconscious process. It initially felt *weird* when they noticed it, but soon this weirdness dissipated.

Deepening friendships

The most significant method of crafting home employed by the women, taking dynamic energy and forethought, was the making and deepening of new friendships at university. Feeling relationally connected not only gave the women people to spend time with, but enabled them to feel safe, valued and a sense of belonging. Danielle described this beautifully: '[We] all do stuff together and it does make you feel right at home and really comfortable, and like you're somewhere you should be.' Parks provides insight into the 'faithing' process of creating a new 'psychological home' through tentative 'probing commitment'[2] in friendships. She writes,

> Young adulthood is nurtured into being most powerfully by the availability of a community that poses an alternative to an earlier assumed knowing, vividly embodies the potential of the emerging self, and offers the promise of a new network of belonging.[3]

At least at first, this network is often within an 'ideologically compatible social group' as the young adult 'seeks alliances with those who share her stance'.[4] Similarly, Webster argues that safety is often found with 'those whom we assume to be like us'.[5] Nicole only wanted to spend time with people who were like her, with shared implicit and explicit assumptions, as a means of keeping herself safe. Her body language shrank as she used the visceral image of feeling 'bulldozed' by people who disagreed with her, demonstrating her feelings of vulnerability. This was an intentional search for familiarity as a means of protecting herself, partly, she recognized, due to having had a difficult gap year. Yet Parks argues that the search for a 'tribe' can result in a narrowing of vision, and even 'a diminished concern for others'[6] as young adults are vulnerable to practices of cynicism and exclusion. Nicole was neither stubborn nor unintelligent, nor did she lack reflection or perception.

Instead, she intentionally sought to keep herself safe from unhappiness, chaos and loneliness.

Making new friends was the most important pastime for the first-year students. Holdsworth argues that most students are consciously aware of 'fitting in', and are reflexive in how they respond to being surrounded by new people.[7] Similarly, Sonya Sharma and Guest suggest that 'fitting in is not something that students go about unconsciously'.[8] While many women found it difficult because of shyness or avoiding drinking alcohol, all were actively considering the most effective means of meeting people in their new environment. For many students this involved careful planning and negotiation, influencing decisions about which events and activities to join, as the previous chapter argued when discussing loneliness. Moreover, several students were wary about 'cliques' from which they felt excluded, or 'fickle' relationships that did not deepen.

While most women recognized that making new friends was 'scary' and made them feel vulnerable, they discussed the positives of being 'forced' to 'go out of my comfort zone and meet new people', because you 'have to ... do more [and] go out'. In turn, they recognized that this resulted in them being more 'confident' and having a range of experiences that they would not otherwise have participated in. The process was made easier because students recognized that they were, as Sarah said, 'all in it together'. Gill Valentine argues that '"family", defined in the broadest sense, still remains a form of relationship that most people strive to create for themselves and are still attached to'.[9] This may be even more evident among those in an unfamiliar environment, since a chosen-family contributes to the building of a psychological home. Courtney described meeting 'a nice group of girls on my course ... I see them around [and] we're constantly spending time with each other, it ... forces you to get closer.'

In their first year, crafting home involved meeting people and making new friends. The closest first-year friends became second-year housemates. The second year saw a deepening in relationships and a focus on nurturing a chosen-family. In his theory of faith development, James W. Fowler argues that, as students 'substitute one family group for another', identity development and change in outlook become difficult.[10] However, the women in this book found that such close-knit chosen-families were places of exploration and becoming, as well as safety. In her first year, Stephanie was determined to meet a range of people sharing her different interests. She joined at least eight different student societies, ranging from dance to Dr Who to Classics. In her second year she had stopped attending most of these societies because her friendship group had deepened. She said, 'Last year I was very worried about making friends ... [now] instead of going to societies I'll just go and sit on [Alexis and Melissa's] sofa.' She reflected that in her interview, she spoke a lot about her friends, more than about other things.

As with Nicole and Courtney, alliances were formed according to the ideological compatibility of friends, especially with other women and/or Christians. Alexis, Melissa and Stephanie's friendship was a prime example, with all three women stating that they had grown in confidence and happiness because of the solid base it provided. Similarly, Amber and Briana shared a house in their second year, together with other women from their church, which 'definitely' felt 'like family'. Amber said, 'My friendships have become better and deeper in the last year, I think this is just because I spend every day with people!' Caitlin's best friends were those that shared her political allegiance or her interest in religion. These friendships had developed because 'as much of a cliché as it is, we want to make the world a better place, and it's ... brought us together.' Meeting these friends helped Caitlin feel 'like it was the place I was supposed to be in ... it was like things started clicking.' Despite early resistance to friendship cliques, these women were orchestrating their own circles consisting of those with whom they felt safe and at home. Ashley was the only student who considered it important to live with a mixed-gender and mixed-faith group, 'having a house where it's not another little bubble'.

Finding their living environment 'comfortable', 'homely' and 'relaxed' (or not) were significant factors in how *at home* the women felt, and in how they went about crafting home. Interestingly, these three words were also used to describe the churches that the women were happiest in, and this link between friendships, home, church and faith is discussed further in Chapter 5. Katz and colleagues find that the word *fam* epitomizes the sense of belonging found in Gen Z relationships with close friends 'in whom you confide and trust, and around whom you can be your most authentic self'. They track the practice of referring to 'families of choice' since the growth of LGBTQIA+ and feminist communities in the 1950s, communities 'united by strong emotional bonds – similar to kinship – but formed on the basis of social, rather than biological, connection'. Similar to these historic groupings, 'where Gen Zers feel an affinity, they find out who they are; when they know who they are, they can navigate social life and relationships with greater confidence.' However, while their research found that 'Gen Zers easily combine online and offline belonging',[11] social media and online communication was referred to surprisingly little by the women in this book, perhaps due to the immediate need to make new friends 'IRL' at university.

In testing means of being true to themselves in their new environment, the women regularly expressed their identity in terms of their relationships. The safety that these new 'families' provided became apparent as the women narrated feeling more relaxed and, as Alexis said, 'a lot more able to, just, be myself'. Vicky said, 'Everything that people say about uni being a place where everyone's just their self and everyone lets them be their self is true.' Danielle reflected with her flatmates, 'It just felt like we could say anything to each other and no one cares ... we end up laughing so much, it's great, it is genuinely like a little family, really comfy.' Feeling supported by her friends, Courtney said, was 'helping me feel more at home', since she had 'people I can feel comfortable around ... to talk to if something does go wrong.'

Yet as new friendships developed, the women were also able to reconstruct their identities, trying out what Herminia Ibarra calls 'provisional selves'.[12] This resonates with Slee, who argues that women 'try out' their transitioning selves with 'like-minded others'.[13] Stephanie reflected that since 'I'm in a different place, I'm with different people, [then] some of them is going to rub off on me.' She continued,

> I was talking to someone, um, cos I've always thought of myself as quite nervous when talking to new people, and she thought, she said she thought I was really outgoing cos I could talk to people, and I was like, 'How did that happen?!' [laughs].

Stephanie was surprised to be perceived as 'confident' by others, but then was able to realize and accept that confidence, owning it for herself. I interviewed Taylor for a second time as a doctoral student, seven years after her initial interview. She reflected upon how her chosen-family influenced her time at university, making her a 'different person'; but more than this, it also increased her confidence to make new friends going forward:

> Because of them ... I'm a lot more confident now... [When you] feel like a normal functioning person who has friends ... you'll have less fuel for the shyness .... Had I not met those people, I don't know how my life would have turned out, and I think I feel more at home [now] because ... of the friendships I made at university.

Anne Phillips refers to mirroring as the process whereby girls 'needed to see an image of themselves reflected back in or by another'.[14] Similarly, Fowler argues that at adolescence, there is a need to have reflected back 'the new feelings, insights, anxieties and commitments that are forming and seeking expression'.[15] Abigail discussed finding ways to be creatively different 'in different situations' due to spending her childhood abroad. She recognized having:

> a lot of parts of me scattered around, so I've got friends in all different countries ... it means I share [different] stories with them ... and perhaps [some] people don't necessarily understand it as easily as they might.

The stories that she told depended on how easily her new friends understood her history and the 'different' and 'scattered' parts of her identities. Due to having had practice and support at this while growing up, Abigail was able to feel at home with different people in different places.

Taylor's metaphor of 'fuel' as the inner-narratives and resources that she accumulated is vivid. If a woman's fuel is primarily made up of negativity, loneliness or trauma, then she may find herself under-resourced. However, if her fuel consists of safe, loving relationships, then the resulting confidence and resilience enable her to craft her psychological home. The women were all working towards this home as new friendships deepened.

Safety in the middle

For Parks, times of 'incubation', 'contemplative pause' or 'lingering' are integral to processes of 'faithing' and identity work.[16] The women found safety in such moments of pause, allowing them to retreat from immediate pressures, and reflect upon their situation 'in the middle'. These pauses took four different forms: use of a 'lockbox'; ambiguity at adulthood; feeling positively in-between; and cognitive dissonance. Each of these strategies contributed to the women feeling psychologically safe amid their traumatic transitions and the extent to which they felt at home, and all the women demonstrated at least one of these four. I take each of them in turn.

First, many of the women described placing parts of themselves – particularly their faith or gender – into an 'identity lockbox', as found among first-year students by Clydesdale: 'Teens can preserve certain identities ... by removing them from interaction and resisting efforts to alter them'.[17] Separating significant identities lessened the impact of the traumatic transitions. Women who kept their religious beliefs safely away from other aspects of their lives described their faith as 'separate from my views', 'a personal thing' or something they 'never really thought about'. They stated that their faith played no role in decision-making, and that their daily life did not impact their religious views – or vice versa. Mary did not 'see any reason' for her view of God to change at university, and Taylor said that she had not 'thought about it enough'.

Placing their gendered identities aside was more common. For many women, their gender was 'unexamined' and thus, John Hull writes, 'does not attract our attention as being debatable'.[18] In their first year at university, both Olivia and Ashley recognized that gender and feminism were important and 'massive', but considered it 'abstract, and not really to do with me', and they were 'not really part of it'. Many women said that gender did not make 'a huge impact on my life' and that they did not reflect upon their gendered selves. Often questions on gender appeared to baffle the women. Mary was 'not really too sure why, I don't really think about it'. The safety of the lockbox allowed the women to explore different identities *in turn* before beginning to integrate them, and it was employed as long as it was useful. Alexis said, 'I've thought about my faith, but I haven't really thought about my gender.'

Second, many women communicated ambiguity about adulthood, as something distant or undesirable. Arnett writes that traditional markers of maturity are seen by emerging adults 'not as achievements to be pursued but as perils to be avoided'. Instead, emerging adults seek independence, spontaneity and 'wide-open possibilities'.[19] This ambiguity was seen in the students viewing themselves as 'girls' rather than 'women'. The title of *girl* was claimed by Briana because 'it's nice to be young' and because 'I don't feel old enough' to be a woman. She saw the title of *woman* as negative, being 'very, kind of, grown up and, like [pause] adult'. Courtney said, 'It sounds older, I don't feel that old.' These responses are of course connected with how the women understood their gendered selves, discussed further in Chapter 6.

Ambiguity at maturing was also expressed by women who did not want to think about their futures or post-university life. Briana discussed this in both her first and second year, although in the second year she thought it was slowly changing: 'I've always hated the idea of growing up, still, I'm getting over that now, but I still don't like the idea that I'm an adult.' Melissa was worried about what might be next for her, getting visibly upset in the interview. It was 'all tied up in being scared about the future … I want a future I can plan, and I don't have that.' Alexis contrasted her student life with the life of 'some general really grown-up person'. While laughing, Vicky said, 'I don't feel like I should be in charge of myself.' In her first year, Samantha feared having 'loads of decisions to make' and said, 'I'm trying not to think about them cos they're really scary.' A year later, she reflected, 'I'm not really sure if I'll ever feel [pause] like an adult.' This fear expressed by the women was real, and so by delaying adulthood they could stay safe, for now at least.

Third, the women expressed a sense of pause as positive, being in liminal space, and delegating decisions and delaying development for their future selves. This delay was understood either as a gap in which to abide for a short time; as being between childhood and adulthood; or as another step in life's progression. Megan focused on 'living life each day' and taking each moment 'in the circumstances'. In her second year, Courtney remembered using this approach when she first arrived: 'let[ting] everything kind of slide' because 'everything is so new' and she could 'relax'. Some women still believed 'in the same way as I did before' or lived 'exactly the same' as they would anywhere, feeling that university had not 'changed me that much'. While Clydesdale writes that this pausing 'diminishes teens' willingness to connect their daily lives to deeper values or larger purposes, or to consider those values and purposes thoughtfully',[20] this was seen as a positive strategy for the women.

One expression of this strategy involved feeling in the 'middle', in 'between' or in 'limbo'. This included not relinquishing childhood selves, despite recognizing that girlhood was 'very young' or even 'childish', while use of the word 'yet' suggested that this letting go would eventually come. It also included feeling suspended between the familial home and the future, or, as Stephanie said, 'between being, sort of, kids and adults'. Taylor similarly described herself as neither 'a little child' nor 'someone with an established life, job and family'. This suspension could feel discombobulating, but the women utilized it to their advantage, as a place without unnecessary responsibility or commitment. The students were in liminal time, at a threshold whereby normalcy could be redefined. Richard Rohr argues that such liminal space is 'sacred': 'the old world is left behind, but we're not yet sure of the new one ... Get there often and stay as long as you can.'[21]

The sense of being in-between allowed a pause in reflection while recognizing that growth was happening subconsciously, even if it could not quite be articulated. Megan thought that her faith and her degree subject would integrate later on, 'but I haven't given that so much thought ... that might come into it later.' Amber said, 'I think I'll change more, but I don't know how', reflecting that university was 'not the final shaping stage, but one of the last ones before I become an adult'. Similarly, Abigail reflected, 'I might realize in a few months' time that, "Gosh I've changed a lot", but I think at the moment I'm right in the middle of it, so I haven't noticed.' Many women expected university to prepare them for whatever was next, even if they could not explain how. Lauren described university as a 'platform ... so that I can go on and do things', while Ashley thought of it as a place to 'build foundations ... that will carry us through the rest of our lives'. To safeguard their vulnerabilities, many women were vague about their development, or regarded growth as something for future consideration. They did not want to leave behind familiar identities or ways of knowing that had served them well until now, but recognized that this would need to happen sometime.

Finally, the women held contradictory beliefs simultaneously, unaware of this cognitive dissonance, and often using mental blocks to avoid confronting these inconsistencies. Hull argues that 'thought-stopping' techniques are a common response to identity transitions as individuals attempt to learn less.[22] Again, the most common examples included protection of gender and faith as key identities. Haley disliked her male friends objectifying women, but shifted her stance to include women who do the 'same thing about men', downplaying sexism among her peers. Three women who attended churches that forbade women's leadership shared conflicted thoughts about it, denouncing the lack of 'equality' while also saying 'it doesn't really matter to me'. Haley said, 'I still don't agree with it and, I dunno, it wasn't something that I was really too fussed about.' Less often, students who attended churches where leadership positions were open to women were similarly contradictory. For example, even though Nicole's priest was 'very good and her sermons are always interesting', Nicole would still 'generally prefer a male preacher'.

Despite experiencing difficult transitions, the women found ways to cope and establish themselves at university through compartmentalizing different aspects of their identity, taking time before embracing adult responsibilities, appreciating their transitional state, and maintaining multiple perspectives even when these appeared to conflict. These creative strategies contributed to their ability to craft home at university.

Inner-dependence

Mary F. Belenky and her colleagues document a significant transformation among women, a shift from external dependence to internal authority. These women developed trust in their personal wisdom; growing 'strength, optimism and self-value'; and a concept of truth as inherently personal and intuitive. Crucially, these women rejected externally imposed answers and recognized this change as genuine development. Their individual voices were strengthened without disconnecting them from others, suggesting a balance between relationship and newfound autonomy.[23] Parks describes 'inner-dependence' as a developmental milestone where emerging adults recognize 'the Spirit within', including themselves 'within the arena of authority'. They value their own authority alongside external sources; have self-compassion; and acknowledge their involvement in 'composing truth and choice'. This emerging inner-dependence is initially 'healthy, vital, and full of promise, yet vulnerable', and requires further maturation before becoming firmly established.[24]

For the women in this book, the independence that came with meeting their own basic daily needs gave them a confidence that they saw as a necessary step in becoming 'grown up'. Many demonstrated a shift in knowing and meaning-making as they began to claim their own experience as valid. Inner-dependent women were better equipped to critically explore their new environment and to negotiate their daily lives with confidence and openness, without relying on others. For most of the women, this began with the excitement of a newfound 'independence', 'freedom' or 'autonomy' at university. Even students who described traumatic aspects of their transitions were enthusiastic at the opportunity to make their own decisions and trust their own experiences as they made home. Stephanie was looking forward to becoming 'more independent' and 'confident in my ability to actually live ... by myself.' Other women already felt independent. Kimberly was glad that at university, 'You learn to, sort of, live by yourself ... [to] manage yourself and your own time and what you do.' For Melissa, university meant 'standing on your own two feet', while Courtney said, 'I have that freedom, no one telling you what you can and cannot do ... it's kind of nice to take responsibility.'

The women were realizing that just as they were learning from others, so too they had something unique to offer, and could trust their own spirited reasoning. They celebrated a noticeable shift inward of what Fowler terms the 'locus of authority'.[25] Amber recognized that at university she was 'more sure in my decisions without having to check them with other people', while Alexis was 'a lot more able to do things by myself and not ask people beforehand, just try and figure things out [myself].' For Haley, the new 'freedom that I've got ... allowed me' to be 'more myself' and 'have my own opinions' without parental influence. Taylor noticed that instead of pretending to be someone different around other people, 'I'll just do me', trusting her own sense of self. For some, their new self-assurance meant that they were more open about their faith, 'just tell[ing] people straight away' about being Christian. These women were beginning to carve out their unique, creative, resilient and hopeful 'own way' – as Alexis and Haley described it – in which to explore both their inner and outward lives from a secure base.

The 11 students who had undertaken some form of gap experience demonstrated more inner-dependence in their first year than other students. Gap experiences involved either taking a year out of, or an extra year in, education, or spending at least a month outside of the family home. As well as in further education, gap experiences were spent in various contexts, including: travelling abroad, volunteering in Christian contexts, paid employment, living with friends, and beginning but dropping out of another university. Gap experiences were undertaken by students of all classes and for a variety of reasons, and were not limited to women from the middle classes. These women had already left home, physically or emotionally, before university, and so even the women whose gap experiences were for 'negative' reasons (like dropping out of university or having to re-sit exams) had begun the work of internalizing authority prior to starting university. They described becoming more self-aware, 'really sure who I was' and 'more confident with myself' during their gap experience, and being able 'to carry that with me to uni'. Danielle said, 'I learnt a lot about myself', which positively influenced her behaviour at university. Haley described 'finding myself' and having experiences that 'opened my eyes' which made starting university easier than 'if I hadn't had that year'. Ashley felt that her gap experience gave her time to 'think' and 'learn about what I liked', making her university transitions 'easier than [for] other people' because she was better 'able to get used to [new] situations', and without which she 'would have struggled' when starting university. Stephanie 'made friends with people and it made me realize that ... [at university] there are going to be people who like you for who you are'. Nicole 'definitely knew' how to survive university because 'I've sort of done the trial and now this is the real thing [laughs]'. Lauren's gap experience had involved 'ongoing growth' so she had 'come to a bit more of a, yeah, a more grounded position'. Abigail had 'grown out of' missing her parents, becoming more independent during her gap experience.

Embracing difference

While students gravitated towards friends with shared interests and backgrounds, they also understood that meaningful community-building required engaging with individuals *different* from themselves, both friends and strangers, and some embraced this. The more students felt at home, the more they felt able to engage with others. This activity, while not safe, fostered students' self-discovery and worldview development, helping them create meaning and faith amid the greater freedom and diversity they encountered at university compared to their previous settings.

Parks argues that higher education has a distinct role in broadening the experiences of students through facilitating encounters with difference. She advocates for educators enabling 'conscious conflict' among students, ensuring that 'one is not left alone with it, overwhelmed by it, or otherwise has to defend against it', but that diversity is held in respectful and relational community.[26] For the women, encounters with difference were sometimes challenging or uncomfortable, and it was this sense of disruption that influenced their formation at university. Samantha was learning that it was 'OK to disagree with people', something that was new for her. Haley said, 'Go out and meet as many people as you can, it makes you a better person ... I'm exposed to different people and different views and stuff, I think that influences me.' For Lauren, 'Finding out new things is really shaping how I see the world and what I wanna do ... Yeah, reading, and chatting to people and, um, and engaging with things.' In Briana's second year, she reflected that, 'I've definitely changed ... I understand more about other people ... I have a bit more of an awareness of people who are more different than me.'

University provided an important contrast for Christian students who had narrow school experiences.[27] Several women reflected that university enabled them to encounter different perspectives daily, contrasted with the 'bubble' of their schools. Sarah enjoyed volunteering in her local community, meeting people from outside the university. In her second year, she thought the best thing about university was 'meeting such a diverse range of people and expanding my worldview ... learning from them and their experiences.'

Danielle, in particular, experienced personal growth through expanding her social circle beyond people 'similar to myself'. Before university, she was 'just hanging around with the same types of people' in a homogeneous social environment. At university, she discovered the value of 'building relationships with new types of people' in a 'diverse place'. This exposure to difference made her 'a lot more comfortable' with herself. She was now actively seeking out diversity, saying, 'I'll go and sit with different people all the time', and appreciated being 'surrounded with people who like different stuff'. She recognized university as a force that pushed her outside her comfort zone by requiring her to 'get to know people that aren't the same as you'. She had developed a more open worldview and greater self-confidence through these diverse interactions. She also recognized a long-term benefit, reflecting that the ability to relate to different people 'helps you later on in life', suggesting that she saw embracing difference as an important new skill, rather than being confined to her university experience.

Some women were keen not merely to *meet* different people, they wanted *friends* who believed differently too, and they enjoyed discussing their different opinions. Vicky was glad to have friends who 'don't have the same worldview on many things'. Stephanie noticed that being 'surrounded by people who are interested and informed' influenced her own growth. She watched coverage of a national election with friends holding a range of political opinions:

> We could ... debate things rather than it just turning into a 'you're wrong, you're wrong, you're evil' ... it was just more, you know, 'I acknowledge you have a point, I might not agree with it, but, and here are some reasons why.'

Both Vicky and Stephanie said that these close encounters with difference influenced their own opinions and made them more confident in their beliefs.

Similarly, Belenky and her colleagues find embracing difference to be significant for women in their first year at university. They argue,

> These conversations occur with special frequency whenever women encounter people who hold and practice beliefs that seem exotic, intriguing, bizarre, alien ... If one can discover the experiential logic behind these ideas, the ideas become less strange and the owners of the ideas cease to be strangers. The world becomes warmer and more orderly.[28]

They name embracing difference 'connected knowing', whereby empathetic learning takes place in relationship. For the women in this book, embracing difference served as both a catalyst for self-discovery, and a framework for interpreting their surroundings. By engaging with different perspectives at university, they simultaneously explored their own identities and developed more nuanced understandings of the world.

Confident awakening

Students in their second year discussed an increased confidence in comparison with their first-year selves, and demonstrated an awakening in their relationship with the world and its structures. The women recognized that they had become more 'comfortable', 'confident', 'settled', 'grown', 'aware', 'happier', in 'control', 'responsible', 'mature', 'assertive', 'likely to speak up', 'stronger', 'together', 'less anxious' and concerned with 'the meaning of things ... [and] the world'. These words are extraordinary when compared with the women's negative feelings when they first arrived at university, described in the introduction to Chapter 2. Here are a few examples expanding on this list:

I feel really settled and like I have a place here. (Abigail)

[I'm] more confident and secure in who I am, and more supported by friends I have made. (Amber)

[This year feels] a world apart! I've really put down roots here. A year ago, I fully intended on moving back [home] when I graduated but now I plan on staying! I'm more confident and far happier in my environment. (Kimberly)

Going into second year, everything feels a lot more comfortable, and you are in control a lot more than before as you have more confidence. (Mary)

[I'm] so much more comfortable and confident! I have a great group of friends, and I feel at home ... I have more confidence to just go for it! (Sarah)

These students were increasingly feeling at home with themselves, with one another, with their futures, and in the wider world. Together they were able, as Parks writes, 'to come to a self-aware and responsible knowing, to their own self-conscious engagement in the imagination – the creation – of a world.'[29] Two students who had been unsure of their own development in their first year, a year later summarized changes that they had not anticipated. University had changed Kimberly 'far more than I expected ... and in different ways than I thought it would', and Taylor was 'a different person than I was when I started university'.

Many examples of demonstrating their newfound voice in their second year were through claiming greater responsibility for, and more confidence in, their studies. Alexis had become 'more confident in seminars and stuff as well, like, I'm much more likely to speak up.' In her first year, Stephanie feared that she 'wasn't going to be very good at [studying]', but since she 'did quite well in my exams' and passed her coursework, in her second year she felt 'much more confident at, sort of, speaking in front of people and working in groups'. She said, 'I'm really enjoying what I'm doing and I'm doing quite well.' Through engaging with her course, Ashley was 'learning a new way to, sort of, approach looking at other people ... and just engaging in the world in a different way.' She was enjoying working hard and 'being challenged'. Part of this was 'being surrounded by people who think differently, and being taught by my teachers to think in a different way'. Exploratory words here – including 'learning', 'new', 'looking', 'engaging', 'different' and 'challenged' – reveal an unfolding of Ashley's sense of self and the world, and her openness to this happening. Demonstrating her innerdependence, she was learning to 'not just accept everything that I'm told'.

Other students demonstrated 'post-traumatic growth'.[30] Hull writes that shocking or dissonant experiences can be learning situations, stimulating new discoveries and 'a realignment of the whole system'.[31] Karen O'Donnell argues that women who experience reproductive trauma undergo a 'post-traumatic remaking' of the self, where there can be no going back to the pre-traumatized state.[32] In particular, Samantha spoke about having grown, perhaps due to – rather than despite – the traumatic experiences in her first year. Leaving home had been a turning point in her development and enabled reflection on her past. She could not 'have got much older staying at home', implying that her growth would have been stunted had she remained with her parents. In contrast, at university she had 'grown up': it had 'changed me' and she had 'developed my own thought a lot more'. Colley argues that women's transitions often follow 'unending and fragmented' processes of closures and openings, with one instance influencing the next as 'zigzag or spiral movements'.[33] Samantha's becoming was not a linear process of development but rather a series of such openings and closures that impacted upon one another. It included her deteriorating then improving mental health, leaving a problematic family home, getting into a serious romantic relationship, and living with challenging new flatmates.

Interdependence and changing relationships

Moving from first to second year, the women's understanding of themselves in relation to others shifted from increased inner-dependence to the recognition that they were not fully independent, nor did they aspire to be. This section explores intentional changes in the women's relationships with parents and families, friends from home, housemates and new friends, and romantic partners. It highlights the women who were increasingly aware of their need for others. It closes by discussing the women's recognition of their interdependence as demonstrated in their chosen-family friendships. Such changes in relationships contributed to growth in the women's confidence, and their crafting of home at university.

Parks identifies a key tension for emerging adults between independence and relationship. Integrating these requires recognizing one's agency in self-formation, and making deliberate choices about commitments. While Western culture has overvalued independence at the expense of 'affectional relation with others', interdependence allows one to hold truth 'as object in dialogue with others' while listening 'with new attention'. Young adult communities evolve from being 'expansive, experimental and tentative' to becoming 'ideologically compatible' groups that support 'a particular form of meaning'. Though these mature communities may maintain diversity in some aspects, they still generally 'hold similar political, religious, and philosophical views'.[34] Interdependence and such intentional change vary from Fowler's stage 4 faith (and beyond) in which the locus of authority is only internal.[35] Instead, authority is seen as shared, and an increased confidence develops alongside a greater appreciation of others.

While the women all remained in contact with their families in their second year, they now rang home less often and were less reliant on their parents for practical support. Van der Kolk describes changing attitudes towards the family home following experiences of trauma. In some cases, he sees that the traumatized individual becomes unable 'to go home again in any meaningful way'[36] due to irrevocable identity shifts. In their second year, some of the women were able to consider the increased distance from their family with increased insight and empathy. Kimberly saw that her father 'struggles with the fact I've grown up' and Megan's family were 'getting used to the fact that I am more independent'. Courtney noticed a link between her own growth in confidence and her ability to be more vulnerable with her parents. She no longer needed to prove herself, making it easier to ask for their support. Ashley felt some responsibility for her divorced parents, worrying about them being lonely and lacking support. She felt a growing appreciation of her parents, recognizing that, 'I'm here living my passions ... I really just hope for them ... that they have chances to, like, live their dream, beyond being parents.'

Students also renegotiated friendships from home. Ashley described a once close-knit group of Christian friends that were no longer in touch, since 'We didn't need it any more ... it's kind of like I've outgrown them.' Ashley recognized that she *needed* different relationships at different points in her development. Similarly, Kimberly had 'drifted' from friends with 'different uni experiences' which seemed incompatible. Danielle had recently parted ways with some friends, realizing 'they are not the kinds of people I want to surround myself with'. These three students recognized that as they were changing, their priorities in their friendships were also different, and saw this as a positive aspect of their maturing.

There were also some intentional changes in the women's romantic relationships. Alexis and Vicky had ended relationships in their first year and had new boyfriends in their second year. Both were happier and reflected positively on the former relationships ending. Alexis felt 'much more comfortable' with her new boyfriend because they 'share a lot more values'. Vicky's previous boyfriend had not shared her passion for social justice: 'He just didn't really have an opinion on those kinds of issues, and that became quite difficult.' In comparison, her new partner 'has an opinion and will challenge mine, which is perhaps one of the most important things'.

These women demonstrated inner-dependence not as independence from others, but as interdependence with healthy boundaries. They relied confidently on family, friends and partners for support, and viewed relationships as influences rather than defining elements, demonstrating a significant shift from defining themselves *as* their relationships. Instead, these women preserved their distinct identities while acknowledging the importance of their connections to others, showing a more mature integration of Parks's 'two great yearnings'.

Olivia was the only woman to explicitly articulate her need for others in her first year, differentiating between 'independent living' and 'emotional independence'. She was content looking after herself in the former, but in 'emotional' decisions she was sure to involve her parents. She also saw complete independence as detrimental to her relationship with God, on whom she wanted to depend. More often, the reaction against total independence came in the second year. Kimberley had 'confidence in my own actions ... with a good network to support me'. Megan was 'very independent ... but at the same time I still like to ask for guidance'. Similarly, Abigail thought, 'I'm sometimes too much of an independent person as I don't always rely on other people and get help from them when I should.' Sarah reflected on being more interdependent than in her first year:

> I am better at making my own decisions, but I rely on my friends to help me through anything major. This is different from when I first arrived ... I didn't know people well enough at uni to talk to them ...

Being totally independent emotionally from people around you probably isn't healthy.

Many women were intentional about both creating and deepening chosen-familial relationships with friends or housemates. Three close friends, Alexis, Melissa and Stephanie, had shared their everyday seemingly unimportant decisions as well as their biggest challenges, and the confidence they gained through feeling known and understood enabled them to grow in self-knowledge and maturity. I have written in more detail about their interdependent friendship elsewhere, where I argue that for them,

> 'Home' was found in relationship: with one another and the other members of their [Christian] student society; through growth in their relationship with God; and through encounters with difference. This home in turn resourced the women in negotiating their multiple overwhelmings.[37]

Alexis, Melissa and Stephanie's friendship is explored in Chapter 6, detailing the importance of gender.

Alexandra, an international student unable to move to the UK at the start of her degree due to the Covid-19 pandemic, recognized that her friends at home provided a depth of emotional support that her family did not. Her conservative mother had been 'actually attacking my friends and my circle' due to their different beliefs, particularly about sexuality. In comparison to her mother, who 'doesn't see me, yeah, she sees who she wants to see', her friends 'see me, like, they know me before I know me'. She 'could be vulnerable and I could be my true self with them'. She considered these friends as 'family':

> Within a family you have the older ones who help the younger ones who bring the fun ... The fact that you could call out people, not in a bad way, but in a way to take responsibility and also acknowledge when something mightn't be going too right ... Yeah, I think that is what makes us a family.

Alexandra contrasted her mother's conditional love with her chosen-family's authentic acceptance. Within her chosen-family, she valued the safe space for vulnerability, mutual accountability and care, and honest communication. She was open to critique within the safety of her new family, unlike the hurtful criticism that she received from her mother.

Being able to choose the friends with whom the women lived was one of the most substantial differences between their first and second year, and generally relationships with (chosen) second-year housemates were significantly more positive than with (assigned) first-year flatmates. Liz Kenyon writes that the creation of home is dependent on such 'significant others', and university friends often take on 'new importance' and develop 'a new level of intimacy' upon living together.[38] Living with true friends was a world away from what Courtney described as the 'forced closeness' she experienced in the previous year. For Abigail, this had 'a huge impact on how settled I feel', and Sarah felt that 'the house feels much more like a home … going back to a house of people you like makes a big difference.' Amber said, 'The people I live with feel more like family than friends … [so] this year feels more like home.' Many women spent more time with housemates than they had done the previous year, including Megan who cooked Sunday lunch each week, fostering an intentional sense of homeliness and fellowship in the friends' shared becoming. Van der Kolk explains the importance of community during traumatic periods, whereby in relationship a person can become someone new, 'giv[ing] us the power to change ourselves and others by communicating our experiences, helping us to define what we know and finding a common sense of meaning.'[39]

The students mentioned here underwent an intentional narrowing of relationships as they became closer to some friends, chose suitable romantic partners, and attempted mature connections with their parents. This involved an intentional focusing of energy and commitment, where safety and home were crafted in depth and rather than disposability or separation.

Conclusion

Chapter 3 has demonstrated how the women were engaged in the processes of crafting a home in which they could thrive. Despite the often traumatic nature of university, the women were able to create safety, partly though chosen-families also experiencing the transient liminality of student life. Making deep friendships facilitated exploration as the women embraced encounters with difference and grew in their own inner-dependence. In their second year, many women recognized their interdependence, and awakened into confident awareness of themselves and the world around them. The movement between safety, exploration and growth broadened the space in which identity work and the crafting of home took place to include a more holistic worldview and a wider diversity of 'others'. The women were beginning to understand their varied experiences with a new coherence, resulting in renewed confidence, a more authoritative voice, and an openness to difference. Their becoming – involving the zigzagging between the hesitant thoughts and deep fears in Chapter 2, and their growth in confidence and trust in their own voice in this chapter – was remarkable.

Notes

1 William Bridges, *Transitions: Making Sense of Life's Changes* (Reading, MA: Perseus Books, 1980), pp. 5, 98.
2 Sharon Parks, *The Critical Years: The Young Adult Search for a Faith to Live By* (New York: Harper & Row, 1986), pp. 61–3, 82.
3 Parks, *The Critical Years*, p. 89.
4 Parks, *The Critical Years*, pp. 89, 66, 92.
5 Alison Webster, *You Are Mine: Reflections on Who We Are* (London: SPCK, 2009), pp. 21–2.
6 Parks, *The Critical Years*, p. 68.
7 Clare Holdsworth, 'Don't You Think You're Missing Out, Living at Home? Student Experiences and Residential Transitions', *Sociological Review* 54, no. 3 (2006), pp. 515, 506–7.
8 Sonya Sharma and Mathew Guest, 'Navigating Religion Between University and Home: Christian Students' Experiences in English Universities', *Social and Cultural Geography* 14, no. 1 (2013), p. 73.
9 Gill Valentine, 'The Ties that Bind: Towards Geographies of Intimacy', *Geography Compass* 26 (2008), p. 2102.
10 James W. Fowler, *Stages of Faith: The Psychology of Human Development and the Quest for Meaning* (New York: Harper Collins, 1981), p. 178.
11 Roberta Katz et al., *Gen Z, Explained: The Art of Living in a Digital Age* (Chicago, IL: University of Chicago Press, 2022), pp. 91–2, 94, 99.
12 Herminia Ibarra, 'Provisional Selves: Experimenting with Image and Identity in Professional Adaptation', *Administrative Science Quarterly* 44, no. 4 (1999), pp. 764–91.
13 Nicola Slee, *Women's Faith Development: Patterns and Processes* (Aldershot: Ashgate, 2004), p. 111.
14 Anne Phillips, *The Faith of Girls: Children's Spirituality and Transition to Adulthood* (Farnham: Ashgate, 2011), p. 156.
15 Fowler, *Stages of Faith*, p. 151.
16 Sharon Parks, *Big Questions, Worthy Dreams: Mentoring Young Adults in Their Search for Meaning, Purpose, and Faith* (San Francisco, CA: Jossey-Bass, 2000), pp. 147–8.
17 Tim Clydesdale, *The First Year Out: Understanding American Teens after High School* (Chicago, IL: University of Chicago Press, 2007), p. 60.
18 John Hull, *What Prevents Christian Adults from Learning?* (London: SCM Press, 1985), p. 54.
19 Jeffrey Jensen Arnett, *Emerging Adulthood: The Winding Road from the Late Teens Through the Twenties* (Oxford: Oxford University Press, 2004), p. 6.
20 Clydesdale, *The First Year Out*, p. 40.

21 Richard Rohr, *Everything Belongs: The Gift of Contemplative Prayer* (New York: Crossroad Publishing Company, 2003), p. 155.

22 Hull, *What Prevents?*, p. 123.

23 Mary F. Belenky et al., *Women's Ways of Knowing: The Development of Self, Voice and Mind*, 10th Anniversary ed. (New York: Basic Books, 1986), pp. 83, 54.

24 Parks, *The Critical Years*, pp. 57–8, 95.

25 Fowler, *Stages of Faith*.

26 Parks, *The Critical Years*, pp. 143–5.

27 Andrew Kam-Tuck Yip and Sarah-Jane Page, *Religious and Sexual Identities: A Multi-Faith Exploration of Young Adults* (Farnham: Ashgate, 2013).

28 Belenky et al., *Women's Ways of Knowing*, pp. 114–15.

29 Parks, *The Critical Years*, p. 164.

30 See, for example, Lawrence G. Calhoun and Richard G. Tedeschi, *Post-traumatic Growth in Clinical Practice* (New York: Routledge, 2013).

31 Hull, *What Prevents?*, pp. 98–9.

32 Karen O'Donnell, *The Dark Womb: Re-Conceiving Theology Through Reproductive Loss* (London: SCM Press, 2022), p. 44.

33 Helen Colley, 'Understanding Time in Learning Transitions Through the Lifecourse', *International Studies in Sociology of Education* 17, no. 4 (2007), p. 438.

34 Parks, *The Critical Years*, pp. 57–66.

35 Fowler, *Stages of Faith*, pp. 178–9.

36 Bessel van der Kolk, *The Body Keeps the Score: Mind, Brain and Body in the Transformation of Trauma* (London: Penguin Books, 2014), p. 13.

37 Jenny Morgans, 'Faithing, Friendship and Feeling at Home: Three Women Encounter University Chaplaincy' in *From the Shores of Silence: Conversations in Feminist Practical Theology*, ed. Ashley Cocksworth, Rachel Starr and Stephen Burns (London: SCM Press, 2023), p. 108.

38 Liz Kenyon, 'A Home from Home: Students' Transitional Experience of Home' in *Ideal Homes? Social Change and the Experience of Home*, ed. Tony Chapman and Jenny Hockey (London: Routledge, 1999), pp. 90–1.

39 van der Kolk, *The Body Keeps the Score*, p. 38; see also p. 7.

PART II

Faith at University

4

Faith Change and Development

This chapter examines the women's religious experiences and evolving Christian faith at university. It demonstrates how some women initially compartmentalized their faith, protecting it by keeping it separate from other aspects of life and postponing spiritual growth until they felt ready. Over time, many developed greater autonomy in their religious praxis, with some experiencing spiritual awakenings. Some women gradually wove their faith into their daily routines, and their conceptions of God shifted to become more expansive. Relationships remained central to their faith journeys, both with God and through connections with Christian friends and family. The chapter concludes by exploring the experiences of women who left conservative evangelical communities.

Separation and delay

Navigating their faith in a new setting, adapting to university life, and forming new relationships left the women feeling exposed and unsettled. In response, many adopted safe approaches to their faith, including separating it from their everyday lives, and creating a dualism between it and the rest of the world. This separation often resulted in a disconnection that prevented Christianity from becoming a realized faith. Several women saw their faith as a distinct part of their identity or even as an extra-curricular activity, rather than something that influenced, and was influenced by, their whole lives. Often, this was because they considered their faith to be 'personal', 'innate' or 'internalized' rather than conscious or visible. In part, this reflects Western trends that assume religion to be a private matter. Mary and Taylor reflected that because they had always been Christian, they had never examined their faith identities, and Danielle chose to keep her faith to herself and practise it alone rather than in a community. Taylor suggested that her behaviour 'could be down to personality as opposed to just faith, I'm not sure, but I imagine my personality is what it is because I've been raised in church, so it's really hard to, kind of, pull the two apart.' Stephanie realized that since her faith had unconsciously 'shaped my upbringing' then it was also likely to be shaping her current behaviour without her noticing, yet this was not something that she was intentionally doing. For these women, support was needed in connecting their faith with the reality of their daily lives.

Nicole spoke of her faith as a distinct extra-curricular activity, considering her faith to be her third priority after her studies and sports activities. However, the Anglican student society that she attended at her chaplaincy was helping her realize that her faith *was* unconsciously influencing her motivations for 'why I do what I do'. She reflected that her faith had 'always been a part of me, so I wouldn't know anything different ... it's just who I am.' In these words, Nicole's faith identity was both a given and something chosen. She felt that her faith, as a core identity marker, could not be considered consciously and so was largely left unexamined. Clydesdale critiques the practice of Christian students placing their faith inside identity lockboxes, 'removing them from interaction and resisting efforts to alter them', which he especially witnessed in first-year students.[1]

Other women recognized that their faith *would* grow or begin to influence their daily lives; however, they delayed such change until some unspecified future point. For Parks, such times of 'contemplative pause' are necessary in emerging adulthood, when some things are not up for negotiation but rather held in creative 'incubation' for a time of 'lingering'.[2] As in other areas of the women's lives explored in the previous chapter, the word *yet* was common as the in-between nature of student life paused their spiritual development. It seemed that the students had an inkling of the invitation to a more rounded faith, while recognizing that they were not yet ready to accept the challenge. The little word *yet* crystallized a powerful awareness of their liminality, and enabled a sense of safety as they resisted any movement in their faith at a time when so much else was changing. For example, Kimberly stated that, 'It would take quite a lot for me to have something that really changed radically what I thought.' Megan reflected, 'I don't think it has [changed, but] I guess as you get older, you're more aware of what you think', expecting her understanding of her faith to grow as she matured. Haley said that university had not impacted her understanding of God: 'I think it will change but it hasn't yet.' Courtney's view of God had 'stayed the same'; however, she thought 'hopefully' it would change at university 'once I've kind of settled in more'. Both Alexis and Mary also used the word *yet* to describe their future plans to become more active in their faith: 'it hasn't been able to happen yet', and similarly, 'it just hasn't quite happened yet'. Sarah emphasized the relationship between needing to feel at home and being able to explore: 'I'm just getting more comfortable with being here and then maybe I'll explore a bit more in the next few months ... I haven't really had the chance yet.'

Many of the women stated that they had fewer doubts about their faith at university than beforehand, suggesting a reluctance to question their spiritual status quo. They lacked the recognition that change may already be occurring, or that it was a process over which they had some control. However, these words also reveal something of the women's perceived vulnerability, desire for safety, and awareness that *one day* they would be ready for growth. Hull argues that it is common for faith and meaning to go uncritiqued during times of change. He writes,

> It would be painful and unsettling to question the things which are the source and ground for the rest of our life ... [especially] during periods of threat to our identity, which are resisted by the creation of clear boundaries between that with which we identify and that with which we do not identify.[3]

The strategies of separation and delay resonate with research with young millennials suggesting that what some called 'Christianity' had little to do with the Christian God. In 2006, Sara Savage and her colleagues found that religious literacy was low for millennial Christians, arguing that their spirituality was better termed a 'Happy Midi-Narrative', reflecting their desire for happiness for themselves and their 'midi' networks of friends and family. The authors discovered fuzziness concerning traditional Christian beliefs, yet a resilience of Christian ideals in the background of millennials' minds.[4] In 2010, Smith found that 'feeling happy, good, better and fulfilled' were the cornerstone of US millennials' 'Christian' faith, in what he terms a 'Moralistic Therapeutic Deism'. God wants people to feel good about themselves and be good to others, and can be drawn upon in times of stress or trouble, but offers no ethical relevance to everyday life.[5] Several women stated that the biggest impact their belief in God had on their lives was in 'just trying to be nice to people' (Taylor) or being 'kind and generous to everyone' (Stephanie). As Clare Herbert writes, such a God demanding that 'everyone ha[s] to be gentle, kind, unassertive, safe and dull' perpetuates a lack of energy or motivation within Christianity,[6] which suited these women in their attempts to feel safe at university. Safely separating faith from the changes taking place around and inside them, and delaying spiritual growth from happening *yet*, contributed to the women's tentative crafting of home. Rather than needing to give conscious energy to their faith, they were able to focus on the consuming daily life management amid university's traumatic transitions.

Christian inner-dependence

Despite the above, many women began to find greater confidence and autonomy in their faith: a Christian inner-dependence. For Parks, beginning to locate 'the Spirit within' involves an inward shifting of the locus of authority in the composing of truth.[7] This transition in consciousness stemmed from what the women described as their newfound 'independence', 'freedom' or 'autonomy' at university. Even students who described traumatic challenges in the transition were enthusiastic about making their own faith decisions and trusting their own spiritual experiences as they crafted home. This Christian inner-dependence manifested through freedom, journeying, and a healthy separation, and I take each of these three related experiences in turn.

First, the absence of immediate parental influence created a liberating environment where students could, in Guest and colleagues' words, intertwine 'the two transitional projects of faith development and the pursuit of independence'.[8] Slee notes that for some women, once the necessity for safety diminishes, security can be 'increasingly internalized … for her selfhood to flourish'. In this process, 'separations' and 'leavings' can be central to 'the freedom to pursue her emerging spiritual path'.[9] Leaving the parental home and establishing a home at university enabled many students to value their own authority in influencing their faith, and to be creative with the new opportunities they encountered. Ashley was eager to think more about the impact of her faith on her time at university and recognized that 'I'm still figuring it out'. Similarly, Danielle was 'learning and trying to understand' more about God, claiming her own spiritual growth for herself. Kimberly put a lot of thought into finding a church that met her needs. She enjoyed the playful process of 'seeing what I like and … what works for me'. Lauren and Briana reflected on their autonomy as they had to 'actively think about' their faith and 'actively go and seek out' a place to worship away from their Christian families. Briana continued that 'my faith has got stronger' because 'I've had to make the choice myself'. This active seeking is very different from the language of safe separation used above. A year later, in her second year, Briana reflected again on this experience, explaining that 'coming away for the first time' was a 'breaking free'. She said, 'it's changing me' including 'becoming … more sure of what I believe and who I am'.

Second, the women's increased autonomy contributed to an understanding of journeying in faith, a process over which they could take ownership. Journeying is a common metaphor for a Christian life, and it has been identified in diverse literature. For example, Alexander W. Astin and his colleagues find that students become 'more actively engaged in a spiritual quest' over their time at university.[10] Several women articulated a sense that their faith was transitioning with them at university, or that they hoped that it would, and saw that this transition was enabling them to explore faith on their own terms. Lauren discussed learning about other faiths at university and 'hoping it'll strengthen my faith, um, I'm not sure, um, but I'm almost hoping it'll challenge what I think.' This is a tentative statement, with 'I'm not sure', 'almost' and two 'um's. Yet Lauren was clear in her repetition of the word 'hoping' that she wanted her faith to deepen. Similarly, Caitlin had an openness in studying theology, including other faiths, which had 'encouraged me to look a lot more deeper [sic] about things' and was 'challenging' what she believed. She thought that while this might be 'scary to some people', she 'really enjoy[s] it … if I change my mind about things, I think that's a good thing rather than something to be scared of.' Courtney also hoped for growth: 'It's good when stuff is changing, it means I'm kind of growing in faith more, and deepen[ing] your understanding so hopefully it changes a bit.' Danielle and Abigail found the metaphor of faith as 'a continual journey' helpful, whereby 'every person's individual journey is theirs'. Abigail elaborated, saying, 'We're designed to keep growing … I think it changes all the time.' She continued, 'It takes time to get to know [God] more, so our understanding changes as we go through life with him.'

Tumi demonstrated the importance of having an internal locus of control. In moving away from her Christian networks at home, Tumi realized how pressure from others made it 'very difficult to have my relationship with God'. At university, she joined but then withdrew from the Christian Union in order to 'know [faith] for myself, not just because that's what everyone else is doing'. She had 'gone through my whole faith … and not even realized that I've not actually had the relationship with God that I've wanted.' Tumi used a journeying metaphor to demonstrate her own beliefs developing, distinct from others' influence: 'To think any differently, or know anything for myself, I think, has been, is going to be, like walking through mud almost, and then getting to the grass where it's not muddy.' In Tumi's metaphor, mud suggests feeling encumbered by inherited beliefs, an uncertain path ahead, discomfort in questioning what she had been taught, and the possibility of slipping backwards. In contrast, movement to the grass represents finding a more authentic understanding of faith and stable ground in her own understanding, with greater freedom of movement and a sense of relief after the struggle. Her use of both the present and future tense emphasized the ongoing nature of her journey and suggested multiple phases of discovery. She described a transition from inherited religious beliefs towards developing her own understanding of faith, with the imagery implying that this was a challenging but worthwhile process.

Third, some women tentatively exhibited patterns of Fowler's stage 4, Individuative-Reflective Faith, and were no longer willing to conform to others' expectations. Instead, a 'demythologizing' took place, whereby symbols previously adhered to were subjected to analysis.[11] This involved separating themselves from the assumptions of others as confidence in their Christian selves grew and they developed an autonomous system of meaning. Briana gave this considerable thought, and reflected on how her beliefs created a boundary between her and her non-Christian peers. While she did not want to 'alienate' herself, she recognized that being Christian at university was 'not normal' but rather 'counter-cultural', and so Christians should not pretend to 'be cool and world-wise'. Christianity was something she was proud of, and she showed no embarrassment at standing out from the crowd due to her faith. She saw this positioning on the edge of student life as an opportunity to rethink her faith, a process that was just beginning:

> It's a really important time to consolidate what I believe ... for me to work out, actually, what do I believe and why, why I'm living like this ... I think it's going to be, or it is being, really important and, um, I think the word is 'formative'.

Melissa's experience was somewhat different. She described her faith as 'personal', and arriving at university she did not speak about it with others or seek out any Christian activities. However, having made like-minded Christian friends at the university chaplaincy, this was changing, and in her second year she was 'much more willing to think about [things] from my perspective as a Christian' because 'it's just sort of part of me now'. She reflected further on how her developing faith related to her wider worldview:

> It's very important to me that I have that clear distinction between what I believe in relation to God, and what I believe is right in relationship to the world ... I don't think those are necessarily disconnected, but, I think, that helps stop you going, 'Well, I must be right about this cos I'm a Christian and therefore I'm morally right.'

This separation in her thought is akin to Richard Holloway's suspicion of Christianity's ownership of moral imperatives, leading to Christians' refusal to act without first finding theological reason for doing so. This, he argues, places rules over reasons, and can result in a failure to negotiate, or even cruelty.[12] Melissa saw that Christians often profess 'quite hateful and upsetting things' by using biblical or moral reasoning which she saw as deeply distressing. Melissa wanted her morality, while inspired by her inclusive faith, to come from within.

Christian awakenings

Maria Harris argues that in connecting with fundamental aspects in their spiritual quest, women experience an *awakening* in the midst of transitions, making room for change to take place.[13] For Slee, awakenings involve the process of continued birthings, each one leading 'to a rearrangement of normal perceptions ... enabling newness'.[14] Many women recognized tentative growth in their fluid Christian identities since arriving at university, awakening from a static or outdated faith into a new Christian becoming. This was usually encouraged by increased engagement with Christian activities. Smith and Snell argue that for a significant minority of emerging adults the search for identity differentiation results in increased religious commitment. They write, 'Religious practices ... help to define, establish and confirm religious identities. Persons who pray regularly become as a result known both to themselves and to others as more faithful religious persons than those who do not.'[15]

Partly, the women's increased commitment was due to greater opportunity to participate in faith activities compared with previously, alongside engagement with Christian peers and the new independence to choose their faith practices for themselves. Many of the women prayed, attended Christian activities and/or read the Bible at least weekly. They saw these practices as contributing to their becoming at university and to their faith being 'strengthened'. For example, Danielle intentionally engaged more with Christian music and books, and Courtney described 'increased exposure' to her faith, saying that now, 'I understand it a lot more, I think about it a lot more.'

Many women recognized the connection between their Christian practice and their shifting identities. Olivia said that, at university, 'I want God to shape [me].' Ashley saw that, 'The Bible and how it's working in my life [is] changing me.' Amber was 'learning more' through increased dedication to her faith and so had 'grown a lot' and felt able 'to put God more at the centre of my life'. While identity development through greater religious engagement was tentative, the women nonetheless recognized that they were awakening into a deeper understanding of their faith.

Women who were in their second year at university showed a newly expanded comprehension of Christianity's diverse expressions, in stark contrast to their limited understanding of the Church when they first arrived. Perrin argues that such growth in awareness at university is common, while the absence of such engagement can be detrimental to faith development.[16] Chaplaincies and Christian student societies were significant in facilitating such awareness. In her first year, Briana had no knowledge of what defined her evangelical Christianity or of different theologies. She viewed the Christian Union (CU) as the obvious Christian society to join and did not see its biases. In her second year, however, she recognized the diversity of theological opinions that existed at university, both within and outside of the CU. She described 'difficult issues' that 'I'd never thought of before and suddenly now I have to make up my mind about them.' For example, she explained that the CU felt unable to work with the chaplaincy because the latter's multifaith engagement was contrary to the CU's attempts to evangelize people from other faiths.

In her second year, Ashley had been to reconciliatory meetings at the chaplaincy to 'resolve issues' between different Christian societies. She had attempted to organize an event 'where all Christians could come together', and the chaplaincy had helped her to realize why this would not be possible.[17] She felt sad that there was 'conflict' between the societies that were 'secluded in our difference, rather than united'. Melissa had enjoyed attending a conservative evangelical youth group at home, but she had disagreed with its theology and not known any alternative. However, finding peers with similarly inclusive beliefs at her chaplaincy helped strengthen her faith and reduce her previous sense of isolation. The process of developing awareness demonstrated here by Briana, Ashley and Melissa mirrors Fowler's theory of stage transition. When a person cannot *assimilate* 'what is to be "known" in the environment' into her existing thought structures due to its contradictory nature, the person *accommodates*, that is, generates new structures of knowing.[18] For the women who encountered such difference, not only was their knowledge of Christianity broadened but their faithing was reshaped. The women's emerging spiritual awareness, manifested through increased participation in Christian activities and recognition of Christianity's diverse expressions, fostered parallel growth in both their religious understanding and personal identity.

The labour of integration

The beginning of this chapter outlined an approach to faith that kept it distinct and separate from other areas of the women's lives. However, in contrast, several women intentionally placed their Christianity in conversation with other parts of their lives. Slee terms this weaving of identities the 'labour of integration'. For Slee, integration is the search for 'an inclusive spirituality', able 'to inhabit every aspect' of life and to 'reconcile' identity conflict:

> The emphasis on the integration of all experience within a holistic faith … is a direct outflowing of the conviction that all things are, at heart, interconnected, and, for many of the women, represented a deliberate choice to move away from dualistic ways of thinking and acting.[19]

Two women recognized that Christian books they were reading were influencing how their faith related to the rest of their lives. Vicky was no longer 'restricting God to quite a set, like, *thing*' but now 'my view of what God is, is more broad'. Danielle said, 'Now I do try to focus everything around being a Christian … whereas back home … [I thought that] my faith and my actual life are completely separate, but now I'm realizing they're actually not.'

In her second year, Ashley had begun to develop her 'relationship with God' through things other than just 'quiet times … and prayer' since 'I don't always find that the easiest thing to do'. That God could be encountered in a wide range of activities was a new discovery for Ashley. In particular, she was meeting God 'through writing', and began to see 'reading poetry and writing poetry' as 'like having a Sabbath with God'. As well as experiencing God in different activities, she also recognized that 'God is within everyone' and so deliberately kept a broad friendship group. Integration was something that Ashley was 'still learning' and she felt that, going forward, 'it will be really beneficial' in her faith development.

The most common area of life where the women demonstrated integration with their faith was their course of study. This is in keeping with the previous chapter, in which I detailed the significance that the women attached to their academic subject, and Chapter 7 where I discuss the women's studies alongside their intersectional identities. Briana sometimes prayed about her essays, saying, 'I'm trying not to separate God and work because obviously I need his help in my work as well [laughs].' Some students said that being a Christian influenced their work ethic, wanting 'to work hard' compared with other 'lax' students, because 'God's given me these gifts so I need to use them.' Other students saw God's influence through their subject material. Amber said, 'I definitely see God in the biology.' She saw her two identities of scientist and Christian as merged, saying, 'I wanna be, like, a Christian biologist.' Lauren's humanities degree was enabling her to 'think a lot more about the basis of my faith' because she had 'to sit and think about … what I believe'. This included thinking 'about power, and how people are treated'. Lauren saw how her faith was interwoven with social issues that she was becoming aware of at university, reassessing and reintegrating her belief system to be able to communicate it. She continued, 'I'm really passionate about trying to, to find out how we can change things and develop ideas, so that we can help other people, so I think it is really tied to my faith.'

The women in this book were all younger than those in Slee's research and thus less experienced in integrating their faith into the rest of their lives. Yet many of the students were clearly beginning to see the importance of transitioning away from a separatist faith to something more integrated. Moreover, as with the women in Slee's study,

> Whether integration remained an ideal towards which they moved or a reality which they had begun to grasp, there was a strong commitment amongst the women to relationship to God as the arena within which to draw together the disparate and contradictory elements within their lives.[20]

God

The women discussed both their understandings of, and relationships with, God. For many, it was important that God was a safe and reliable source of comfort, protection and guidance, and had a plan for their lives that they did not need to understand. Kimberly was 'at peace with the idea that God will take me where I need to be, and that I don't need to worry about it', giving herself permission to be passive in her decisions. Megan was struggling with her academic work and took solace in remembering that 'God's there to keep you going.' She believed strongly that 'God's got a plan, and you've got to go with it even if you don't like it.' She drew on a popular poem about Jesus carrying Christians during their most difficult experiences, saying, 'I was thinking of that idea of the sort of footprints in the sand, and actually that's God carrying you through, and I thought, "You've just got to trust, trust God a bit more."' Early in Olivia's first term, she had thought, 'This is horrible!'

Her grandfather was unwell and she 'realized how lonely I was'. In this unsettling time of change she recognized that 'We just have to rely on God.' She began to think of God as her 'strong foundation ... cos anything can be ripped away.' For Taylor, God was 'someone that you can turn to whatever, in whatever situation you're in ... [and] come to if you're feeling sad.' Caitlin described God as 'my shoulder to cry on, my [sighs] just, yeah, the reason why I get up in the morning.' Tumi saw how 'God has quite literally protected me ... he's still helped me'.

It was not surprising that many women relied upon God as a source of comfort given the traumatic nature of the transitions that they were experiencing. In keeping with this uncertainty, some felt more reliant on God at university than previously. Samantha recognized her increased need for God's 'help ... cos I'm away from home and I have more things [that] need praying about'. For Ola, 'being at home just made me slack off', while being at university she had 'no one else to depend on ... I can't do it [alone], so I'll have to go to God.' In each of these quotes, God is framed in personal, relational terms rather than abstract theological concepts. These women had developed intimate, personalized and safe understandings of God who was an active presence in their daily lives.

David G. Ford and colleagues find that the Bible verse most 'memed' among emerging Christians is Jeremiah 29.11: '"For I know the plans I have for you," declares the Lord, "plans to prosper you and not to harm you, plans to give you hope and a future."' Perrin argues that use of this verse demonstrates a need for reassurance amid the uncertainty underpinning emerging adulthood.[21] Tumi found that this verse calmed her fears during the Covid-19 pandemic:

> I can't sit and stew on 'why?', I just have to trust that God, you know, 'he knows the plans that he has for us, like, plans to prosper us and not to harm us', you know, you do just have to trust in that, in his grace ... I can lean on God's mercy, there's no one else I can lean on.

Other students reflecting on the Covid-19 pandemic also asked God 'why?' Ola wondered why she was completely isolated in a new country: 'So it was just me asking God, "Why, why is this happening?"' Caitlin had been unwell with Covid and was still struggling with her health. She 'was like, "Why, God, is this happening?" like, getting a bit frustrated with God.' Conversely, Taylor did not find herself angry at God during the pandemic. While she reflected that her experience of Covid-19 was not 'nearly as bad as it's been for others', she could not 'imagine feeling angry with God because no matter what happens [pause], he's there to help you rather than, you know, make it worse', perhaps unconsciously echoing Jeremiah 29.

Nicole and Chloe both sought comfort in God during a time of bereavement.[22] Nicole recognized an elderly friend's death as an unexpected answer to her prayer that she be comfortable. Chloe 'grew up with so much pessimism' about God that when her grandmother died, she wondered, 'How could he do stuff like this? ... Even though I believed in God, I was like, "How?!"' Coming to terms with her grandmother's death helped Chloe to realize that God did not cause suffering or control the minutiae of her life. She described other ways that God had changed for her:

> I always just had the idea that ... we kind of owed stuff to God or, like ... going to church is something that you had to do ... But as I've got older, I realized, I think to me God is someone that just knows everything that's happened to me and understands me and is seeing everything [bad] before, like, as injustice.

Like Chloe, other women narrated a tentative awakening in their relationship with, or understanding of, God, especially in their second year as they settled into feeling at home at university and were less concerned with stability. While Taylor referred to God as 'scary', she began to focus less on the 'splendour and majesty' of God and more on the 'friend aspect'. Lauren had become more 'grounded' in God; Amber and Mary had felt the relationship grow 'deeper'; and Amber and Samantha felt 'closer' to God than before. Tumi said, 'I don't know ... what God is for me', which made her feel 'stupid and really silly', but she was 'on a journey of realizing'. She could see that through the 'mistakes that I've done ... he's still taught me a lot ... I'm very much still learning.'

Melissa discovered that divine connection was not about 'acting in the right way you should to go to heaven', but simply believing in God. Her student society had helped nurture an authentic 'relationship [and] connection with God'. As their connections with God evolved, Melissa and Ashley both reported feeling more 'comfortable', which proved essential to feeling at home in their spiritual journeys and daily lives. In her third interview, Ashley explained that she was beginning to feel that 'You can't run away from God ... by nature of being a human being made in the image of God, you know, God is already aligned with you.' Since leaving behind her evangelicalism, she was open 'to exploring ... who God is and how God shows up in the world, and what that means for us ... in a way that ... allows God to meet us in our humanity more than I had given credit for.'

Taylor and Alexandra described something of the ambiguity of God's nature. Taylor experienced God as 'close, but also far away'. Alexandra described how 'God is up there and ... God is also within, God is also around, and God is also in everybody.' For Alexandra, God's personal nature influenced her ethics and 'how you treat people ... because God is basically in everything.' Caitlin saw ambiguity between her 'really good personal relationship' and her conservative 'church relationship' with God, saying, 'I didn't know how to make that click.' She left the church and became involved in her university chaplaincy to marry the two more closely.

Lauren's view of God transformed after missing the grades to study medicine despite believing it was her calling. While initially seeming to defer all decisions to God, she developed a collaborative approach to decision-making with the divine. Astin and colleagues suggest that Christian students are resilient in difficult situations and do so with equanimity, perhaps more so than their peers.[23] This equanimity became a powerful resource in the women's intense transitions. Lauren said,

> [God] let me fail ... It kinda changed how I see my relationship with God so that was really helpful, but it was a hard lesson to learn when ... everything disappears ... I kind of realized I shouldn't be [studying medicine] ... even if I got the grades.

This unexpected God was not safe. Instead, the relationship involved conscious participation and prayer, which resulted in Lauren recognizing a new vocation to study humanities.

God's justice was an aspect of the divine that many women named as important, like Chloe above who understood that God saw the injustice of her past experiences. Alexandra expressed this aspect of God most clearly. As a queer woman of colour and a theology student from the Caribbean, Liberation Theology resonated with her experiences. A 'core ... tenet' of her faith was 'the God of liberation ... that God is my friend'. She looked to the God of Exodus who liberated the Israelites, including Miriam as 'a rebel ... advocating with the God of justice ... there on the front lines'. She also quoted Micah 6.8: '"to walk humbly and love kindness and walk humbly with God, to do justice and love kindness", yeah, that Scripture, it resonates a lot'.

In my first two rounds of interviews, none of the students referred to God with any pronouns other than he/his. However, in the third round, many of the women discussed the gender of God, or gave open responses when questioned, and two women assigned God with the pronoun 'they'. It is difficult to know why this discrepancy arose. Perhaps there had been a shift in Christian conversations about the nature of God, or perhaps increased discourse around transgender rights and pronouns made the topic more live. The inclusion of more queer women in my research might also explain the change. Recent interviewees demonstrated greater familiarity with intersectionality, diversity and inclusion in general, compared to those interviewed earlier, including in their faith and gendered experiences, and so perhaps this reflected a difference between Gen Y and Gen Z. However, this is speculative.

Juliana Claassens argues that 'the language and metaphors we use for God greatly affect the world we live in.'[24] Yet Nelle Morton notes that the God 'we create' through 'unexamined language' in worship is detached from women's experiences.[25] Mark J. Cartledge demonstrates that patriarchal language used to describe God impacts Christians' theological and ethical beliefs, including influencing the exclusion of women from positions of leadership.[26] Scriptural metaphors for God – including God as friend, midwife, mourner, weaver, embodied, mother and liberator – not only incorporate feminine imagery, but could also serve as powerful resources supporting Christian women's spiritual exploration and becoming, yet largely they were not mentioned by most women. Taylor recognized that although she always referred to God as male, this was due to 'conversations with others and through Scripture ... so that's the image I have of him and ... that's been in my head for my whole life.' While she did not think it was 'wrong', she could not 'imagine ... thinking of God as she'. For Chloe, God's gender was 'a concept' since 'he's not, like, human, he's something different'. While she usually prayed using male language for God because 'I grew up with it', it was important to her that 'he can understand women and girls perfectly, I don't think of him as a man.' Both Taylor and Chloe reflected on how they had always heard God referred to and addressed, and how this had failed to help them imagine God beyond these confines. Neither had been exposed to expansive imagery and language used for God in Scripture, let alone in feminist liturgies.

Refuting a problematic image of God discussed further in Chapter 7, when Caitlin became a Christian in her teens she realized that the 'scary ... portrayals of God ... where he's got a long, scraggly white beard and he's this old looking man' were false. Instead, she experienced God 'more as an, an energy and as a love, and as a, something that powers me, rather than something that's got gender attached to it ... just ultimate love'. She continued:

> I would happily pray to a Father God or Mother God, anything, I'm comfortable using anything like that ... I see God as a father *and* a

mother, not one or the other, definitely as a parent, but also encompassing other roles such as a friend and a companion ... God is my friend above anything.

Sallie McFague's model of God includes the metaphor of friend, emphasizing 'mutuality, respect, acceptance of differences, cooperation, solidarity, attraction, perseverance, tolerance, gift-giving, delight, sacrifice, constructive criticism'.[27] This metaphor speaks to the significance of supportive female peers reported throughout this book.

Alexandra had given a lot of thought to the gender of God, partly through theological study, and discussed how she experienced the different persons of the Trinity. Rejecting parental imagery, she found it 'difficult to connect to the Father God ... [and] Mother God'. She related instead to 'the "I am that I am" ... from the Old Testament' as 'a being, an entity, that is, that *just is*, and also that has characteristics of both feminine and masculine'. While she accepted the male gender of Jesus, she disliked 'how we sometimes glorify ... Creator God as a man'. For Alexandra, 'the Spirit has always been a feminine energy to me'. Referencing Genesis 1, she said, 'It stems from *Rumah* ... where the wind of God went over the waters.' She continued: 'I feel Spirit and Spirit is nurturing, Spirit is encouraging, Spirit is an advocate. And, not that women only embody those qualities, but that's the way I perceive Spirit to be.' Because of the association that Alexandra made between the Holy Spirit and the feminine, she said, 'I do connect to Spirit a lot more than the Creator God and sometimes Jesus.' She explained that her image of the Holy Spirit inspired how she understood herself and how she related to the world:

> How Spirit moves is just how I visualize, like, a woman dancing within [laughs] ... I am Spirit, Spirit is me, but also Spirit is around me ... we use Spirit to go out and to, like, create and to speak and to do, and acting in accordance with Spirit is something that I relate to.

In Ola's interview, we had a fascinating exchange about God's gender. Even though it was not something that she had thought about before, and she laughed at the idea of God being female, she came to an important realization that echoed Mary Daly's words from 1973: 'If God is male then the male is God.'[28] When I asked what she thought about the gender of God, she responded, 'I don't know if God is male ... but then, Jesus was a man on earth, so, probably, yeah ... but that doesn't affect how I feel about him.' She described God in traditional stereotypically male terms, although she also mentioned God as a friend:

I don't want to say this big guy in the sky [laughs], but ... he sort of is, but then he's ... my father, he's my friend, and he is sovereign, he guides me through everything and he created the world ... and he has everything planned out.

When I asked if she ever thought of God as female, she replied:

Not really, no [laughs]. I think if God was a female [laughs] it would be a bit, this is just me joking around, but he could be a bit more emotional, cos women are quite, more ... we're not really logical, we're more emotions-based.

I followed up with another question, asking if she would find it easier to connect with God if the divine was portrayed as more emotional and like a woman. Ola thought:

It would probably help to relate more with God ... [But] I might end up trying to misuse that to justify whatever I do ... if I thought God was more woman, I'll just ... try to behave like I'm God and almost use it as an excuse.

I then asked if men are 'tempted to behave like God because they are male and God is male?' She replied:

Yeah! [laughs] Definitely some, some men, yeah, I think I have seen some men who are like, 'Oh God does this, and why do you think he created man first?' and think they are, I mean they are sort of 'superior', but not really, we're all the same, but ... yeah, I think some are tempted to do that.

Ola recognized that if she were to consider God as female, then that would enable her to feel 'superior', in the same way that she saw men considering themselves to be like God. She drew the connection between how people speak about God and how the personhood of women is considered. Ola realized that the patriarchy, in portraying God solely as male, justified women's inferior position and raised the status of men. Though she did not directly criticize this, she found that androcentric divine attributes made it harder to relate to God or see herself as reflecting God's image. The gender used for God mattered.

Marcella Althaus-Reid's queer theology challenges patriarchal orthodoxy, arguing that Christians must 'betray' oppressive ideologies to rediscover God. She contends that conservative views on gender and sexuality imprison God 'in the closet', while queer theology 'liberates Godself' and recognizes God as inherently dwelling in the margins.[29] These aspects of Godself were being realized and recognized by some of the women in this book, while others lacked the experience and the resources to know that such questioning was possible. Equally importantly, however, for the women's traumatic transitions God was safe and unchanging, provided support and guidance, and had some control over or a plan for their lives.

Christian friends and family

Supportive Christian relationships with friends, family and mentors offered both emotional security and a stable foundation for the women to explore and develop their faith independently. Christine D. Pohl writes that safe communities are needed in order 'for people to take the risks that are necessary for growth and transformation'; while for Wendy M. Wright, spiritual growth 'is possible only when we are most deeply related to others'.[30] Slee argues that close relationships are often a context for Christian women in '"coming home" to themselves, to truth and to God'. In her research, women's close friends 'were those who, perhaps more than any other, represented a freely chosen commitment of love and availability.'[31] It is this *chosen, loving commitment* to one another that enabled the women in my study to explore their faith with confidence, which in turn influenced their Christian identity. For Briana, there was correlation between supportive relationships, faith development and identity growth. She described how 'talking about faith' and 'praying' with friends that she saw 'every day' had 'helped me', had 'definitely changed' her faith and had 'changed me'. Some of Melissa's best friends were Christian and so she felt able 'to be more outspoken amongst them'. She found it 'easier' to have difficult conversations because she knew that there would still be 'that support of niceness and lovingness and kindness'. These conversations enabled her to nurture her faith while also hearing the experiences of others.

Churches and Christian student societies were 'moral communities' in which students encouraged each other to explore together their religious beliefs.[32] At first, bonds were made by the women with those who were considered similar, and this created safe spaces to test new ideas. The women felt freer to explore or debate their faith at university than previously due to these new bonds and the sense of freedom that university provided, where, as Olivia said, 'It's easier ... I can meet up with Christians a lot more.' In these moral communities, students reported that they: felt able to 'strengthen my faith' (Kimberly); were 'praying and chatting with people' (Lauren); were 'doing more related to my faith' due to extra 'support' (Sarah); and 'had discussions on what we believe' (Stephanie). In these traumatic transitions, Christian student societies created a home from home through a sense of community and the strengthening of religious identity in a transforming connection with self and others.[33] Victor Turner writes that such communities experience a strong sense of bonding during liminal times. He refers to this feeling as 'communitas': an immediate, temporary and potentially transformative means of experiencing human connection.[34]

As well as in these chosen, loving relationships, exploration also took place through encountering people whom the women experienced as different to themselves. Edward Croft Dutton, expanding Turner's theory of communitas, writes about Christian student societies at an elite university: 'The very structure of the university ... forced students together with people from very different backgrounds and with very different ideas, challenging their social position and bringing their worldview – and thus identity – into question.'[35]

Astin and colleagues argue that encounters involving diversity are the most transformative for emerging adults' spiritual life, whereby 'students become more caring, more tolerant, more connected with others, and more actively engaged' during their time at university.[36] Kimberly liked the 'people that I meet that challenge what I've come to accept'. For Briana, this included those 'who have never met Jesus', and for Danielle those who 'ask me questions'. Courtney said that she shared her faith straightaway, 'at the beginning' of a new friendship, and this gave her confidence to examine why she was a Christian. For some students, this involved speaking with Christians with different beliefs to their own. Olivia was 'interested in other people's opinions so I can learn about it'. At university, Haley's faith was transformed by being 'exposed to ... different people' and 'embracing new things'. Unlike her judgemental home church that rejected homosexuality and other religions, she became 'more open' and 'accepting', embracing differences through her expanded social networks. Nicole found value in engaging with 'other people that have similar or contradictory ideas', recognizing that all these encounters contributed to her growth: 'At university there's other people to bounce ideas off and question you and therefore by being questioned you then have to delve deeper, into actually what do I think, what do I believe.'

Many women discussed the importance of having Christian mentors. Parks calls for higher education to include 'multiple mentoring communities',[37] including both religious and academic 'spiritual guide[s]'.[38]

Christopher Moody argues that university chaplains walk alongside students at critical moments, similar to midwives calling forth new life.[39] Anne Phillips also uses the midwife metaphor to describe identity formation in transitional times. She finds that pre-teen girls are 'both birthing and being birthed into a new identity',[40] and benefit from supportive adult relationships in informal, safe settings.

Several women stated that they appreciated the chance to explore together with trusted Christian adults at university, who were most often chaplains or church leaders. Lauren appreciated 'having a chaplain there who's just … to help you'. Alexis, Melissa and Stephanie agreed that the personality and theology of the chaplain affected whether they attended the chaplaincy, suggesting the importance of the teaching and encouragement they received. Samantha received 'a lot' of pastoral care from a religious Brother at her church. Courtney valued the mentoring she received at her church prayer group as both supportive and challenging. Although this perhaps demonstrated a lack of boundaries where she 'can't hide', she found the group helpful for her own development:

[If there's] a question that I, kind of, don't want to think about or … makes me, kind of, feel uncomfortable, like, I have to answer and I have to, kind of, think about it, which is really good, they're willing to challenge me but they're also there to support me.

Sarah lamented a lack of support for this reason. She said, 'with more input … and more support, I feel like I could probably spend more time thinking about stuff and actually developing a bit more.'

The significance of close Christian friendships in the women's faith exploration is perhaps unsurprising. Yet exploration was enabled and supported through a multiplicity of relationships, including close friends, Christian peers with whom they both agreed and disagreed, and Christian mentors. This exploration enabled spiritual growth and contributed to the students' crafting of home at university.

Post-evangelicalism

Out of the 26 women that I interviewed, 17 of them had engaged with some kind of evangelical activity at some point. Of these, six departed from their evangelical communities, citing conflicts with the religious teachings or how these teachings were practised, with some reporting psychological harm from these experiences. This section highlights some of the women's voices as they reflected on these former communities.

David W. Bebbington identifies evangelicalism by four traits:

Conversionism, the belief that lives need to be changed; *activism*, the expression of the gospel in effort; *biblicism*, a particular regard for the Bible; and what may be called *crucicentrism*, a stress on the sacrifice of Christ on the cross.[41]

Of course, it is not only evangelical spaces that can cause harm, as is shown by Lisa Oakley and Kathryn Kinmond in their important work on spiritual abuse.[42] For example, Chapter 7 demonstrates harm caused in many different Christian settings by theologies that reject queer identities. Yet it is evangelical communities that the women in this book had left behind.

Olivia Jackson, researching those who 'deconstruct' evangelical faith, explains that evangelicalism goes beyond church attendance, and 'is a culture with its own language, music and celebrities; an industry with its own merch; an all-encompassing way of life'.[43] Perrin discusses the 'kaleidoscopic' term *evangelical* as a descriptor in identity and theology, particularly as it is used and understood by emerging adults: 'For many it has become pejorative, synonymous with a hardline absolutism that disregards other types of Christian spirituality. However, this is often a caricature, since churches that hold to Bebbington's quadrilateral are so diverse.'[44]

Of Bebbington's model, the women critiqued all four positions, but were especially concerned with conversionism and biblicism. Conservative theologies questioned by the women included exclusive atonement theories, the limiting of women's roles, and queerphobic attitudes. These latter two, along with experiences of evangelism, are explored in later chapters. The women also expressed feeling unable to ask questions openly and experiencing pressure to conform in both belief and behaviour.

Taylor's home church was mainstream Anglican, then at university she had joined the Christian Union (CU) to make friends. She said, 'I didn't really know what it would be about. Of course, I now know it's about evangelism.' Despite not agreeing with their conservative theology, she also became involved with an independent evangelical church 'to meet other Christian students'. This importance placed upon the building of relationships above a church's theology was common, and understandable given that the women were away from support networks.

Taylor recognized that her faith had been both broadened and challenged by these spaces. When I interviewed her again years later, she reflected upon the church's confusing and 'uncomfortable' Calvinistic theology, with the acrostic TULIP:

T for total depravity, so everyone is completely sinful and there's nothing we can do to stop that. U for unconditional election, you have been picked to be saved ... L for limited atonement, which is, Jesus died to save some people, but not everybody. I for irresistible grace ... you are saved whether you like it or not ... And then P was perseverance of the saints, but I missed that lesson so I still don't know what it is! [laughs]

Taylor's recitation of the TULIP definitions, including her lack of knowledge about P, demonstrated that she never subscribed to this theology herself, but rather held these beliefs at arm's length while going along with them at church. She remembered rejecting double predestination after questioning prayer's purpose in such a system. She found it troubling that some believed Jesus died only for select people, preferring universal salvation over the idea that most are predestined for hell. She said, 'I think Jesus died for everyone!' This cognitive dissonance eventually became too much for Taylor. With some courage, she left both the CU and her church to be able to explore her faith more openly. She was worried about being shamed for leaving, or having someone 'reach out to me and go, "Where did that one go?! Bring her back!"', which was not what she wanted. After moving to a different city, she settled into another mainstream Anglican church where she felt more at home. In contrast to unquestioning belief, Taylor now felt 'comfortable not knowing' anything for certain. Instead, she felt able to 'focus on that faith, saying love your neighbour and God, [rather] than the teeny little things that separate us.'

Caitlin also joined the CU to make new friends: 'Because I was like, "Oh they're Christians", I'd never met a Christian my age.' While the evangelical 'style of worship didn't really speak to me', due to her teetotal lifestyle influenced by growing up around alcoholism, she valued their alcohol-free social activities. Caitlin quickly bonded with CU members who became her closest friends. However, she soon realized that the society had a conservative stance on sexuality which, as a queer student, she found upsetting. She experienced clear social rejection after coming out as queer, with some members actively avoiding interaction and physical proximity. Moreover, Caitlin's girlfriend was a Muslim, in direct contrast with the CU's aim to convert people of other faiths to Christianity. She said, 'I think some of them genuinely see people of other faiths, especially Muslims, as almost subhuman.' Eventually, realizing 'I can't do this anymore', she described leaving the CU as 'hard' and 'traumatic':

I felt sort of guilty about it, but at the same time it was hard to put myself in a position where I knew I was continually getting hurt ... you can't really deny that they hold bigoted beliefs, some people in the CU ... so it's hard to sort of see the people who are maybe more open and less hardline.

Although Caitlin was 'sceptical' about the chaplaincy due to what she had heard from the CU, she became increasingly involved after speaking with a chaplain.

Melissa had attended a weekly evangelical youth group as a teenager, where 'lots of people had [conservative] views on abortion and gay marriage'. They also preached conversionism, to the point of saying 'Catholicism is wrong'. Melissa 'loved the atmosphere', yet while she made some 'lovely' friends she felt an emotional 'barrier' between them. She criticized teachings that emphasized guilt and proper behaviour 'to go to heaven', rather than fostering a relationship with God. This left Melissa feeling inadequate as a Christian, when 'all you need to do is believe'.

Coming to university, she attended the Anglican Society at the chaplaincy with her flatmate Alexis. Since then, 'I've realized actually that's not everyone's theology [laughs].' Melissa thought that the society was 'brilliant' because 'it is more liberal'. There, she found a community where she felt at home and was able to be herself. As for Caitlin and Melissa, Shelly Rambo finds that university chaplaincies are safe, unpressured spaces for those who have experienced harm or isolation elsewhere.[45]

Ashley was an evangelical student and joined the committee of a conservative student society. Interviewed twice as an undergraduate, Ashley was consistently open to questioning faith but disappointed by the lack of space for discussion. After graduating, she worked for the organization that ran the society, until becoming disenchanted and leaving some years later. Interviewed again eight years after she started university, she had recently left the organization and was rethinking her faith and her worldview. She was undertaking what is commonly called 'deconstruction', defined by Jackson as 'an intentional examination of one's core faith and beliefs, leading to a profound change'.[46] Deconstruction of evangelical faith is something that has gained much attention in recent years, with authors such as Rohr in the US, and the Nomad podcast based in the UK.[47] Ashley experienced common criticisms that Jackson observes among deconstructing Christians, namely that they 'want to sin', are 'bitter' or 'were never really saved'. She writes, 'the negativity ... seems to come from a place of feeling threatened as much as a concern for our salvation'.⁴⁸ For Ashley, deconstruction felt 'unsettling' and like 'trauma', 'because you don't want to put yourself in a context where you're not sure or don't feel safe'. But it also involved 'reconstruction', as she felt 'better equipped and more loving in terms of how I approach people with my faith' and was 'more accepting of myself'. She said, 'I'm reconstructing my sense of self and my sense of God in a way that is much stronger ... because it has more room for flexibility.'

Looking back on her faith at university and in the years afterwards, Ashley saw that 'how God made me ... was having to be squeezed out in order to fit the mould.' This violent metaphor could be understood as spiritual abuse, as Ashley's sense of self was diminished. Spiritual abuse is defined by Oakley and Kinmond as 'coercion and control ... in a spiritual context', including 'enforced accountability, censorship of decision making ... pressure to conform ... [and] requirement of obedience'.⁴⁹ As well as being 'squeezed', Ashley was told that she 'needed ... other people around me who believed the same thing as I did, in order to affirm that what I was doing was good and correct.' Her community acted as gatekeeper, controlling 'my relationship with God, everything about God ... and whatever they told me was of God or was God, was what I believed.' Whenever she disagreed with their beliefs, she would think, 'But these are the people who I trusted and who introduced me to God in the first place, so I want to trust that they know what they're talking about.'

Ashley used a metaphor of being 'unmoored' to describe the challenge of leaving the community and the positive impact this had on her faith:

> I had this image ... of being in a boat ... and then actually finding that when I'm pushed over and in the ocean, that it's still very scary, but actually this thing that I had been afraid of – the ocean and uncertainty – is actually the place where I meet and encounter God even more. So, I thought I knew God on the boat, in that safety and security and I *did*, because I could see God, but now it feels like I'm more, like, *in* life with God.

Ashley was unsure whether she would attend church again, and missed 'finding community and home', yet she was enjoying 'having this freedom to go deep with God' which included engaging with websites, literature and podcasts as well as talking with trusted friends. For now, exploring in 'freedom' was the priority.

While there were many differences in these women's stories, there were some parallels. For example, while in these conservative spaces, the women did not know about (or were told to dismiss) Christian communities with inclusive theologies. They also found these networks emotionally difficult to leave due to having made close relationships, but also due to pressure or fear of judgement. All had expressed their disagreement while *within* their evangelical spaces, but knew that questioning was not permitted, as Jackson writes, 'as though no learning or human development were permissible and certainly not a sign of faith'. She explains that such communities are easy to commit to initially, but then difficult to leave. She writes, 'When the evangelical bubble is your entire world, the threat or risk of losing that keeps people compliant and leads them to ignore a great deal of harm.'[50]

Kathy Escobar has produced a helpful model of faith deconstruction, emphasizing, as Ashley did, the process of reconstructing or 'rebuilding' faith by embracing the values of mystery, diversity and freedom.[51] The women named here had all found other people or spaces to facilitate this rebuilding through exploring the freedom and mystery of faith. However, while some who leave conservative churches explore other denominations, this is not universal, partly because evangelical communities often instil scepticism towards other expressions of Christianity.

Conclusion

Perrin, in her research with millennials, suggests that for emerging Christians' faith, the path is unmarked due to cultural shifts resulting in Christianity no longer being the 'de facto worldview'. Instead, these young Christians have to find their own way, and have 'little choice but to take responsibility for owning or disowning a religious identity'. She finds that confidence in this identity often does not develop until the early thirties.[52] Most of the women in my research were at least a decade younger than this, and were away from home and support networks for the first time. It is unsurprising that they were thus tentative in their faith development. In fact, given the circumstances, many of the women in this chapter demonstrate remarkable awareness, courage and resilience in being able to ask questions, integrate their faith, and hope that their faith would begin to influence their daily life. Nevertheless, the need for safety and being 'comfortable' was key.

The next chapter goes on to explore the different Christian spaces and activities in which the women participated. Safety is again a common requirement for the women, yet, as with this chapter, there are plenty of signs of exploration and growth.

Notes

1 Tim Clydesdale, *The First Year Out: Understanding American Teens after High School* (Chicago, IL: University of Chicago Press, 2007), p. 60.

2 Sharon Parks, *Big Questions, Worthy Dreams: Mentoring Young Adults in Their Search for Meaning, Purpose, and Faith* (San Francisco, CA: Jossey-Bass, 2000), pp. 147–8.

3 John Hull, *What Prevents Christian Adults from Learning?* (London: SCM Press, 1985), pp. 54–5, 157–8.

4 Sara Savage et al., *Making Sense of Generation Y: The Worldview of 15- to 25-Year-Olds* (London: Church House Publishing, 2006).

5 Christian Smith, 'On "Moralistic Therapeutic Deism" as US Teenagers' Actual, Tacit, De Facto Religious Faith' in *Religion and Youth*, ed. Sylvia Collins-Mayo and Pink Dandelion (Farnham: Ashgate, 2010), p. 44.

6 Clare Herbert, 'Who Is God for You?', *Feminist Theology* 23, no. 1 (2000), p. 28.

7 Sharon Parks, *The Critical Years: The Young Adult Search for a Faith to Live By* (New York: Harper & Row, 1986), p. 58; See also James W. Fowler, *Stages of Faith: The Psychology of Human Development and the Quest for Meaning* (New York: Harper Collins, 1981).

8 Mathew Guest et al., *Christianity and the University Experience: Understanding Student Faith* (London: Bloomsbury, 2013), p. 131.

9 Nicola Slee, *Women's Faith Development: Patterns and Processes* (Aldershot: Ashgate, 2004), pp. 124–5, 151.

10 Alexander W. Astin, Helen S. Astin and Jennifer A. Lindholm, *Cultivating the Spirit: How College Can Enhance Students' Inner Lives* (San Francisco, CA: Jossey-Bass, 2011), p. 10.

11 Fowler, *Stages of Faith*.

12 Richard Holloway, *Leaving Alexandria: A Memoir of Faith and Doubt* (Edinburgh: Canongate Books, 2012).

13 Maria Harris, *Dance of the Spirit: The Seven Steps of Women's Spirituality* (New York: Bantam, 1989).

14 Slee, *Women's Faith Development*, p. 39.

15 Christian Smith and Patricia Snell, *Souls in Transition: The Religious and Spiritual Lives of Emerging Adults* (Oxford: Oxford University Press, 2009), p. 236.

16 Ruth H. Perrin, *Changing Shape: The Faith Lives of Millennials* (London: SCM Press, 2020), p. 35.

17 Conflict management and mediation is a significant role of modern chaplaincies. See, for example, Sophie Gilliat-Ray, *Higher Education and Student Religious Identity* (Exeter: University of Exeter, 1999), p. 4.

18 Fowler, *Stages of Faith*, p. 49.

19 Slee, *Women's Faith Development*, pp. 154–5, 157.

20 Slee, *Women's Faith Development*, p. 159.

21 David G. Ford, Joshua L. Mann and Peter M. Phillips, *The Bible and Digital Millennials* (London: Routledge, 2019); Perrin, *Changing Shape*, p. 8. Biblical quotation from Jeremiah 29.11 NIV (this is the version usually quoted).

22 David E. Balk, 'Grieving: 22 to 30 Percent of All College Students', *New Directions for Student Services* 121 (2008), p. 9.

23 Astin, Astin and Lindholm, *Cultivating the Spirit*.

24 Juliana Claassens, *Mourner, Mother, Midwife: Reimagining God's Delivering Presence in the Old Testament* (Louisville, KY: Westminster John Knox Press, 2012), p. 4.

25 Nelle Morton, *The Journey Is Home* (Boston, MA: Beacon Press, 1985), pp. xxi, 210.

26 Mark J. Cartledge, 'God, Gender and Social Roles: A Study in Relation to Empirical-Theological Models of the Trinity', *Journal of Empirical Theology* 22 (2009), pp. 117–41.

27 Sallie McFague, *Metaphorical Theology: Models of God in Religious Language* (London: SCM Press, 1983), p. 182.

28 Mary Daly, *Beyond God the Father: Toward a Philosophy of Women's Liberation* (Boston, MA: Beacon Press, 1985), p. 19.

29 Marcella Althaus-Reid, *From Feminist Theology to Indecent Theology: Readings on Poverty, Sexual Identity and God* (London: SCM Press, 2004), pp. 4, 102, 143, 146.

30 Christine D. Pohl, *Living into Community: Cultivating Practices that Sustain Us* (Grand Rapids, MI: W.B. Eerdmans, 2012), p. 4; Wendy M. Wright, *Sacred Dwelling: A Spirituality of Family Life* (London: Darton, Longman and Todd, 2007), p. 86.

31 Slee, *Women's Faith Development*, pp. 123–4, 72.

32 Damon Mayrl and Jeremy E. Uecker, 'Higher Education and Religious Liberalisation Among Young Adults', *Social Forces* 90, no. 1 (2011), pp. 181–208.

33 See, for example, Edward Croft Dutton, *Meeting Jesus at University: Rites of Passage and Student Evangelicals* (Aldershot: Ashgate, 2008); Kristin Aune, Simon Perfect and Ben Ryan, 'Building Bridges or Holy Huddles? Student Religious Organizations in British Universities', *Journal of Diversity in Higher Education* (27 June 2024).

34 Victor Turner, *The Ritual Process* (New York: Aldine Publishers, 1969).

35 Dutton, *Meeting Jesus at University*, p. 3.

36 Astin, Astin and Lindholm, *Cultivating the Spirit*, p. 10.

37 Parks, *Big Questions, Worthy Dreams*, pp. 158–9.

38 Parks, *The Critical Years*, p. 134 see also p. 177.

39 Christopher Moody, 'Spirituality and Sector Ministry' in *Chaplaincy: The Church's Sector Ministries*, ed. Giles Legood (London: Cassell, 1999), pp. 15–24.

40 Anne Phillips, *The Faith of Girls: Children's Spirituality and Transition to Adulthood* (Farnham: Ashgate, 2011), p. 166.

41 David W. Bebbington, *Evangelicalism in Modern Britain: A History from the 1730s to the 1980s* (London: Unwin Hyman, 1989), p. 3.

42 Lisa Oakley and Kathryn Kinmond, *Breaking the Silence of Spiritual Abuse* (Basingstoke: Palgrave Macmillan, 2013).

43 Olivia Jackson, *(Un)Certain: A Collective Memoir of Deconstructing Faith* (London: SCM Press, 2023), p. xiii.

44 Ruth H. Perrin, *The Bible Reading of Young Evangelicals: An Exploration of the Ordinary Hermeneutics and Faith of Generation Y* (Eugene, OR: Pickwick Publications, 2016), p. 6.

45 Shelly Rambo, 'Making a Case for College and University Chaplaincy: Howard Thurman as Guide', *Journal of Pastoral Theology* 34, no. 1 (2 January 2024), p. 44.

46 Jackson, *(Un)Certain*, p. xvii.
47 Richard Rohr, *Everything Belongs: The Gift of Contemplative Prayer* (New York: Crossroad Publishing Company, 2003); Nomad Podcast, www.nomadpodcast.co.uk/, accessed 30.06.2025.
48 Jackson, *(Un)Certain*, p. xiv.
49 Oakley and Kinmond, *Breaking the Silence*, p. 21.
50 Jackson, *(Un)Certain*, pp. xv, 74.
51 Kathy Escobar, *Faith Shift: Finding Your Way Forward When Everything You Believe Is Coming Apart* (New York: Convergent Books, 2014), p. 129.
52 Perrin, *Changing Shape*, p. 152.

5

Christian Spaces and Activities

This chapter examines the diverse churches, Christian student societies and chaplaincies that shaped these women's university faith experiences. I then discuss students' faith practices during the Covid-19 pandemic, before exploring three expressions of faith that the women found impacted upon their time at university: evangelism, listening to sermons and volunteering.

Churches

Most of the students, with just two exceptions, attended a church in their university town at least irregularly. These churches encompassed a variety of denominations and traditions, as follows:

- Anglican evangelical (2 students);
- Anglican mainstream or liberal (6 students);
- Catholic conservative or mainstream (2 students);
- Independent open evangelical (4 students);
- Independent conservative evangelical (6 students);
- Methodist mainstream or liberal (3 students);
- Presbyterian (1 student).

Measuring students' church affiliations is not simple. For example, Generations Y and Z display loose denominational ties and scant religious knowledge, with higher mobility necessitating changes in church attendance. As Guest and his colleagues note, denominational loyalty has become less important than a broader Christian identity.[1] Many of the students would not have known which of the above descriptions their church fitted into. Catholic students provided an exception here, but even in Methodism – traditionally a denomination with a strong identity – one student held her affiliation lightly, despite her mother being a minister. Reflecting the opinions of many students, Sarah said,

Different denominational differences can end up being more of a hindrance than a help in certain situations. I wouldn't put my preference of Methodism ahead of working together with other Christians, as in the end we all share the same core values and beliefs.

Rather than denominational allegiance, Guest and his colleagues argue that church *attendance* is a good measure of students' religiosity. Analysing data from 4,500 students across 13 universities, they argue that a distinctive feature of university life is how students must navigate between two concurrent contexts, and so develop a schema from the regularity with which students attend church both at university and at home outside of term-time.[2] They find that this categorization 'can be used for ... the identification of a clear and strong set of correlations with variables associated with Christian practices like prayer and Bible reading, as well as Christian belief and moral conviction.'[3] Their schema places students into five distinct groups:

- Active Affirmers: consistently frequent attenders at university and at home (25.9 per cent);
- Lapsed Engagers: students who attend church frequently during vacations but less so during term-time (9 per cent);
- Established Occasionals: infrequent attenders during vacations and term-time (13.9 per cent);
- Emerging Nominals: infrequent vacation attenders who do not attend at all during term-time (16.2 per cent);
- Unchurched Christians: consistent non-attenders (30.9 per cent).

Of the students in my study, 19 students (73 per cent) could be described as Active Affirmers. This high number reflects my methods of recruiting students from churches and Christian student societies, who were thus more likely to be regular attendees. Three were Lapsed Engagers, with one Established Occasional, and one Unchurched Christian. None were Emerging Nominals. There was no correlation between the regularity of a woman's church attendance and her church denomination/tradition. Two students did not fit neatly into these categories, and attended church more regularly at university than when visiting their families. Caitlin and Melissa had never consistently attended church at home, and had only developed a coherent faith at university. Their Christianity was very much a part of their university identity, and was fostered and nurtured by their student Christian friends.

While the label of 'active affirming' is a helpful one for understanding patterns of faith commitment,[4] there are other ways of denoting emerging women's faith. For example, while many of the women were Active Affirmers in church attendance, their faith in other aspects sometimes looked more like 'passive negating' or 'active delaying', as the previous chapter showed. Thus, this book is largely more concerned with the everyday praxis, emotions and experiences of these Christian women than in external markers of commitment and attendance.

While many of the women attended church at university, the processes for finding and settling into those churches were varied. Sometimes finding a church was intentional, while at other times quite accidental. For those students who were intentional in their 'church search', many first looked for similarities with their home church, wanting the church to feel familiar. Most students arrived at university having only previously known one church context, and without the experience to understand the breadth of Christianity. This limited experience was the women's one point of comparison for finding a new church. For example, Taylor decided not to continue attending one church because 'it was too different from church at home', and Danielle worried about trying a new church because 'it will not be like my one back home'. Instead, the women chose churches that were 'like my one at home', 'similar', the 'same' and 'familiar' especially in the sense of community or the style of worship. Only one student, Amber, said that she valued aspects of her church that differed from her previous congregation: 'It's a bit more charismatic than I'm used to ... it's important to try new bits that like disturb you.'

Second, it was often *people* rather than doctrine or worship that attracted them to a new church. As well as homesickness, 'friendsickness',[5] and what Kimberly called 'oldlifesickness' in Chapter 2, many women experienced *churchsickness* upon arriving at university, missing the comfort of friends or familiar others. Danielle had come from a church that was 'a proper little community ... you knew who needed care'. Kimberly missed having 'a really good network of people' around her, and Haley 'always had people in my church to talk to'. Courtney found it important to keep in touch with 'good friends back home who kind of keep me rooted [in my faith]'. The women contrasted feeling part of a familiar community with attempting to get to know people in their new church, and not knowing anyone well enough to seek advice or discuss their difficulties. The attempt to make friends was a primary reason for choosing to stay at a particular church, and in their second year some of the women had begun to feel 'supported' and were able 'to play more of a role' in their church as it felt more like home.

Many students' first church visit at university was either recommended by or accompanied by a friend, suggesting the influence of peers and the initial reluctance to try a new church alone. All the women thought it was important to attend a church where there were at least some other students, dismissing churches that 'no other students go to'. Some preferred churches that were 'family-friendly' with 'a wide range of other ages'. Others chose their church because it was simply 'full of students'. Courtney said, 'I want there to be students but it's also nice to actually speak with adults', and so found a church where there were 'families and kids, and there's old people as well'. She did however change from attending the morning service to the evening since it had higher student attendance. Despite enjoying the diversity of her church, she recognized that at church, 'It's easier to be friends with people who are like you.' Similarly, Briana reflected that at church it 'was amazing to find Christians who feel exactly the same way as me'. Caitlin valued both her close student friendships and the age diversity at her church, feeling 'a sense of belonging ... because I have this community of people ... and they look out for me'. She continued, 'It's really nice to have almost friendships with people who are across such different age ranges ... having all these people looking out for you and that genuinely care about you in a deeper way rather than just your uni mates.'

In terms of faith development, Fowler considers the replication of, and reliance upon, familiar Christian contexts as stagnation, 'making any genuinely individuative move as regards identity and outlook difficult' and 'sanctifying one's remaining in the dependence on external authority and derivative group identity of stage 3'.[6] However, the tendency to seek out and create a Christian 'family' can be interpreted positively. For example, such relationships are important for forming and testing out provisional selves in community.[7] If and when young adults' faith develops into Fowler's stage 4, such relationships are also necessary in the development of inner-dependence, including 'an internal panel of experts'[8] who begin to make informed choices and to take responsibility.

Practising their Christian faith offered many students a sense of continuity between home and university, both maintaining and emulating links with home. The words that the women used about making home at university more broadly, as seen in Chapter 3, were 'homely', 'comfortable' and 'settled'. These were the same words that the women used when describing the church that they had chosen or were looking for. Comments included:

I came to this [church] and I just felt really at home. (Abigail)

I just find it really homely ... like a family. (Amber)

It feels more like home than other churches. (Courtney)

It feels comfortable because it is what I know. (Sarah)

Interestingly, finding a new church was something that the students chose for themselves, linked with the importance placed on 'freedom' explored in the previous chapter. While some women like Haley tried a particular church because it was 'recommended ... by people at home', the women spoke very little about experiencing family pressure to find a church at university. Rather, the search for a church was an autonomous strategy for feeling safe and at home.

Third, for a small number of women, questions of theology or praxis were important in choosing a church, including: worship or sermon style, women's leadership roles (see Chapter 7), and the approach to evangelism. For example, Abigail said, 'I really liked the worship, the talking, the preaching, so yeah, it felt like, "I'll settle here".' Some students had to compromise on some of their criteria in favour of others that were less negotiable. For example, Taylor chose making new friends over theological stance, Alexis chose theology over worship style, Kimberly chose theology over 'however nice and friendly it was' and Olivia chose making friends, and emphasis on the Bible, over the worship style and 'doctrine'.

For many of the women, however, choosing a church was a straightforward and even accidental activity based on new relationships, in keeping with Fowler's stage 3 whereby individuals' 'values and self-images, mediated by the significant others in their lives, have largely *chosen them.*'[9] James E. Côté argues that many emerging adults experience 'default individualization',[10] which fits some of the women's experiences. For example, Olivia said, 'I never really decided to stay [at my church], it just kind of happened, and like the more I went, the more I got involved with the community, and the more [pause] I just ended up there.'

Danielle also appeared to give searching for a church little thought: 'I'm quite lazy and wait for it to come to me, because I am nervous about that kind of stuff.' 'Lazy' is a harsh word for Danielle to use about herself; it is more likely that she lacked confidence and felt vulnerable about positioning her lesbian identity in Christian contexts.

As the previous chapter details, Taylor found herself attending a large student church because she 'wanted to meet people'. When I interviewed her in her first term, she assumed that the church was Anglican and that women were able to preach there. However, the church was a conservative independent evangelical church which denied women any leadership roles. Like many other large evangelical churches, Taylor's church made it 'a priority to appeal to the student population to a point where this becomes central to their shared ethos', and, Guest and colleagues continue, to connect church with student life.[11] As with Taylor's church, conservative congregations aimed at students are often covert in describing their doctrines and practices, especially to newcomers, and Perrin finds that sometimes only the leadership might know the doctrinal stance held by a church.[12] In recent years, campaigns for churches to be transparent about their theologies of sexuality and gender have been run by the Student Christian Movement (SCM) and Women and the Church (WATCH), arguing that a lack of clarity is either intentionally or accidentally deceptive.[13] Since students arrive at university knowing very little about the diversity of the Christian faith, they can find themselves at churches in which they do not fit, like Taylor, or, like Danielle, feel unable to find a church at all. This is just one reason why church attendance cannot be the only measure of a student's faith. Nonetheless, settling into a church was an ongoing process for most of the women in this research, especially as relationships deepened.

Christian student societies

Many students were involved with a Christian student society, a student-led organization attached to their university's Student Union. While four students did not regularly attend any Christian student society, the rest attended eight different societies:

- an Anglican Society (AngSoc, 4 students);
- a Catholic Society (CathSoc, 2 students);
- Christian Connections, affiliated with the national Student Christian Movement (SCM, 1 student);
- the Christian Union (CU), affiliated to the national Universities and Colleges Christian Fellowship (UCCF, 7 students);
- GIFT, a Pentecostal society (1 student);
- Love Ur Uni, an evangelical society affiliated to a national body of the same name (1 student);[14]
- a Methodist Society (MethSoc, 3 students);
- the Navigators (Navs), an evangelical society affiliated to a national body of the same name (2 students).

The most popular societies were the CUs, with seven of the students regularly attending, and another five students having attended at least once. CUs were thriving in all three of the universities in this book, and are described by Guest and colleagues as 'the largest and most visible Christian group at most universities'. They find that:

> CU members are far more activist in their faith than all other types of Christian student; they attend church more often, frequently meet in small groups for prayer and Bible study, have more close Christian friends, and volunteer more often.

Yet, the authors continue, while CUs attempt to include diverse expressions of evangelicalism, in reality this creates 'increasing pressures', due to its 'rigorously conservative' interpretation of Christianity and its mission.[15] UCCF determines a doctrinal basis of faith that all CUs are expected to follow, and supplies regional workers to support local CUs and their leadership committees. UCCF states that the primary aims of the CUs are 'to help everyone at uni engage with the life-changing message of Jesus' and to enable students 'to reach their friends with the gospel'.[16] However, when they first arrive at university many Christian students find themselves attending CU activities while unaware of their proselytizing mission.

Despite the CUs' active and well-funded efforts at proselytizing, very few students actually convert to Christianity at university.[17] This finding is supported by Dutton, who suggests that CUs at more prestigious universities tend to be distinct and transitional in nature, with a stronger emphasis on conversion. He proposes that 'a high level of conversion experience' correlates with the 'questioning of identity' that is particularly common at elite academic institutions.[18] Students who appear to convert at university are often actually 'reconverting' from a non-evangelical (and thus considered unacceptable) form of Christianity, as an act of bonding and communitas. In non-elite universities, Dutton finds, CUs are less structured, less central to the identity of their members, and less likely to hold conservative views about a number of different issues.[19]

CUs represent around 10 per cent of Christian students, while the evangelical approach of the CUs, as Guest and his colleagues argue, 'may irritate or embarrass, offend or alienate other Christians'.[20] Among the five students who initially joined the CU but later left, both Alexis and Caitlin cited disagreement with the emphasis on evangelism as a reason for departing. Kimberly thought that while evangelism was important, the CU 'sometimes go a bit overboard with it, and it's a bit aggressive'. Both Abigail and Kimberly said that they 'get quite annoyed by the CU' 'because women can't be in leadership', and Caitlin rejected their conservative stance on sexuality. Researching a comparable evangelical student organization in the US, Alyssa N. Bryant observes that, 'the culture embraced normative masculinity, essential gender differences, and separate roles and expectations for men and women'.[21] She continues, 'the construction of gender roles and norms was both purposeful and directed by deeply embedded beliefs about the essential natures of women and men'.[22] These are attitudes that I explore in Part III of this book. Nathan R. Todd and his colleagues argue that the distinctiveness of conservative beliefs about gender and sexuality contribute to the presence of societies as student subcultures, clarifying who is 'in' and who is 'out'.[23]

The students who did not remain in the CU all joined other Christian societies. For Caitlin and Alexis, it was important that their student society reflected their inclusive theologies. Caitlin helped found a new society affiliated with the Student Christian Movement (SCM), and Alexis joined AngSoc, both of which were attached to their university's chaplaincies which themselves had long-term connections with SCM. Founded in 1889, SCM is the oldest organization of Christian students in the UK, and was instrumental in the founding of other significant organizations including the World Council of Churches (WCC) and the National Union of Students (NUS). Guest and his colleagues state that 'in its heyday, SCM was a remarkable influence not only among students, but upon the wider church, with a pervasive influence in society and across the globe.' However, at the time of writing, only a few students demonstrate a visible, engaged liberal Christian practice, indicating SCM may face ongoing recruitment challenges.[24]

Aune and her colleagues find that student faith societies are primarily sources of intra-community bonding, 'helping students feel at home on campus, creating friendships and strengthening religious identity'. Yet they are also 'resources of bridging ... creating relationships with people outside the group', especially through volunteering, multifaith work, and to some extent evangelism.[25] Elsewhere, I write about friends who attended AngSoc, and demonstrate the society's function of *bonding* where Stephanie 'immediately felt welcome', while Melissa found it 'easier to talk to' other students due to shared theological perspectives. As I have written, 'Attendance at the chaplaincy society was a primary site for identity growth, both together and with God, and these relational processes were woven together in enabling and resourcing their crafting of home at university.'[26]

The *bridging* role of the society was met through engaging with strangers and maintaining friendships despite disagreements, participating in multifaith initiatives and ecumenical volunteering.[27] However, with all the women that I interviewed, it was the experience of bonding that was the most important aspect of attending a student society. More than anything else, the students needed to feel safe and supported, and Christian societies provided this space particularly through close friendships.

For many women, their Christian student society enabled them to make their deepest friendships where, as Sharma and Guest write, 'students' imaginaries of family extend, where they experience and cultivate intimate ties that become "home"'.[28] Not only were societies spaces in which to foster deep friendships, they also facilitated identity security as the students felt able to be themselves and share the difficulties they faced; both of which were important factors in the creation of safety and the crafting of home, as Stephanie demonstrates: 'They were just really nice and welcoming, it did, I just felt quite safe there ... yeah that, that's it, it's just somewhere that feels like home.' Abigail appreciated Navs as 'a secure kind of place ... a support group'. Because the other society members were also evangelical Christians she felt 'a little freer, because I know that there's a lot of common ground'. Through Navs, she had 'made friends that I feel at home with'. At GIFT, Danielle felt 'comfortable and a bit more, like, safe' knowing that there were other Christians 'to talk about stuff, like, God-related'. Mary attended CathSoc because of 'the people your age, they're all at university ... it's like the social aspect'. Lauren found it 'easier' to 'be myself' at MethSoc, and was able to ask friends 'Can I have a chat?' when she needed someone to talk with. Several women said similar things about the CU. Comments included:

> People are more welcoming ... it's just warmer. (Amber)

> When I'm there it's like they look out for you. (Haley)

> People really care about your week ... you're just more comfortable. (Olivia)

> All my close friends I've met at CU, which just shows how valuable CU is. (Tumi)

Briana attended the CU 'more for the friends and for the fellowship than for God', while Stephanie recognized that AngSoc 'was as much [about] the people as the faith'. Discussing bridging and bonding in Christian student societies, Guest and colleagues reflect that university 'depends upon bonding social capital between peer groups ... Close community may be a barrier to integration, but also a precondition of survival in the longer term.'[29]

Gilliat-Ray argues that the student-led committees of faith societies often prepare the next generation of faith leaders in Britain.[30] Of course I do not know, for most students, how they went on to practise their faith after university, or whether they took on leadership roles. However, many of the students became involved in the leadership committee of their student society, and some found the experience transformative, including Ashley who did go on to be a Christian leader in her twenties (as explored in the previous chapter). It was important for Ashley that, at Love Ur Uni, she was 'learning more skills, that will be valuable for me, outside of the university'. She was also learning about different expressions of Christianity. She was 'disappoint[ed]' when the CU's doctrinal statement created 'conflict' and an 'unwillingness to work with other societies', while other societies 'were unwilling to hear about evangelism'. The university chaplaincy became involved with helping these different societies understand their differences, which Ashley found beneficial.[31]

Briana experienced an awakening in her understanding of her faith, partly because her place on the CU committee led to some difficult conversations about gender roles, broadening her understanding and enabling her to consider her own beliefs. Having come to university believing that her faith and church were typical of Christianity, her eyes were opened to different expressions of Christianity and different theologies, giving her confidence in exploring her own beliefs. She said, 'I've grown a lot in my relationship with God, grown more as a person, like confidence-wise, like knowledge-wise ... in terms of Christian matters as it were, I've grown with that.'

As with research by Guest and colleagues, the depth, homeliness and comfort that the women found in these 'sites of refuge' was unmatched in any other social group, demonstrating a 'blurring [of] familial and friendship boundaries' and a sense of belonging in 'surrogate families'. These Christian friendships are one way in which 'students model, embody and convey religion'.[32] While only four students said that *most* of their friends were Christian, a higher number found that their *closest* friendships were with other Christians. The women found that Christian friendships were more 'real' and 'deep' since sharing the same faith led to a more 'natural' 'connection' than in other communities. Samantha thought that Christians 'have really similar values, so it sort of inevitably leads to better friendships'.

Among Christian societies, as also reported by Guest and colleagues, the CU was 'the most highly visible Christian subculture', yet should not be assumed typical of contemporary Christianity at university, or the 'group where most Christian students are to be found'.[33] Ashley critiqued the 'push' for Christian students to attend their CU, emphasizing that 'there are so many other groups and they all have a different way of allowing you to express your faith'. Yet, Guest and colleagues continue, 'declining student interest and support has resulted in decline in funding for denominational societies and the long-term decline of SCM.'[34] Since I conducted my research, AngSoc and MethSoc merged to form a new SCM group. It will be interesting to see what the future holds for student expressions of liberal Christianity that go beyond the overt proselytism of the CUs.

Chaplaincies

In her creative foreword to *A Handbook of Chaplaincy Studies*, edited by Christopher Swift and colleagues, Linda Woodhead imagines a new 'Future Religion' taskforce with the mandate of re-engineering the British religious landscape. This taskforce discerns four functions of religion: meeting people's spiritual needs; offering communitas; serving society; and 'hold[ing] up a higher vision'. The group pays attention to the multifaith nature of Britain, and assesses both the public and private nature of religion. Weighing up the odds, the taskforce makes some surprising discoveries. The taskforce decides that chaplaincy offers the best model of religious provision to serve the British people, and easily meets all four religious functions identified through its 'healthy partnership' with society and 'ability to grow and adapt to changing socio-political conditions'. Woodhead's conclusion to this imaginary scenario is that 'When it came to rebooting religion, the Future Religion group found in chaplaincy a "stub" on which it was able to grow the kind of religion that Britain today really needed.'[35]

Published in 2015, the *Handbook* came amid a tide of new academic interest in chaplaincy,[36] including in higher education.[37] Of course, important literature on chaplaincy existed previously,[38] but renewed attention to the work of chaplaincy has both recognized its current relevance and – as Woodhead states – points to its necessity in the future of British faith.

In 2008, almost 90 per cent of higher education institutions had a university chaplaincy.[39] A 2019 report finds that 'the older the university sector, the more chaplains there were', from an average of 13 chaplains at traditional elite universities to 4.9 chaplains per university in the Cathedrals Group.[40] The role of chaplains has changed significantly in the past few decades, having moved away from 'an extension of the parish model'[41] and providing Anglican worship and spiritual support for Christian students. After interviewing 367 higher education chaplains, Aune, Guest and Jeremy Law find that chaplains' primary aims include:

- pastoral care and well-being, especially listening to those in need;
- religious and spiritual provision and support, including multifaith work and space for exploration;
- presence, that is, 'placing being ... before doing and activity ... because the former essentially leads to the latter';
- mission or witness, communicating the richness of God's love, including occasional evangelism;
- prophetic, including seeking justice and 'raising profound questions';
- building relationships and community.[42]

Simon Perfect discusses the interaction between 'a chaplain's physical presence and their accompanying presence – the latter meaning their role in being alongside people in their journey, and "being around" and emotionally available even when not literally present.'[43]

An emphasis on presence is framed in theological terms as being incarnational. Ben Ryan argues that:

> The incarnation is made more significant by the constant encounter between God and humanity in the life of Jesus. In the same way, chaplaincy's greatest theological tool is its ability to encounter people ... Incarnation is the model of chaplaincy that seems most theologically robust, and true to what chaplains do in practice already.[44]

Elsewhere, Ryan frames the prophetic as 'critical feedback', making the surprising observation that: 'This may seem like a role which shouldn't appeal to an organization – tantamount to trouble making. Yet stakeholders time and again subverted that expectation and praised the chaplain for being able to speak up and keep an organization honest.'[45]

With over 50 per cent of 17- to 30-year-olds participating in higher education in England in 2017–18, and almost 57 per cent of those being women,[46] university chaplaincies are an essential space for the church to build relationships with the younger generations. Thus, higher education chaplaincy is good, both for universities as they increasingly recognize the need to support students' well-being, and for the Church in its mission to be present with emerging adults. Chaplaincies and faith provision are also useful for universities in their recruitment. Lauren, for example, chose to attend her particular university in part because of its chaplaincy and Methodist Society, demonstrating the importance of her faith in her education.

Several authors note that university chaplaincies act as safe places of 'refuge'[47] or 'haven'[48] for students, where they can feel at home away from the depersonalizing and destabilizing effects of university life. Jane Speck writes that chaplaincies are a space where students are able to 'let go and let be ... where we can all find nurturing and rejuvenation'.[49] As Guest and his colleagues write, 'Given that most Christians will not join the CU and only half are going to church at university, chaplaincies seem best placed to explore creative re-engagement with the Christian majority, on their own terms.'[50]

Of the students in my research, 22 had had some interaction with chaplaincy. Nine attended chaplaincy-affiliated societies supported by chaplains – AngSoc, CathSoc and MethSoc – and these students understood chaplaincy's function. They often hung out at the chaplaincy and took some ownership over the spaces, freely using kitchen facilities and common rooms. For example, Sarah described the chaplaincy as 'a nice space' to have 'a cup of tea and [do] some work'. Both AngSoc and CathSoc hosted Sunday worship in the chaplaincy alongside social events; thus some students regarded these spaces as their *church* as well as student society. Three students not involved with these societies also saw the space as somewhere they could go to relax or catch up on work. Tumi described the chaplaincy as 'just a good safe space', and Alexandra considered it 'integral to the "at home" place ... [with] a sense of belonging'. Caitlin described the chaplaincy as where 'you can be yourself 100 per cent and people just will accept you', and where she could 'drop the mask once in a while'.

For all these students, plus two who could not physically visit their chaplaincy due to Covid-19 restrictions, being able to talk with a chaplain had a significant positive impact upon their time at university. Lauren reflected on how important it was for her to have 'a chaplain there who's ... [available] to help students'. Lauren, Mary and Melissa said that they would speak to their chaplain 'if I had a major problem', 'depending on what it was', 'cos I really like our chaplain', while Nicole said, 'She's one of the closest people, like, members of staff, that I've got to know'. Stephanie had spoken to a chaplain 'for advice on ... an issue I was having', and Samantha reported, 'he's helped me'. Alexandra attended mindfulness sessions led by a chaplain, and Chloe had 'redeveloped' and 'become more comfortable' with her faith through conversations with her chaplain. Caitlin spoke to a chaplain after a friend's suicide attempt, and he was able to 'help me through the process'. Tumi described her chaplain:

You just trust them, and they've made the space for you, for students, and that's lovely ... I think she does just have a heart for students and, and, you know, for their faith to be vocal and for them to have a chance to speak up.

Sacha Pearce and Jan Collis argue that, in encountering people on the margins of faith communities, chaplains are at the 'heart of human experience',[51] while Sharma and Sheryl Reimer-Kirkham find that chaplaincies operate at the edges of their institutions.[52] For bell hooks, edges are both 'sites of repression and sites of resistance', enabling being a part of the body while also being outside of the body, resulting in creativity and transformation.[53] In such an act of resistance, Perfect observes that chaplaincies particularly serve students experiencing isolation, including international students and LGBTQIA+ students who may feel marginalized in other religious spaces,[54] partly because of their emphasis on hospitality and inclusivity. For the students who interacted with their chaplaincy, the feeling of safety and home was significant as it both enabled them simply to be, and provided extra support. Many of the students engaged with their chaplaincy saw themselves as on the edge of the university, feeling distinct from what Holdsworth names the 'mythical student',[55] or marked as outsiders by their faith. Several students also felt at the margins of Christianity, through having felt unwelcome in other Christian spaces, or due to being new to Christian community, yet they were able to belong at the chaplaincy. It was significant to them that chaplaincies were integral to their university, and this helped them to feel as though the university was invested in both their well-being and their faith needs. Rambo describes chaplaincy as a means by which 'universities can attend to other ways of knowing, more associated with embodiment, intuition, and imagination', not merely 'academic endeavour'.[56] She continues, 'if students feel a sense of safety and belonging, they can activate inner resources to live with intention and have more clarity in ethical decision-making'. In this, 'the chaplain does not perform a rescue operation, they ... clear room for students to wrestle with what they are experiencing'.[57] Chaplaincies thus help students both in surviving their time at university, and in thriving in the adult world beyond their studies.

There were, however, areas of controversy or conflict apparent in how some students discussed the chaplaincy. Students from the CU, and those who did not attend any of these societies, knew very little about their chaplaincy. Many members of their CU were, as Caitlin said, 'a bit sceptical of chaplaincy because ... CU's practices were obviously very evangelical, very different to chaplaincies.' Despite the CU at the redbrick university meeting weekly in its chaplaincy space, CU students there understood themselves as hiring, rather than owning, it. Olivia would not consider the chaplaincy as 'somewhere to go', not even for free hot drinks or a comfortable place to work. Briana said, 'I don't really know anything about it actually', and Taylor thought, 'I'm not sure why I'd come.' The CU at this university also did not have a relationship with any of the chaplains due to the former's doctrinal statement; thus CU students 'would be more inclined to go to my church than the chaplaincy' if they wanted spiritual support. Amber and Danielle said that they would not go to speak with a chaplain 'because I don't know them' and they would not 'go and see a stranger'.

Hesitancy about chaplaincy was especially noticeable among students at the more elite universities, reflecting Dutton's findings mentioned above that CUs at less privileged institutions tend to be more relaxed.[58] At a post-1992 university, Ola thought that the CU and the chaplaincy 'work[ed] hand-in-hand', and she used the chaplaincy space when she wanted to 'chill' or 'have lunch'. Tumi was actually introduced to the chaplain through 'our staff member at CU'. She thought, 'That's important for the CU, I think, to have a good relationship with [the chaplain], and she can tell us, you know, the different things that are going on in the religious space of the university.'

Chaplaincies have an important role in supporting community cohesion, including informing ecumenical and multifaith conversations, and generally increasing awareness within and between faith communities. Several students found the chaplaincy helped them encounter a breadth of Christianity with which they were previously unfamiliar, including Caitlin who 'felt at home within the more traditional Anglicanism' that she encountered in chaplaincy services.

Multifaith work was a common point of tension between chaplaincies and CUs. Briana said, 'We don't generally do stuff, um, with the chaplaincy, I think we, we kind of avoid doing any interfaith stuff because, being an evangelist society we don't, kind of, collaborate.' Chaplaincies often have chaplains, facilities and activities that cater for a range of faiths, and Christians that emphasize proselytizing over dialogue or relationship can be wary of spaces in which people of different faiths come together. More than this, chaplaincies often hold multifaith events, building community across faiths,[59] which five students discussed attending. Again, the post-1992 university CU was more relaxed, hosting a multifaith event jointly with the chaplaincy. Tumi recognized the importance of making all faiths visible on campus and considered the chaplaincy the best space for this. She said, 'It was really nice to just speak, just have a conversation amongst people from different religions

... it was great that [the chaplain] allows that space.' James Walters and Margaret Bradley observe chaplaincies building 'the credibility of the Church within the secular world' and holding 'a space open within a highly suspicious secular environment', both of which are integral to making Christianity visible outside church boundaries.[60] Nonetheless, chaplaincies distinguish between incarnational mission and proselytism, which they necessarily avoid.

As with student faith societies, chaplaincies play a part in developing future Christian leaders, with both Caitlin and Alexandra exploring possible vocations to ordained ministry in their different denominations. Alexandra attended a vocations group where she encountered 'the difference in leadership positions' and 'different types of ministry' in churches.

For many students, chaplaincies were places of deep encounter – with themselves, with others, and with God. Despite their limited reach, with many students unaware of chaplaincy services or their potential benefits, chaplaincies proved to be deeply transformative for the students who connected with them.

Faith spaces and the Covid-19 pandemic

Following from the women's experiences of the Covid-19 pandemic explored in Chapter 2, this section considers the women's faith and engagement with Christian spaces during the pandemic. When the UK government announced the first national lockdown in March 2020, churches closed for at least four months, including for private prayer, worship gatherings, weddings and funerals. The subsequent relaxation of restrictions, followed by further lockdowns, changes in UK policy, and a system of local lockdowns dependent on infection rates, resulted in confusion and uncertainty for the country. Churches attempted to adapt as best they could to these moving goalposts. For Helen Froud, 'this interruption of shared experience' was akin to 'exile', which 'interrupt[ed] the warp and weft of the community's conversations with one another'.[61] Even when churches were permitted to open, they felt like different spaces than before the pandemic, 'with booking required, one-way systems, hand sanitisation stations, distanced seating, no singing, no after-worship gathering and with the need to wear masks.'[62]

Joshua Edelman collected data with colleagues about how faith communities responded to the restrictions imposed during the pandemic. They demonstrate the many ways that church provision moved online, especially through posting pre-recorded services, live-streaming services, and the use of video conferencing platforms to host services. While there is much to be celebrated in how churches inhabited virtual space, the authors observe: 'deep-seated dissatisfaction with digital worship during the pandemic ... They are perceived as less meaningful, less communal, less spiritual, less effective ... An overall sense of community has been markedly lacking and deeply missed.'[63]

I interviewed seven women during the Covid-19 pandemic. Six of these expressed dissatisfaction with virtual church, feeling that embodiment and physical relationship were too important to sacrifice. Physical aspects of church that the students particularly missed included receiving Holy Communion, engaging with sermons and meeting people. Some examples:

> I really hated watching online churches, it just felt so boring and isolating. (Ashley)

> I feel a bit, I think, [of] online fatigue now. But I think I would really like to go in person ... if it's online I feel so disconnected. (Chloe)

> We couldn't go into the church, and I was like, 'What's even the point of attending if it's online?' (Ola)

> I never really logged into my church to listen to the online sermons because it just felt more like paying lip service ... than actually getting the experience. (Taylor)

Caitlin stated that being unable to attend church affected her mental health. She said:

> I just can't engage with online church ... I was really struggling with that ... It's made me understand how important physically going to church is for me ... it's the thing I look forward to most out of the week, and just on the psychological level, when that was taken away from me, it was really crushing.

Caitlin had planned to be baptized during a Sunday morning service, but due to restrictions she chose to have a small ceremony with just two friends present, rather than delaying it until churches could re-open fully. She felt that she had made the right decision, but had missed out on a significant celebration of her faith with her community.

Only Alexandra benefited from online engagement with her church during the pandemic. In fact, Alexandra became involved in new initiatives as her church responded to Covid-19, including supporting vulnerable women, providing outreach with young people, and leading a Bible study group.

While Ola found it difficult to connect to a local church, she took advantage of the global move online and engaged with virtual content from a church based in the US. Inspired by the church's female pastor (discussed further in Chapter 7), Ola felt encouraged by their online services and podcasts. As it was online, Ola was free to engage as much or as little as she wanted, with little risk or pressure, which she found easier and safer. It became an important space for Ola to encounter new perspectives and explore her own beliefs. While she had no personal relationships there, she felt motivated and involved in something beyond herself. As Edelman and colleagues report: 'Online engagement has also led to a re-thinking of community as a naturally bounded geographical phenomenon. Instead, participants are increasingly able to seek out ... communities which best align with their own religious outlooks and spiritual needs.'[64]

In the absence of being able to meet in person, students sought this embodiment and relationship elsewhere. Several reported being intentional about having more time to 'sit with my faith', to 'think about God and ... my values', and 'to turn to God'. Chloe found the physical freedom from her conservative childhood church liberating, and felt able to 'independently ... think about God myself ... and how I want to live my life'. Alexandra made time each morning 'to centre myself', including listening to music and 'sit[ting] with God'. Caitlin 'tried to do morning and evening prayer, sort of, sat in front of candles or, with like physical presence, like, I started praying rosary more.' Ashley 'started to do Sabbaths together' with a close friend via video call during the pandemic, which she described as 'beautiful'. They would share 'the things that we were reflecting on ... learning or growing', reading Scripture and praying together. She described these calls as 'influential' for her faith because they 'had this love and support for one another to, kind of, make meaning'.

A report by Caroline Nye and Matt Lobley echoes some of these women's words, finding that many people were 'praying more, feeling closer to their faith, God, family and local communities' during the pandemic.[65] This is perhaps surprising given the global crisis, yet it reflects many people's increased free time and desire for connection. As Alexandra said, she felt too busy pre-pandemic 'to actually sit with my faith'.

Alexandra's morning devotions, Caitlin's rosary and candles, and Ashley's weekly video conversations enabled the women to find ritual and meaning outside of their church communities, and provided a physical, embodied and relational space for spiritual nurturing. Edelman and colleagues found that the 'lack of embodied collectivity' resulted in the innovation of new rituals 'that drew worshippers' attention to the physical, relational and embodied nature' of worship, which they may not have previously prioritized.[66]

Aside from churches and personal devotions, both Ola and Tumi were involved with their CU during the pandemic, including as part of the leadership committee. They developed embodied ways of connecting with the student community, including delivering care packages, which were important as much for the relational connection as the package contents.

Chaplaincy was also a space for connection and community during the pandemic. Perfect observes that university chaplaincies became more accessible and innovative, while chaplains saw 'increases in requests for pastoral support'; facilitated 'talking about big issues of meaning and mortality'; and 'generate[d] new forms of community'. Chaplains saw their role as 'encouraging hope'.[67] Alexandra, Caitlin and Chloe each regularly met a chaplain for one-to-one support during the pandemic. Chloe's grandmother recently died. Unable to travel to the funeral because of the restrictions, Chloe was asking questions about death, heaven and God. Her chaplain helped her 'become more comfortable' in her faith, 'slowly just dipping my toes in and just feeling comfortable in, I feel I know God exists.' Alexandra attended her chaplaincy's online activities, including mindfulness, multifaith events, and a discussion for queer Christians. Feeling isolated in her studies due to not being able to travel to the UK, chaplaincy involvement meant she began to feel at home at university.

As restrictions lifted, Alexandra continued to attend hybrid events (both in person and online) at her church and the chaplaincy. Most of the students who were involved with online Christian activities, however, left these behind, including Ola who no longer engaged with the American church but instead committed to her local church.

Andrew Village and Leslie J. Francis report that during the Covid-19 pandemic, a national survey found that 69 per cent of Church of England churches offered live-streamed or pre-recorded online services, and 92 per cent of participants had accessed services online. While accessing online church was not gendered, they found variation with age, observing that worshippers under 40 reported less satisfaction with online services than those aged 40–60. They argue that this finding was contrary to other research finding that 'one in three young adults between the ages of 18–34 had accessed an online or broadcast religious service during the previous 4 weeks'.[68]

This would perhaps be more aligned with what might be expected of students who are 'digital natives' and would probably have had the necessary computer equipment and internet access. However, as Village and Francis argue, 'online provision is unable to mitigate isolation or loneliness'.[69] Nye and Lobley echo this, with under-45s stating 'that they coped less well' and were 'more likely to feel further from their church' than over-65s.[70]

More research is needed into the impact of Covid-19 upon Christian emerging adults' engagement with church, both during the pandemic and in its ongoing legacy. The long-term effect of the pandemic upon church engagement is yet to be seen.

Evangelism

In the women's Christian spaces, they encountered practices that prompted them to rethink what they believed, and how they lived out that faith. The first was new exposure to, and encouragement to carry out, evangelism. Almost all the women mentioned discussing their faith with non-Christian students, and many overtly considered this to be 'evangelism' or 'mission'. Yet evangelism was particularly discussed by members of the CUs. Evangelism was emphasized at CU meetings to a greater extent than any of the women had encountered before, and for most it was completely new and came as a surprise. Taylor didn't know when she joined that evangelism was the society's priority, and Olivia 'hadn't actually realized that was the function of CU'.

The women discussed three different approaches to sharing their faith. The first approach to evangelism was more confrontational 'cold contact'[71] evangelism, with the aim of converting strangers. None of the women were expressly told to preach in public places or approach strangers on campus. The closest example was 'water bottling', whereby CU students distributed bottles of water outside nightclubs and attempted to engage people on questions of faith, which four students said they had done. Amber described it as a 'really good, like, a practical way of showing my faith', and Olivia reported that 'I did have a good, a few good conversations with people, like, actually about Christianity.' Dutton argues that such confrontational evangelism is more common at elite universities, posing a pronounced threat to students' identities, and 'has the effect of monitoring and controlling the behaviour of group members'.[72]

The second approach involved discussing faith with friends and inviting them to attend Christian events, sometimes called 'friendship evangelism'.[73] Examples include the CU's 'Events Week' involving external speakers addressing various topics, alongside free food, with the intention of inviting non-Christian friends; and a book that CU members were encouraged to read with their flatmates. However, many students recognized, as Mike Booker and Mark Ireland write, that evangelistic efforts were dependent upon relationships and 'cannot in themselves be the time when most relationships begin',[74] and so struggled to engage with these initiatives. For example, Kimberly attended Navigators because she preferred 'relational evangelism' to what she perceived as these 'overboard' and 'aggressive' methods.

Third, some students considered it important to be a visible witness to Christianity on campus. Amber hoped that people 'know I'm a Christian and they see from my behaviour', whereas she hadn't invited friends to events because 'I don't really wanna shove it under their noses.' A particular example of this kind of evangelism involved remaining sober amid the drinking culture. Olivia stated that not getting drunk was 'such a good time to witness', Kimberly thought of refraining from alcohol as being 'a representative of my faith', while Haley considered staying sober to be 'showing people ... straight away that I was a Christian'.

Briana was practising a mixture of the latter two methods in an incarnational approach to evangelism, saying, 'If you go and preach at them, they won't respect that [pause]. I think if you live, try and live by it, they see what a difference it's making in your life.' She described really enjoying the 'emphasis on mission ... I really like talking about my faith ... talk[ing] to your classmates and things, so I think I've become a lot more evangelistic.' A year later, Briana reflected that her experiences of evangelism, rather than converting others to Christianity, had shaped her own faith development at university, especially 'when I got asked questions ... I had to work out what I believed.'

It was not only members of the evangelical societies that were considering their approach to evangelism for the first time, and many women reflected upon how to relationally share their faith with integrity. Lauren had discussed her faith with her flatmates and 'they wanted to come to church to see what it's all about'; Megan's flatmates were 'keen to have a chat about it'; and Sarah had 'good conversations' about her faith with new friends. However, some students were more hesitant. Mary said, 'I don't really talk about it very much, oh, unless someone brings it up.' Nicole wished that she felt more confident and equipped to talk about her faith. Her lack of confidence meant that she did not discuss her faith 'because I don't understand enough'.

In encountering the CU's expectation to assist in the conversion of other students, some women felt guilty that they were not 'good' at evangelizing and wished they could be 'better' at sharing their faith. This made students uncomfortable, hindering rather than enabling them to feel at home. In keeping with Guest and colleagues' research, many students were ambiguous about evangelism at university, and this applied to evangelical as well as other Christians. They write, 'In practice many pay lip service to an activity that is proving increasingly awkward, difficult and culturally alien.'[75] Sometimes, a cheerful attitude to evangelism appeared rehearsed rather than personally owned. Olivia seemed enthusiastic yet simply quoted what she had been told by the CU, adding the word 'apparently', suggesting that her experience was different to what she had heard. She stated that university was a good 'opportunity to just evangelize and get to preach the gospels' because at university 'you have to talk about Jesus cos people are so open-minded, apparently.'

In their facilitated gathering, Alexis, Melissa and Stephanie discussed evangelism together in some detail as something they felt 'strongly' about. Melissa had heard 'horror stories' about CUs, and believed that cold contact evangelism was 'arrogance' suggesting that Christians are 'superior and [so other people] should listen to you'. Alexis moved from attending the CU to AngSoc because the CU taught 'you should just go up to people randomly and talk to them about religion', but she did not believe in 'shoving it in people's faces'. They believed it was wrong to convert people of other faiths to Christianity, and enjoyed attending multifaith events. Yet Melissa's friends at home had noticed that she had 'become a lot more comfortable in saying I'm a Christian [and] speaking about my faith', so her reaction was not against discussing Christianity per se. Moreover, the friends were concerned about the reputation of Christianity and wanted others to know their faith was inclusive and welcoming. They feared that evangelists were 'actually driving people away' from Christianity because people would believe that 'all Christians are crazy'. Alexis, Melissa and Stephanie's attitude was in keeping with that of other emerging adults, believing that individual choice and authenticity are more important than doctrinal orthodoxy.[76] Like students in research by Guest and colleagues, the women were 'aware of how resistant the wider student culture is to strident forms of religion'. In this way, the evangelistic praxis of the CU tended to 'irritate or embarrass, offend or alienate other Christians'.[77]

Aune and her colleagues argue that, as well as functioning as intra-group bonding, evangelism can actually be a means of bridging with other groups and building new relationships. They write,

Work inviting non-members to events is evidence of building bridges for communication that did not exist before. When ... students step away from their safe spaces to create conversations with students they do not know, this is evidence of building bridges.[78]

Moreover, contrary to the opinions of the students in my research, they argue that, 'Faith sharing should not be seen as necessarily antithetical to interfaith work.'[79] This might in part be due to the lack of evidence of students successfully converting others.[80] The authors identify a 'tension between creating community among religious students ... and how religious students express their religion publicly'.[81] This tension was keenly felt by many of the women. However, they renegotiated evangelism, using it as a means to explore their own beliefs and adopting subtle, personally comfortable methods of sharing their faith.

Sermons

The second practice that the women discussed was the experience of hearing sermons with different content or styles than they had previously encountered. Perhaps unexpectedly, more than two-thirds of the women discussed the importance of sermons in exploring their faith, and preaching was often a significant factor in choosing their church at university. The students were open to, as Briana said, 'obviously learn things' through sermons, including encountering beliefs that they might never have heard before or might not agree with. Walter Brueggemann regards preaching as 'a chance to let the practice of mercy touch the reality of God's displaced orphans',[82] and many of the women experienced sermons as similarly pastoral and affirming in being away from home for the first time. They also heard relevant teachings and ethics in sermons that they had never previously encountered in public worship. Taylor thought that sermons were 'the words of someone who's had ... a lot more, teaching in terms of religion than me, so their words are worth listening to'. She saw sermons as 'the main body of the church experience'. When unable to attend during the Covid-19 pandemic, hearing sermons in person was the aspect of church that she missed most.

Examples of sermon topics that students found helpful in exploring their faith included: 'the peace of God', God's love, relating the Bible 'to real life situations', 'what it is to be a Christian in the modern world', issues 'relatable to people my age', 'God wants you to enjoy life not necessarily just follow all these rules', 'human rights', 'putting [the Bible] into context and not telling you what to believe', and current political issues. Tumi heard a sermon where she thought, 'I can see the love of God here, I can see the way they want to show me the love of God'. In Ola's church, members of the congregation were in 'life groups … [that] talk about the sermon on Sunday', and she found this regular opportunity helpful both in her faith development and in developing a sense of belonging.

Kat, Olivia and Taylor attended the same student-oriented independent evangelical church. Kat and Olivia appreciated the church's biblical expositions, where the preacher would explain a passage verse-by-verse. Olivia contrasted this style of preaching with sermons at home, after which she would wonder, 'I don't actually know what I was meant to learn from that.' Hull critiques what he considers a simple pietistic address that discourages questioning.[83] However, for some students, such sermons presented the Bible in a new way that felt clear and accessible. Kat and Olivia were both present for a sermon extolling a conservative theology of the role of women, which they disagreed with but said helped them to 'appreciate both sides of the Christian argument'. However, due to the didactic nature of the preaching, Taylor felt unable to ask questions or 'refute something from the Bible'. Taylor was confused by hearing contradictory sermons, saying both 'God judges you by how many souls you've managed to net', but conversely that 'God's already picked who's going [to heaven], you make no difference.' Some years later, Taylor was able to critique this preaching with language that she did not have at the time, and understood that she had some choice in her beliefs: 'People have so many different opinions, I don't know who's right, I'm just going for the one that feels best.' She did not feel that the sermons at this church resourced her to explore her faith or to own what she believed.

As with evangelism, Alexis, Melissa and Stephanie discussed sermons together in detail. They agreed that the sermon content at AngSoc was significant, and Melissa thought, 'If I disagree with what [the chaplain is] saying in the sermon, I'm not gonna keep coming.' In fact, the sermons had been a primary reason why she had continued attending AngSoc, having been surprised to find a peer group that shared the same liberal theology as her. Alexis particularly valued sermons emphasizing that 'You can't make God love you any more, because he already does', and discussing queer justice. Melissa was struck by a sermon which was 'The first time [for] anyone to have been actually, "You're not a failure" … that made me understand the idea of "God loves you" much more than anything else.'

The significance of sermons for the women is interesting when seen alongside literature arguing that young people are under-resourced in navigating religious life.[84] Taylor's concern with 'refuting' the Bible must be heeded, since sermons had shut down exploration rather than resourcing her in a life-giving faith. Yet, through a balance of confirming God's love and introducing new theological ideas, sermons encouraged the students to consider issues of meaning and purpose in their own lives and in relation to the world around them, and were a valued means of faith exploration.

Volunteering and social justice

Many women were engaged in some kind of social action. Different studies both in the UK and the US suggest that emerging adults most committed to volunteering also tend to be regular church attenders.[85] Astin and his colleagues find that 'One of the surest ways to enhance the spiritual development of undergraduate students is to encourage them to engage in almost any form of charitable or altruistic activity.'[86]

Melissa's belief that 'one of the best ways to practise your faith is through helping other people' and 'trying to make the world a better place' was common, perhaps spurred by the fallout of economic austerity in the UK at the time, and encouraged by 'gap experiences' (see Chapter 3) whereby students had encountered people in need. Contexts for volunteering or campaigning were broad, including: retirement housing, foodbanks, conservation projects, refugee charities, children's education or health, uniformed organizations, international development, homelessness projects, feminist campaigns and anti-war protests. Little distinction was made regarding whether a project or campaign was Christian or not; rather, engagement was understood as unconditionally offering support for those who most needed it. For Olivia, volunteering was 'a way to respond to God's love for us'. She believed that giving up her time 'to love other people' was more valuable than donating money. Samantha viewed her commitment to environmentalism as showing that Christians must be 'responsible for everything we do'. Lauren said, 'I wanna help people, I think that's about my faith, and about my faith and its relation to social action.' Stephanie agreed that social action was 'what I think religion should be about, it's not about "I'm right and you're wrong", it's sort of working together to improve people's lives.'

Other students saw their commitment to social justice as a covert alternative to cold contact evangelism, whereby other people were, as Jerry Persha argues, more likely to 'listen to the witness of a genuine life of service and love than to the words of a proclaimer'.[87] These students did not necessarily declare their faith, but rather showed God's love simply by doing good. In her second year, Courtney felt more able to 'direct my thoughts and everything, my energy, towards others'. She found herself thinking 'less about me and more about others, like how my relationship with God is shown to others, even if they don't necessarily know about it.' Vicky said, 'I'd rather do the things that show that love, than talk to somebody about why I think that God loves them.' Melissa thought that helping others was 'more important' than evangelism. She said, 'That's the way of displaying my faith to God ... that's no one else's business as to why I'm doing it.' For Melissa, her commitment to justice included campaigning for same-sex marriage in the church, spreading God's love rather than 'hatred ... because otherwise you just see the Christians with terrible banners and slogans.'

Some students' commitment to helping others came specifically from how they understood the nature of God. Ashley felt that God was against violence and 'cries out against it'. Abigail believed, 'Jesus does want me to go to the people who have been quite broken hearted', including the biblical imperative to care for refugees.

In recognition of her interdependence with people on the margins, Vicky spoke passionately about her 'conscious decision' to work with those stereotyped as 'poor', 'rubbish' or 'scroungers', realizing her privileged position to 'champion' them. She was involved in several different projects, both at university and at home:

> That's been a conscious decision ... taking the things that Jesus said literally, like feeding people who need food, and like looking after people who are vulnerable ... doing as much as you can to demonstrate that there's a God that loves everybody and that they need to know about it.

Similarly, Alexandra thought that 'God would want us to advocate for people who aren't given the opportunity to advocate for themselves.' She continued, 'social justice ... can't be separated from faith because it's what God is like, it's what God calls me to do.' Caitlin believed that 'to be a Christian is inherently a political act' since 'the teachings of Jesus, you can't read them in a non-political way'. She continued: 'I don't understand how people [pause] read the Bible and yet forget to love their neighbour or forget to serve the poor and the most needy in society when that is the core truth of Jesus' teaching.'

While not shared by all the women, students across various religious traditions were committed to volunteering and social justice, and this commitment was a significant and widespread factor in how women interpreted and practised their faith at university.

Conclusion

The first half of this chapter demonstrates the importance of the women's Christian communities, including churches, student societies and chaplaincies. Within these spaces, the students were able to build meaningful and significant relationships, encounter new ideas and craft a home for themselves at university. In these spaces, the students' faith identities were relationally nurtured through the chosen-families that they fostered. As Katz and her colleagues argue: 'Postmillennials' emphasis on identity is intensely social ... To find out who you are also means finding out where you fit ... Finding your *fam* is intimately connected with finding your identity.'[88]

These spaces also introduced many of the women to theologies and expressions of Christianity different from their own, broadening their understanding and enabling them to consider their own beliefs. Perrin argues for the benefits of such a broadened awareness, while a 'lack of exposure to alternative theological traditions can have long term consequences for faith development'.[89] I discussed the women's mixed experiences of faith during the Covid-19 pandemic, and the impact of being prevented from physically engaging with these important spaces.

I then explored evangelism, listening to sermons and social justice. While the students also briefly discussed Holy Communion, prayer, reading Christian books, listening to Christian music, as well as multifaith engagement, it was these three practices that the women most engaged with and that impacted upon their faith at university. Even those who were uncomfortable with 'evangelism' were able to faithfully articulate their concerns and still found ways of sharing their faith. In hearing pastorally affirming sermons that related the Bible to their lives as emerging adults, the women were able to locate themselves within the life of God's story, and feel confident in navigating this journey. In engaging with social action, the women practised their faith in publicly altruistic ways that reminded them of their responsibilities as citizens and as Christians. These activities helped the students move from simply feeling safe and secure in their Christian communities to exploring new ideas, trying out new practices and owning their faith for themselves.

Notes

1 Mathew Guest et al., *Christianity and the University Experience: Understanding Student Faith* (London: Bloomsbury, 2013), p. 37.
2 Guest et al., *Christianity and the University Experience*, p. 38.
3 Guest et al., *Christianity and the University Experience*, pp. 38–9.

CHRISTIAN SPACES AND ACTIVITIES

4 See, for example, Ruth H. Perrin, *Changing Shape: The Faith Lives of Millennials* (London: SCM Press, 2020).

5 Jennifer L. Crissman-Ishler and Staci Schreiber, 'First-Year Female Students: Perceptions of Friendship', *Journal of Higher Education* 63 (2002), pp. 441–62.

6 James W. Fowler, *Stages of Faith: The Psychology of Human Development and the Quest for Meaning* (New York: Harper Collins, 1981), p. 178.

7 See, for example, Sonya Sharma and Mathew Guest, 'Navigating Religion Between University and Home: Christian Students' Experiences in English Universities', *Social and Cultural Geography* 14, no. 1 (2013); Herminia Ibarra, 'Provisional Selves: Experimenting with Image and Identity in Professional Adaptation', *Administrative Science Quarterly* 44, no. 4 (1999), pp. 764–91.

8 Fowler, *Stages of Faith*, p. 179.

9 Fowler, *Stages of Faith*, p. 154, emphasis my own.

10 James E. Côté, 'Emerging Adulthood as an Institutionalized Moratorium: Risks and Benefits to Identity Formation' in *Emerging Adults in America*, ed. Jeffrey Jensen Arnett and Jennifer L. Tanner (Washington, DC: American Psychological Association, 2006), p. 92.

11 Guest et al., *Christianity and the University Experience*, pp. 159–60.

12 Ruth H. Perrin, *The Bible Reading of Young Evangelicals: An Exploration of the Ordinary Hermeneutics and Faith of Generation Y* (Eugene, OR: Pickwick Publications, 2016), p. 5.

13 See Student Christian Movement, 'Honest Church', https://www.movement.org.uk/get-involved/honest-church, and Women and the Church, www.womenandthechurch.org, accessed 4.10.2024.

14 This student society is given a pseudonym due to its small size, to protect the anonymity of this student.

15 Guest et al., *Christianity and the University Experience*, pp. 147–8, 197.

16 UCCF: The Christian Unions, https://www.uccf.org.uk, accessed 5.10.2024.

17 Guest et al., *Christianity and the University Experience*, pp. 83–112.

18 Edward Croft Dutton, *Meeting Jesus at University: Rites of Passage and Student Evangelicals* (Aldershot: Ashgate, 2008), p. 30.

19 Dutton, *Meeting Jesus at University*, p. 13.

20 Guest et al., *Christianity and the University Experience*, pp. 206, 157.

21 Alyssa N. Bryant, 'Negotiating the Complementarian Gender Ideology of an Evangelical Student Subculture: Further Evidence from Women's Narratives', *Gender and Education* 21, no. 5 (September 2009), p. 549.

22 Alyssa N. Bryant, 'Assessing the Gender Climate of an Evangelical Student Subculture in the United States', *Gender and Education* 18, no. 6 (2006), p. 629.

23 Nathan R. Todd et al., 'Christian Campus-Ministry Groups at Public Universities and Opposition to Same-Sex Marriage', *Psychology of Religion and Spirituality* 9, no. 4 (November 2017), pp. 412–22.

24 Guest et al., *Christianity and the University Experience*, pp. 145–7.

25 Kristin Aune, Simon Perfect and Ben Ryan, 'Building Bridges or Holy Huddles? Student Religious Organizations in British Universities', *Journal of Diversity in Higher Education* (27 June 2024), p. 1.

26 Jenny Morgans, 'Faithing, Friendship and Feeling at Home: Three Women Encounter University Chaplaincy' in *From the Shores of Silence: Conversations in Feminist Practical Theology*, ed. Ashley Cocksworth, Rachel Starr and Stephen Burns (London: SCM Press, 2023), p. 105.

27 Morgans, 'Faithing, Friendship and Feeling at Home', p. 107.
28 Sharma and Guest, 'Navigating Religion', p. 71.
29 Guest et al., *Christianity and the University Experience*, p. 197.
30 Sophie Gilliat-Ray, *Higher Education and Student Religious Identity* (Exeter: University of Exeter, 1999), p. 33.
31 Gilliat-Ray argues that chaplaincies often hold such a mediatory role (*Higher Education*, p. 33).
32 Guest et al., *Christianity and the University Experience*, pp. 114–17.
33 Guest et al., *Christianity and the University Experience*, pp. 156–7.
34 Guest et al., *Christianity and the University Experience*, p. 161.
35 Linda Woodhead, 'Foreword: Chaplaincy and the Future of Religion' in *A Handbook of Chaplaincy Studies: Understanding Spiritual Care in Public Places*, ed. Christopher Swift, Mark Cobb and Andrew Todd (Farnham: Ashgate, 2015), pp. xviii–xxi.
36 See, for example, Sophie Gilliat-Ray, Muhammad Mansur Ali and Stephen Pattison, *Understanding Muslim Chaplaincy* (Farnham: Ashgate, 2013); Ben Ryan, 'A Very Modern Ministry: Chaplaincy in the UK' (Theos Think Tank, 2015); Victoria Slater, *Chaplaincy Ministry and the Mission of the Church* (London: SCM Press, 2015); The Methodist Church, 'Chaplaincy Essentials: A Resource for Nurturing Chaplains in the Essential Skills for Their Work' (Trustees for Methodist Church Purposes, 2015); Jeremy M.S. Clines and Sophie Gilliat-Ray, 'Religious Literacy and Chaplaincy' in *Religious Literacy in Policy and Practice*, ed. Adam Dinham and Matthew Francis (Bristol: Policy Press, 2015), pp. 235–54; and John Caperon, Andrew Todd and James Walters, eds, *A Christian Theology of Chaplaincy* (London: Jessica Kingsley, 2018).
37 Rowan Clare Williams, *A Theology for Chaplaincy: Singing Songs in a Strange Land* (Cambridge: Grove Books, 2018); Kristin Aune, Mathew Guest and Jeremy Law, 'Chaplains on Campus: Understanding Chaplaincy in UK Universities' (Coventry University, Durham University, Canterbury Christ Church University, 2019); Simon Perfect, 'Relationships, Presence and Hope: University Chaplaincy during the COVID-19 Pandemic' (Theos Think Tank, 2021); Shelly Rambo, 'Making a Case for College and University Chaplaincy: Howard Thurman as Guide', *Journal of Pastoral Theology* 34, no. 1 (2 January 2024).
38 Christopher Moody, 'Students, Chaplaincy and Pilgrimage', *Theology* 89, no. 732 (1986), pp. 440–7; Giles Legood, *Chaplaincy: The Church's Sector Ministries* (London: Cassell, 1999); Simon Robinson and Mike Benwell, 'Christian Chaplaincy in the Post-Modern University', *Modern Believing* 41, no. 1 (1999), pp. 31–43; Peter McGrail and John Sullivan, *Dancing on the Edge: Chaplaincy, Church and Higher Education* (Chelmsford: Matthew James Publishing, 2007); Jeremy M.S. Clines, 'Faiths in Higher Education Chaplaincy' (Church of England Board of Education, 2008); Paul Ballard, 'Locating Chaplaincy: A Theological Note', *Crucible* (July–September 2009), pp. 18–24; Miranda Threlfall-Holmes and Mark Newitt, *Being a Chaplain* (London: SPCK, 2011).
39 Clines, 'Faiths in Higher Education Chaplaincy', p. 4.
40 Aune, Guest and Law, 'Chaplains on Campus', p. 16.
41 Ben Ryan, 'Theology and Models of Chaplaincy' in *A Christian Theology of Chaplaincy*, ed. John Caperon, Andrew Todd and James Walters (London: Jessica Kingsley, 2018), p. 80.
42 Aune, Guest and Law, 'Chaplains on Campus', pp. 36–9.

43 Perfect, 'Relationships, Presence and Hope', p. 9.
44 Ryan, 'Theology and Models of Chaplaincy', pp. 91–2.
45 Ryan, 'A Very Modern Ministry', p. 39.
46 Alison Kershaw, 'More than Half of Young People Now Going to University, Figures Show', *Independent*, 27 September 2019, https://www.independent.co.uk/news/education/education-news/university-students-young-people-over-half-first-time-a9122321.html, accessed 18.10.2024.
47 Moody, 'Students, Chaplaincy and Pilgrimage', p. 445; Guest et al., *Christianity and the University Experience*, p. 114.
48 Guest et al., *Christianity and the University Experience*, pp. 138–45; McGrail and Sullivan, *Dancing on the Edge*, p. 24.
49 Jane Speck, 'King's College London' in *Being a Chaplain*, ed. Miranda Threlfall-Holmes and Mark Newitt (London: SPCK, 2011), pp. 34–6.
50 Guest et al., *Christianity and the University Experience*, p. 207.
51 Sacha Pearce and Jan Collis, *Creating Space: Story, Reflection and Practice in Healthcare Chaplaincy* (Durham: Sacristy Press, 2022), pp. 10, 13.
52 Sonya Sharma and Sheryl Reimer-Kirkham, 'In Plain View: Gender in the Work of Women Healthcare Chaplains', *Social Compass* (2022), p. 13.
53 bell hooks, 'Choosing the Margin as a Space of Radical Openness', *Framework: The Journal of Cinema and Media* 36 (1989), pp. 21, 23.
54 Perfect, 'Relationships, Presence and Hope', p. 32.
55 Holdsworth, 'Don't You Think You're Missing Out'.
56 Rambo, 'Making a Case for College and University Chaplaincy', p. 42.
57 Rambo, 'Making a Case for College and University Chaplaincy', pp. 44–6.
58 Dutton, *Meeting Jesus at University*.
59 See, for example, Williams, *A Theology for Chaplaincy*; Andrew Todd, 'Responding to Diversity: Chaplaincy in a Multi-Faith Context' in *Being a Chaplain*, ed. Miranda Threlfall-Holmes and Mark Newitt (London: SPCK, 2011), pp. 89–102.
60 James Walters and Margaret Bradley, 'Chaplaincy and Evangelism' in *A Christian Theology of Chaplaincy*, ed. John Caperon, Andrew Todd and James Walters (London: Jessica Kingsley, 2018), pp. 148–9.
61 Helen Froud, 'Returning from Exile? Reconciliation Within the Church after COVID-19', *Practical Theology* 14, no. 1–2 (4 March 2021), pp. 123, 128.
62 Froud, 'Returning from Exile?', p. 125.
63 Joshua Edelman et al., 'British Ritual Innovation under COVID-19' (Manchester Metropolitan University; University of Chester; Arts and Humanities Research Council, 2021), p. 113.
64 Edelman et al., 'British Ritual Innovation under COVID-19', p. 108.
65 Caroline Nye and Matt Lobley, 'COVID-19, Christian Faith and Wellbeing' (University of Exeter, 2020), p. 13.
66 Edelman et al., 'British Ritual Innovation under COVID-19', p. 109.
67 Perfect, 'Relationships, Presence and Hope', pp. 10–11.
68 Andrew Village and Leslie J. Francis, 'Lockdown Worship in the Church of England: Predicting Affect Responses to Leading or Accessing Online and In-Church Services', *Journal of Beliefs & Values* 44, no. 2 (3 April 2023), pp. 2–3, 12, 14.
69 Village and Francis, 'Lockdown Worship in the Church of England', p. 3.
70 Nye and Lobley, 'COVID-19, Christian Faith and Wellbeing', p. 13.

71 Dutton, *Meeting Jesus at University*, p. 86.

72 Dutton, *Meeting Jesus at University*, p. 87; see also John Hull, *What Prevents Christian Adults from Learning?* (London: SCM Press, 1985), pp. 98, 127–8.

73 See Mathew Guest, *Evangelical Identity and Contemporary Culture: A Congregational Study in Innovation* (Milton Keynes: Paternoster, 2007); Floyd Schneider, *Friendship Evangelism* (Eastbourne: Monarch, 1989).

74 Mike Booker and Mark Ireland, *Evangelism: Which Way Now? An Evaluation of Alpha, Emmaus, Cell Church and Other Contemporary Strategies for Evangelism*, 2nd ed. (London: Church House Publishing, 2005), p. 73.

75 Guest et al., *Christianity and the University Experience*, pp. 120, 153, 207.

76 See, for example, Sylvia Collins-Mayo, 'Choosing My Religion: Young People's Personal Christian Knowledge' in *Religion and Knowledge: Sociological Perspectives*, ed. Mathew Guest and Elisabeth Arweck (Aldershot: Ashgate, 2012), pp. 149–63.

77 Guest et al., *Christianity and the University Experience*, pp. 153, 157.

78 Aune, Perfect and Ryan, 'Building Bridges or Holy Huddles?', p. 29.

79 Aune, Perfect and Ryan, 'Building Bridges or Holy Huddles?', pp. 34–5.

80 Guest et al., *Christianity and the University Experience*, pp. 83–112.

81 Aune, Perfect and Ryan, 'Building Bridges or Holy Huddles?', p. 4.

82 Walter Brueggemann, *The Practice of Homefulness* (Eugene, OR: Wipf and Stock, 2014), p. 23.

83 John Hull, *What Prevents Christian Adults from Learning?* (London: SCM Press, 1985), p. 124.

84 See, for example, Collins-Mayo, 'Choosing My Religion'.

85 Christian Smith and Patricia Snell, *Souls in Transition: The Religious and Spiritual Lives of Emerging Adults* (Oxford: Oxford University Press, 2009); Perrin, *Changing Shape*.

86 Alexander W. Astin, Helen S. Astin and Jennifer A. Lindholm, *Cultivating the Spirit: How College Can Enhance Students' Inner Lives* (San Francisco, CA: Jossey-Bass, 2011), p. 147.

87 Jerry Persha, 'Toward Developing an Adequate and Comprehensive Understanding of Evangelization' in *The Study of Evangelism: Exploring a Missional Practice of the Church*, ed. Paul W. Chilcote and Laceye C. Warner (Cambridge: W.B. Eerdmans, 2008), p. 321.

88 Roberta Katz et al., *Gen Z, Explained: The Art of Living in a Digital Age* (Chicago, IL: University of Chicago Press, 2022), p. 93.

89 Perrin, *Changing Shape*, p. 35.

PART III

Identities at University

6

Being Women

This chapter focuses directly on the impact of gender upon the women's everyday lives at university. It begins by exploring four post-feminist claims that were common in the women's lived experiences. The prevalence of gender essentialism, dismissal of gender's significance, and focus on both femininity and youth constrained the women's self-perceptions and undermined their capacity to challenge misogynistic attitudes. The chapter then investigates the women's encounters with lad culture and perspectives on feminism, revealing that despite ubiquitous sexism, many did not consider feminism necessary. The final section explores the significance of female relationships in the students' experiences of feeling at home at university. There are some hints in this chapter at the students' experiences as Christians; however, I leave discussing the intersection between the women's faith and gender to the next chapter.

Slee and Helen D. Cameron place the biblical parable of the prodigal son in feminist dialogue with Marilynne Robinson's novel *Home*.[1] Leaving home, they write, 'has very different connotations, resonances and associations for women than it does for men'.[2] This chapter investigates some of these connotations, resonances and associations from the perspective of these emerging women at university.

First, I offer an introductory note about feminism's history. Following the first wave of feminism focused on women's suffrage in the nineteenth century, the 1960s brought the second wave, expanding its remit to societal gender norms. From the 1990s, the third wave addressed the position of women in politics, media and business as well as home life. The fourth wave, emerging in the 2010s, emphasized intersectionality, rape culture, transgender rights and online safety. Each successive wave built upon the previous movements, progressively broadening the scope of feminist critique, challenging social structures and expanding understandings of gender dynamics. Post-feminism originated in the 1980s as part of a backlash against feminism, and has in many ways grown in popularity. These distinct waves are not uncontested, and Annemarie Vaccaro writes that 'postmodernist feminism would problematize the notion of a single category of feminists, or a uniform feminist identity'.[3]

I understand feminism to be a recognition that the personal is political and that the eradication of patriarchy would benefit all. Feminism incorporates the intersectional critique of hierarchies of power, including the systems and structures that exclude or constrain women.

Post-feminist essentialism

The women lived and studied in a post-feminist society. Lewis and her colleagues list some of the cultural norms that define post-feminism, including:

> an emphasis on individualism, choice and empowerment; the revival and reappearance of 'natural' sexual difference; ... the emphasis upon self-surveillance with constant monitoring and disciplining of women's bodies; ... the resexualization of women's bodies and the retreat to home as a matter of choice.[4]

Nicole, more than other students, articulated most of these views. After saying that she 'definitely' was not a feminist, she went on to qualify what she believed:

> I've heard about ... [guys] calling girls names ... but I haven't had it done to me ... I'm like, 'You shouldn't treat women like that' so in that sense, I am slightly feminist, but then in the other sense I'm not [laughs] ... I don't like being treated as someone's piece of meat ... One of the boys [said] ... 'We shouldn't go for equality, we should go for fairness' which I thought was brilliant ... because women and men have different bodies, the way that they're wired is different.

Here, Nicole's opinions are shaped by her *individual* experience and choice; by the idea that women are 'wired' with different 'hormones'; and by having been sexualized, like 'meat'. Nicole had also recently made the decision that if she had small children in the future, she would leave her work. It is noteworthy that Nicole took her cue from a man that 'fairness' was better than equality or feminism without questioning his motivations.

Redfern and Aune argue that post-feminism communicates 'that gender differences are hard-wired into us as a product of evolution'. While chromosomally, women and men are about 5 per cent different, media and popular culture 'encourage[s] viewers to see these differences as "real" and essential in nature'.[5] The women in this book considered differences between women and men normal and unquestionable. Sometimes they were considered in subtle cultural and social terms, such as Sarah recognizing that they were 'programmed into you since you're tiny'. Other times, stereotypical traits were presented as biological fact. Women and men were understood as having different experiences, pressures, bodies and roles. The women were aware, although often subconsciously, of their gendered selves and experiences. Sadly, the most common female traits expressed by the women were negative. They considered women mean, judgemental, catty, 'back-stabbing', 'moaning' and likely to 'be a bitch'. Being in all-female groups was 'a lot of hard work' because women get 'offended ... really easily'. The students anticipated other women would display these 'innate' characteristics, yet none saw themselves this way, and often experienced the reality of being with other women surprisingly positive. Thinking further about women's judgemental traits, Nicole saw that her female friends 'can be absolutely awful [laughs] to themselves, and other people.' She recognized that first and foremost, women were critical of *themselves*, presumably in terms of their appearance and abilities, before extending the same criticism outwards. Althaus-Reid observes the patriarchy discouraging women from supporting one another, including in Christianity, due to fear of losing power, arguing that, 'If united, they could find the strength that is needed to fight against the several faces of oppression that women suffer.'[6]

Kimberly recognized that her female friends could be 'harder to read', preferring to spend time with male friends whom she considered more straightforward. Vicky thought 'girls don't react well' when she was 'honest' and would 'say how I think things are'. Lyn Mikel Brown and Carol Gilligan argue that adolescent girls learn to withhold their true self through dishonesty, because 'to say what they are feeling and thinking often means to risk ... losing their relationships' since honesty in girls is considered 'selfish', 'rude' or 'mean'. The authors find that becoming autonomous and aware is often accompanied by silencing and being unable 'to convey or even believe in one's own experience' as girls disassociate from themselves and others. They conclude that 'women's psychological development ... is inherently traumatic'. The students in this book had learned to distrust themselves and other women, critiquing their female peers rather than the 'inescapably political' structures that made women's 'dishonesty' necessary.[7]

There were, however, positive traits associated with being women, most of which were relational, including the ability to 'form close' and 'deep relationships'; being 'pastoral' and 'caring'; being 'emotional' and able to talk about 'emotions' and 'difficult issues'; 'openness' to others; and being better 'at communicating'. Other characteristics ascribed to women included facing 'more pressure' on their appearance; 'having to choose between a career and having a family'; being more inclined 'to keep the kitchen tidy' and to 'think it's dirty'; and struggling with being less 'confident'. Many of these traits are explored further in this chapter. The following chapter explores the women's academic context, where they witnessed themselves to be more 'stressed' about academic work; and their religious context, where women were considered less 'natural leaders' than men.

Post-feminist denial

When asked directly about gender, the women revealed their gendered identities as unexamined, unimportant, and safely protected from the rest of their lives and selves. This was despite elsewhere demonstrating the daily importance and influence of gender. Often women shifted between these two dissenting views simultaneously, maintaining their safety in cognitive dissonance. For example, Briana said, 'I find girls easier to get to know … it doesn't matter to me … I do find girls generally easier to start a conversation with, or, I dunno, get to know deeper but no, it doesn't matter.'

Students said that being female did not make 'a huge impact on my life' (Briana); 'has not really had an impact on uni' (Danielle); did not influence 'how I try and approach a situation' (Kimberly); or did not affect 'anything I do or any decision I make' (Alexis). Stephanie said, 'I don't think my gender defines me.' Courtney thought, 'It doesn't really matter … I am who I am.' Sarah wanted being female to not 'be such a big deal'. In making friends, she thought 'personality and how I relate to a person' were 'far more important' than 'the person's gender'.

Many of the responses to questions about being women suggested that the students had previously given their gendered lives little consideration and were thinking aloud as they spoke. The phrase *I don't know* was repeated often, particularly in these quotes by Haley, Amber and Alexis respectively: 'I don't know about the woman thing … I don't know, sorry, I don't know'; 'I don't know … I don't know … I don't know … but yeah it's different [being a woman]'; 'I don't, I don't really know, I never really thought about it … I don't know.' Haley and Olivia admitted, 'It's not something that I've really thought about', 'I just don't really think about it.' Stephanie and Mary said, 'I'm not quite sure.' Stephanie asked for clarification: 'What do you mean?'; and at the end of Haley's interview, she said, 'I was trying to work out, like, "Why are you asking me this?"'

Other women responded to questions about gender with the assumption that women's gendered experiences were understood as *negative*, and then resisted this understanding. Taylor said, 'I wouldn't think, like, "Should I do this? No, girls don't do it".' She did not 'feel I am being stopped from doing anything because of my gender'. Danielle was 'not that kind of person, like, "Oh, I'm a woman, I can and can't do this".' Ashley thought that 'I've had a lot of choice … [it's] not like I've been limited.' For Stephanie and Kimberly, this meant rejecting women's inferiority: 'I can do the same', 'we're just as good as anyone else'. Similarly, Megan was 'not constantly like, "Oh, I'm a woman, so I've got to do this".' However, she added that she did not 'understand what problems' she might face in her future career in law, suggesting that she anticipated facing gender discrimination. These responses, while demonstrating that the women resisted being considered inferior to men, suggest that this was the dominant gendered narrative they encountered. It is also notable that, in these six women's responses, four of them switched to speaking *of* themselves in a conditional sense, rather than *as* themselves, presented using double quotation marks. They externalized an oppressed woman that they feared becoming and wanted to establish a safe distance from her.

Christina Scharff finds that women draw on post-feminist discourse to suggest that feminism is redundant, while demonstrating awareness of gender inequality. Rather than looking to feminist resources, inequalities are individualized, and the person must navigate them alone.[8] This 'aggressive individualism',[9] as Angela McRobbie terms it, replaces feminism as an ideology by which the women understood their world. For Lewis and her colleagues, post-feminism places the 'co-existence of feminist values … alongside the re-articulation of traditional expectations', presenting a reality in which the patriarchy is already obliterated. Instead of structural change, 'it is the women who have to self-improve'.[10]

The need for safety amid the women's emotionally traumatic transitions at university meant that their loyalty to the patriarchal system was in some ways unsurprising. Subscribing to the assumption that equality had been achieved released them from having to critically engage. Hull writes that cognitive dissonance takes place when a person's beliefs are challenged, such as in transitional periods, leaving them feeling vulnerable. When faced with competing beliefs, students seek psychological *safety*, such as by using 'thought-stopping techniques' to intentionally 'learn less'.[11] These students consciously and unconsciously employed such tactics.

Post-feminist femininity

A vocal influence in second wave feminism, Judith Butler argues that women 'daily and incessantly' 'put on' their gender 'with anxiety and pleasure'. For Butler, gender has no biological origin, but is contingent on social practices, and is 'a performative accomplishment' which people 'come to believe and to perform in the mode of belief'.[12] Thus, femininity was understood as a prescribed concept, without clear parameters yet confirming women's subordination. Post-feminism influences the performance of gender by reclaiming and redefining femininity. Gill notes that femininity shifted from idolizing motherhood to becoming 'a bodily property' whereby a 'sexy body' is a key source of women's identity. Popular culture establishes the mainstream narrative for emerging women's bodies as 'requiring constant attention, discipline, self-surveillance and emotional labour', while, 'feminism is set up as a policeman, disallowing women the pleasures of traditional femininity'. Femininity requires women to internalize the male gaze and adopt 'pre-feminist ideals' which are '(seductively) repackaged as post-feminist freedoms'.[13]

In their adolescence, Melissa and Samantha had experienced what could be termed identity crises concerning their gendered, 'feminine', selves. In both of my interviews with Melissa, she discussed how 'damaging' she had found the media's dichotomy between femininity on the one hand, and intelligence and 'wanting to climb trees' on the other, witnessing 'hatred against femininity'. While being 'quite feminine', Melissa wanted to broaden its definition:

> I like the colour pink and I like pretty dresses ... but femininity is associated with people being weak and stupid and silly ... I definitely felt a sense of, I couldn't be feminine and ... valuable as an intelligent woman.

Melissa described a painful internal conflict between self-expression and societal prejudices. While enjoying traditional femininity, she was acutely aware of negative stereotypes, and as an intelligent woman she felt torn. The word 'valuable' demonstrates the positioning of women's worth in their bodies rather than their minds, while traditionally feminine traits are devalued in professional or academic settings. While expressing the pain of navigating this harmful binary, at university Melissa felt that being 'girly' was no longer 'a barrier to being considered clever anymore', which was 'just fantastic ... I've just been able to embrace it.'

When Samantha 'was younger ... gender was quite a problem'.

She reflected on 'being bombarded' by media images of unattainable femininity, feeling overwhelmed and under assault by unrealistic bodily ideals. She struggled to 'find out what femininity was for me ... I couldn't possibly look like that.' She experienced this as a form of violence against her developing sense of self, actively interfering with her ability to form her own identity or find an authentic form of femininity, feeling powerless in the face of these expectations. Samantha went on to reflect upon her changing relationship with modesty, detailed in Chapter 7.

While both women criticized the portrayal of femininity, they accepted the *construct* of the feminine, and wanted to find a way to authentically embrace it. Most women accepted narrow standards of gender performance in their appearance (for example, Samantha cherished her long hair). The women understood and experienced their bodies as sites of femininity. Alexis, Melissa and Stephanie talked in their facilitated gathering about trying on new clothes, and joking that there should be 'classes [on doing] makeup and hair', fearing getting their appearance *wrong* somehow. Women experienced pressure to 'look a certain way', 'about my looks', 'to look nice', to 'fit in', 'to look pretty' and to examine 'how they dress'. Briana recognized 'greater pressure from society put on girls than boys', including the need 'to have a lot of clothes', 'designer clothes', and regularly a 'new wardrobe' of clothes. For Amber and Nicole respectively, being 'seen as an object' and the pressure 'to look good' were the worst things about being women. Olivia experienced 'temptation ... to wear a really tight dress' and have 'good photos of you put up on Facebook'. Megan was 'angry' about the media's 'commercialization' of beauty, and the demand that women 'show their bodies'.

This dominant narrative of femininity impacts upon girls from a young age. It is normal for even preadolescent girls to be unhappy about their body shape, especially wanting to be thinner. Lauren saw that girls she volunteered with through Girlguiding[14] 'had problems with body image'.

Despite common references to femininity, the women struggled to define it, and some spoke about subverting its rules. Stephanie mainly wore skirts because she was 'worried' about being 'taken seriously' studying 'a male-dominated subject', so thought, 'Right, I'm gonna prove, not only can you do it whilst being a girl, but you can do it whilst like wearing a skirt.' Wearing skirts enabled Stephanie to demonstrate her femininity and her identity, while rejecting the dichotomy opposing femininity with intelligence, proving that studying engineering was as 'girly' as wearing skirts. Danielle reflected on the intersection between her sexuality, gender and physical appearance, and performed her lesbian identity so that 'it is very obvious from my image that I am gay'. Because of her 'butch' short hair and piercings, 'people don't put me down for being a girl'. This representation of her sexual orientation 'makes me feel comfortable and it's part of my character'. Femininity assumes heteronormativity, and, as Elisa S. Abes writes, 'heterosexism suggests the appropriate appearance for a woman'.[15] Danielle attempted to escape from its constraints by becoming *male* in appearance (and sexual desire). Kimberly said, 'There are definite gender roles that are expected, I don't follow them cos maybe it's the rebel in me [laughs].' Although Alexis described 'pressure to look nice', she 'can't always be bothered, so it's not an overriding pressure'. These examples demonstrate the differentiation between perceived women's and men's appearance, even when these perceptions do not necessarily fit.

One of the women casually discussed her weight. Discussing choosing outfits, Tumi decided not to 'wear my shorts just because I have gained a little bit of weight, so they are a bit tighter ... but I can't change that I've gained weight [laughs].' However, I read pressure to be thin as a subtext in many of the women's statements about looking good or pretty. More often, they expressed how their clothing influenced how confident and comfortable they felt. Alexis and Nicole did not wear 'skimpy stuff' because they were 'self-conscious' and 'not particularly confident'. Kimberly saw low body-confidence as 'a big issue' for her female friends, echoing Redfern and Aune who argue that only one in ten women are happy in their appearance.[16] The women recognized that their bodies were not neutral, but were disputed sites of conflict. Sometimes this was sexualized. Amber saw a balancing act between looking 'pretty' and 'slutty', and was glad that her friends did not wear 'tight clothes'. Ashley, however, resisted the relationship between women's clothing and perceived promiscuity, and was saddened by women blaming themselves when harassed by men on nights out, saying, 'I wish I hadn't worn this.' Samantha agreed: 'It's so easy for that to become, "It was so-and-so's fault, she was raped because she was dressed like that," because it's never an excuse.'

There is no unmarked territory for woman's clothing choices. Everything makes a statement, whether *butch*, *slut*, *designer* or *feminine* and, as in the next chapter, *modest*. The time and energy that the women felt pressured to spend on their appearance was significant, with women judging themselves and one another; and feeling judged by society's and the media's male gaze. Yet Gill argues that 'this labour must be understood nevertheless as "fun", "pampering" or "self-indulgence" and must *never* be disclosed'.[17]

Post-feminist girling

In contrast to narratives of feminism as old and outdated, post-feminism spotlights youthfulness as desirable and necessary for full participation in society. Yvonne Tasker and Diane Negra argue that, in media culture, 'the highest profile post-feminist franchises have centralized girls and girlhood, fusing empowerment rhetoric with traditionalist identity paradigms'. They refer to the 'girling' of femininity, finding that 'girlhood is imagined within a post-feminist culture as being for everyone'.[18] Examples include the movie *Mean Girls*; pop music artists Britney Spears and Avril Lavigne; Christina Aguilera's song 'What a Girl Wants'; the sports initiative This Girl Can; and the perfume Good Girl, which also has sexual overtones. Gill argues that the 'girlification' of adult women is the flipside of a media culture that promotes female children as its most desirable sexual icons, with 'sexually provocative' clothing and even stationery 'aimed at the pre-teen market'.[19] Ashley criticized girls being made aware of 'themselves as sexual beings ... desirable from a younger age and in a ... predatory sense'.

The categories of *woman* and *girl* are neither fixed nor neutral.[20] However, with a few notable exceptions, the women uncritically referred to themselves and their peers as *girls*. *Guys* was the most common term for male peers, while also considered a gender-neutral term for any group. Nicole and Samantha referred to themselves as *girls* even though it 'sounds very young' and 'I know I'm not a child'. Vicky, however, noticed a shift between her first and second years, noticing that when starting university she referred to herself as a girl because 'everything was a bit all over the place', associating girlhood with uncertainty. When asked whether the term *woman* applied to them, the students felt that it had connotations with a maturity that they did not yet feel. For example, Nicole discussed her *future* self when referring to herself as a woman. Avoiding the title of *woman*, some students said:

> I don't feel old enough ... I still don't like the idea that I'm an adult. (Briana)

> It sounds older, I don't feel that old. (Courtney)

> I still don't think I feel properly 'grown up' enough! (Sarah)

Maturity markers attached to *woman* included being 'married' or 'professional'; being taken 'seriously'; and being 'strong, independent'. Other attributes included the traditional gender role of 'housewife, kitchen, cooking, cleaning'; and 'how they look', such as being 'curvy' or not being 'small'.

Different approaches to how the women identified themselves enabled them to stay safe in this 'in-between' time (described in Chapter 3), excusing them from having to make decisions about their futures. This included 'girling', but also the women's use of both *girl* and *woman*, or neither, to refer to themselves. Taylor said, 'a girl is a little child, and a woman [is] someone with an established life', while she was neither. Megan preferred the term 'young woman', adding, '"girl" sounds childish, but at the same time saying "woman" sounds very grown up and I don't think I'm there yet!' Amber thought that she was 'somewhere in-between', although in her second year she felt 'less like a "girl"' than the previous year, demonstrating a process of maturing. Mary said, 'I don't really think about it', and she and Sarah thought of themselves as 'both' *girls* and *women*.

In deciding between *girl* and *woman* Lauren said, 'I don't really know', it depended on 'certain situations' and 'who I am with'. In their facilitated gathering, Melissa and Stephanie agreed that the terms were contextual. Melissa started referring to herself as a woman 'when I was 15' because she wanted to be 'taken seriously', while '"girl" tends to be frowned on a lot in society ... seen as inferior to masculinity'. She discussed the discrepancy between terminologies for men and women, finding that although teenage boys are called *guys* rather than *boys*, '"guy" doesn't have the same connotations as "girl"'. However, the friends used the term 'girly' to refer to 'that sort of conversation' where 'you're not holding anything back, you're just, like, "Yeah, I'm gonna tell you everything".' Stephanie discussed associating different identities with different contexts, saying, 'With friends I tend to be more like a girl, like, "girls' day out", "girly talk", "girls' house".' However, on her (male-dominated) academic course, she used the term woman because it was harder 'to be taken seriously ... like, "I am professional ... I do know what I'm talking about".' As an engineering student, she had to be 'grown up' with 'responsibilities' in 'an adult environment', whereas with her friends, 'you don't have to be grown up ... [or] prove yourself.'

Feminists have critiqued the term 'girl' for belittling women's autonomy, as Melissa and Stephanie state themselves. However, Jennifer Baumgardner and Amy Richards reflect that 'second wave feminists fought so hard for all women not to be reduced to a "girl" – they didn't lay claim to the good in being a girl'.[21] Anne Phillips argues that this unfair attitude results in women acquiring power at the expense of girlhood.[22] While I am researching emerging women, not girls, these women are on the cusp of adulthood. If being girls offers students an opportunity to be themselves and – as Chapter 2 showed – claim their silly or childlike identities, then remaining girls is a necessary step in creating safety at university; as long as they are also empowered in their womanhood.

Lad culture[23]

By assuming equality and undermining women's lived experiences, post-feminism ignores gender as a lens through which to assess the world, and largely the women in this book explicitly accepted the irrelevance of gender. However, lad culture and rape culture were the greatest exceptions to this rule and infiltrated the women's gendered awareness. Yet even when awareness of lad culture contributed to the women's feminist conscientization, many women utilized the norms of post-feminism and Christian student subcultures to distance themselves from the problem.

Lad culture is a term specific to the UK, but the sexual harassment at universities to which it contributes is a global problem. Lad culture refers to behaviour that assumes women's sexual availability, ranging from 'everyday sexism' and so-called 'banter', to sexual violence, and consisting of consumerist and competitive attitudes towards women and sex. It is considered to be an inevitable aspect of student life, particularly its nightlife.[24] Less acceptable but still prevalent, *rape culture* involves: the normalizing and even celebration of rape; 'jokes' about rape; blaming women for rape; or trivializing the impact of rape upon women. While both terms are contested, including by feminists, they emphasize the pervasiveness of gendered violence, refusing to sideline harassment or rape as isolated individual experiences.[25] Carolyn Jackson and Vanita Sundaram discuss the 'elastic' nature of lad culture, making it difficult to define and challenge. They argue it is 'everywhere … its ubiquity and normalization contributed to its invisibility'. Lad culture is mischaracterized as an individual rather than social problem, which 'minimizes and trivializes' it, 'masking the scale' of the problem.[26]

Much has been written about lad culture and sexual harassment on university campuses in the last 20 years. In 2010, the National Union of Students reported that 68 per cent of female students encountered sexual harassment on campus,[27] while Phipps and Geraldine Smith find that 25 per cent of women students have been subjected to unwanted sexual behaviour.[28] Almost all the women in my research had direct experience of lad culture. Examples included: name-calling, harassment from men driving past them in cars, 'banter' and 'laddish' behaviour, witnessing male students celebrating the number of women they had slept with, being treated as 'an object' or 'a number', and arguments about misogynist song lyrics. Derogatory language experienced by the women was likely influenced by pornography, including 'slag' and 'get your tits out'.

Most of the women's experiences of lad culture involved alcohol. As explored in Chapter 2, many of the students had an ambiguous relationship with the university drinking culture, and often women's faith and student identities were perceived to be at odds. Some women were teetotal, with most enjoying alcohol 'without being drunk'. Encounters with lad culture were either in nightclubs or pubs, or upon meeting drunk students while out in the night-time. University drinking cultures are often fraught with competitive attitudes towards women; exacerbated by student events and nightclub promotions glamorizing heavy alcohol usage and promising sexual activity. Kimberly was followed while walking home by a group of rowdy male students shouting and wearing 'beer boxes on their heads', resulting in her changing her route for safety, saying, 'As soon as I saw them, I sort of made a plan in case anything happened.' Lauren was 'harassed a lot', and she had been 'assaulted ... in a nightclub'. Mary found that in clubs some men 'think that they can do whatever they want'. When dancing in a club, Ashley described a man 'pick[ing] me up from behind, and I was ... so angry ... I pushed him away and he flew back.'

While Ashley's primary response was anger, other women explicitly named their fear, noting how 'aggressive' and 'scary' some 'lads' could be. As these women recounted, lad culture correlates directly with rape culture so that it is difficult to differentiate them. Lauren reported male students saying, 'I'd rape her.' Courtney reflected,

> Guys in general, when they drink are ... not very good at understanding when a girl is saying 'no', they kind of don't take the seriousness of it ... it's that feeling of vulnerability ... like, 'You are like bigger and stronger and you could do whatever.'

About some male students in clubs, Vicky said, 'They're just really forceful ... and you can't really move.' She shared the 'horrendous ordeal' of a friend being raped at a party, with no consequences: 'That guy is still walking around campus ... she would recognize him if she saw him and ... like the rapist doesn't even get arrested [sighs].'

However, despite all that the women said above, some went on to trivialize or normalize experiences of lad culture. Several women repeated, 'I don't know', feeling ill-equipped to engage with it. They lamented the prevalence of harassment, rarely reporting it since nothing would be done. After describing her experience of being picked up, Ashley said, 'Fortunately I've not had anything, apart from weird groping ... or people trying to grab you ... which I am really thankful for.' Olivia described lad culture as 'normal club behaviour' and Nicole thought it has been 'over-sensationalized'. Discussing 'banter', Haley said, 'I don't like it, but, I don't know, [it's] just their own opinion I think, I'm sure women do the same thing about men.' When I asked Sarah how an incidence of name-calling had made her feel, she responded, 'I don't know, I've never really experienced anything', seemingly comforting herself in order not to feel upset by, or need to act upon, what had happened. Perhaps this downplaying reflected the women's refusal to be labelled as victims, and resilience in the face of trauma. Or maybe it demonstrated fear at naming the extent of the problem since that would debunk the myth of equality and unravel their post-feminist assumptions. It is possible that there were a range of motivations at play. Nevertheless, Ashley being 'thankful' and considering herself 'fortunate' for *only* experiencing being groped, grabbed and physically picked up is a damning reflection of what emerging women have to consider normal. Sexual harassment is tolerable when fear of sexual assault is so pervasive.

In her first year, Stephanie's internal dialogue oscillated between conflicting views. While she did not 'want to justify it' by saying, 'They're just objectifying girls but it's all good', she continued, 'but ... I think they're all nice people and ... in the same way, girls might discuss a guy who's hot.' In her second year, however, she became bolder, and had confronted some male friends behaving offensively. She said, 'We don't want to seem like bitches but we [pause] we have to say something.' 'Bitching' here meets the definition proposed by Deborah Jones, as the 'expression of women's anger' that is 'privatized: women's oppression is not discussed as a general concept, but in the relating of specific, personal complaints.' Women's bitching is the means of complaint most acceptable to patriarchal structures because it does 'not expect change'.[29] In the absence of other options, bitching was all the women could do to share their concerns. Otherwise, they remained silent and downplayed their experiences, even to themselves.

Many women excused experiences of harassment by *othering* lad culture through the lens of their faith, utilizing post-feminist tropes to position the problem outside of their own Christian subculture. For example, some women said they intentionally made personal choices to avoid social groups or physical spaces where lad culture might be present. This involved staying 'at home' rather than going to nightclubs, spending time solely in Christian 'circles' or 'more girl-heavy environments', not being 'involved in sports teams', or choosing carefully 'people who I've gone out with'.

Post-feminism presents being anti-sex as the only alternative to hyper-sexualization, effectively eradicating space for critique.[30] The women demonstrated three core aspects of post-feminism in their responses to lad culture: the sexualization of women is normal (while Christianity is counter-normal and prudish); personal choice is emphasized over women's collective empowerment; and the individual can shape her own world. Examples of this final point include: 'I've managed to avoid that'; 'The guys I've met have been pretty decent'; 'It's just not been part of my experience'; and 'For me, that hasn't been an issue.'

However, as Bryant shows, university Christian contexts are not excluded from the normalizing of male experience, and thus from sexist behaviour.[31] Briana was the only woman to discuss lad culture *within* her Christian student subculture, yet was reluctant to criticize it and her thoughts were inconsistent:

> In Christian circles, there's a joke about lad culture ... it can be very destructive, like, 'Oh they're such a lad', meaning that they're cool ... There are concerns that people are condoning lad culture, I'm not sure ... it's like, boisterous, slightly picking on girls in a fun, teasing kinda way, it's not anything particularly serious ... That doesn't bother me ... it's not just girls, it's on boys as well ... and I personally really like that.

Briana oscillated between three different viewpoints: thinking that lad culture is a 'destructive' concern; 'really liking' it for being 'cool'; and not being 'bothered' because it's not 'serious'. She did not overtly name what Ashley called the 'intense' and often hypersexual nature of romantic engagement within these subcultures. Gendered behaviour and power dynamics in these spaces were normalized through humour and 'banter'. While Briana was aware of its 'concerns', she chose to accept and even enjoy it.

Irrespective of how the women positioned themselves regarding lad culture, many expressed concerns for their physical safety. The ubiquitous expectation of encountering lad culture meant that the women worried about their physical safety, feeling 'weak', 'vulnerable' and 'a bit scar[ed]' because 'I am a woman.' Samantha was 'anxious to go out after dark alone', and Kimberly would stay in when unable to guarantee friends to travel home with. The women were attuned to the injustice of needing to police their own freedom in this way because of their gender. Walking alone at night, Nicole thought, 'If I was a guy, I wouldn't feel as wary.' Courtney said, 'It annoys me ... I should be able to feel like I can walk through anywhere at any time.' American women students have identified poor night-lighting and inadequate safe transportation on campus as 'institutional sexism', since these safety issues disproportionately affected them compared to their male counterparts.[32] The injustice of women's lack of safety has received feminist attention over many decades, yet women's right to move around freely is still contested.

These women had a complex relationship with lad culture and its impact. While many felt fear and anger at sexual harassment, they often minimized these experiences. Some avoided engaging with lad culture rather than critiquing it. Donna Freitas suggests that faith can help counter problematic university gender dynamics,[33] but this requires critical involvement with the issue. The post-feminist narrative that gender equality is achieved, along with neoliberal individualization, means that many women lacked the resources and vocabulary to challenge 'laddish' behaviour. In the previous section, Ashley and Samantha critiqued blaming women for harassment. Similarly, women cannot be blamed for lad culture, nor can they bear sole responsibility for eliminating it.

Feminism

In keeping with post-feminism, many women in this study avoided identifying themselves as feminists. When asked what they thought about feminism, several expressed an attitude akin to what Linda R. Hirshman has termed 'choice feminism',[34] emphasizing personal choice over women's empowerment. Prioritizing choice results in the inability to critique or condemn behaviours and systems that discriminate against women. Lewis and colleagues write that 'moderate feminism ... has such wide appeal largely because it abstains from radicalism, exclusion and judgment', while 'the glorification of choice obscures the politics of choice'.[35] Choice feminism is deemed *acceptable*, yet is devoid of political power, restricting possible change.[36] Yet the students often considered individual choice to be the priority in considering feminism.

Jonathan Dean finds that British national media portrays 'a safe unthreatening form of feminism ... [while] curtailing its more radical political dimensions'.[37] As Scharff writes, 'feminism is taken into account but also forcefully repudiated', while the 'mythic construction of "the feminist"' is radical and excessive.[38] Most of the women in my research claimed a version of feminism for themselves, with caveats. Many women were keen to reject the 'stereotype of feminist' or 'strands of feminism' which went 'too far' by insisting, for example, that 'women are better', that women 'don't like men' or 'want power over men', or 'want to put them in a farm [laughs]', or that 'it doesn't matter if we walk around topless'. Briana did not think that 'some feminists go about it in the right way', adding 'I wouldn't say, "Oh, I'm a feminist", even though I am.' Vicky considered herself to be a 'liberal feminist' rather than 'someone who's like really radical and believes in really crazy ideas'. Two women said that they were 'not not' feminists.

Other women could not see the direct relevance of feminism for their own lives. Olivia said, 'It's more of an issue in other countries ... what [do] people campaign against? ... I feel like it's not particularly important to me.' For Danielle, 'It's not something that I really think about in terms of, like, my life.' In her first year, Ashley saw the necessity of feminism 'in an abstract sense and in other women's experience, never in my own'.

Some women rejected feminism regardless of the inequalities they saw. Megan was not feminist 'despite what I said about how I feel about the adverts'. She continued: 'page three, that kind of thing, that does make me angry but ... not everyone sees that as a bad thing and that's up to them ... everyone's got their own view'. Megan here presents an intentional disengagement from her anger as a way of protecting herself, enabled by the belief that everyone's individual choice is valid, no matter how discriminatory.

In keeping with post-feminist tropes, whereby, as Porter argues, 'support for women's equality is not connected to an embrace of feminism',[39] the majority of women insisted on equality over feminism. For example, Haley was not 'someone that's, like, for women's rights' but thought 'women should be equal'. Alexis said, 'everyone's equal and should just get along ... that's what I think about feminism'. Courtney considered herself 'partly, ish' a feminist, but 'would definitely ... believe in equal rights'. The women often mentioned men alongside women, or wanted to 'forget about' 'whether you are male or female' and instead just 'treat each other as human beings'. Olivia took this further, saying, 'I always think with feminism, like, why is there no "menimism" campaigns, like, men should have equal rights too'. Sarah thought that 'it would just be nice if everyone could just like be equal' but 'drawing attention to it ... makes it worse' because 'it's just normal to treat everyone the same'. The false supposition that equality is *normal* is a common critique of post-feminist thought; however, this was widely believed.

Many women in this study *were* aware of gender inequalities and recognized gendered experiences. However, this awareness did not necessarily result in subscribing to feminism. Rather, the women resisted connecting their experiences of sexism with structures of power, subscribing instead to individual femininity which, Gill argues, required them 'to work on the self rather than to work with others for social and political transformation'.[40] To name gender inequality as a lived reality for women would: impede their sense of safety by admitting the scale of the problem; mark them out as different from their peers; and be an admission that change was necessary, perhaps resulting in them needing to act at a time when the creation of safety was the priority. Melissa, however, gave another reason why identifying as a feminist was counter-intuitive and even something that could impede women's empowerment: 'If you say, "as a feminist I believe this", people say, "Oh well you're feminist, they're crazy" and use that to invalidate your argument'. By referring to themselves as feminists, the women felt that they would be aligning themselves with the mythical radical feminist who simply hates men.

However, some women actively embraced feminism, demonstrating nuanced understandings of gender issues and experiencing feminist awakening as they gained critical consciousness about gender inequality. Sometimes, this was facilitated by their university experiences, while for other students, feminism was embraced *despite* university and without knowledge of feminist discourse. For some women, this was a tentative process, such as for Courtney who was just beginning to realize 'how different it is to be a woman'.

Elements of this 'becoming' chime with other research into Christian feminist conscientization. Harris likens women's spiritual journeys to a dance, the first step of which involves awakening '*toward* something', beginning with 'their deepest inner selves' as different aspects of experience are connected, leading to a new dawning. This involves women 'waking slowly' due to fear of losing their previous selves.[41] Slee argues that awakenings are continuing birthings, each one leading 'to a rearrangement of normal perceptions ... enabling newness'. Each awakening involves disrupting and dismantling the previous step.[42]

Feminist awakenings often followed an experience of a loss of voice, and a confrontation with their own pain. Hull argues that experiences of dissonance can kindle 'a realignment of the whole system'.[43] The most articulate and reflective women in awakening had survived a previous rupture, including Melissa and Samantha's adolescent struggle with femininity, and Stephanie's wrestling with being in a female minority on her course, outlined earlier in this chapter. Abigail recognized that 'women have been seriously disadvantaged' when witnessing girls and boys being treated differently during her childhood in Uganda. Lauren saw gender inequality while working during her gap year. An 'inspirational woman' that she worked with encouraged her to think, 'I need to challenge this.' Beforehand, she had thought 'there's no problem with female representation in society', but she became 'passionate', 'engaged' and 'fiercely feminist'. She described her gender as 'important to me', saying, 'I'm really proud to be a woman, I'm proud to be able to do the things I do as a woman, and be able to fight for things.'

Vicky recognized the need to influence 'policy changes and ... cultural attitude' while rejecting post-feminist claims of equality because women 'got the vote'. She began to 'object to people using "girl"' to refer to her. Thinking of herself as a woman reflected her growing inner-dependence, feeling more 'able to make your own decisions and being confident in them'. Other women's feminist awakenings involving intersecting identities and faith are presented in the next chapter.

Feminist becoming was entrenched in the women's relationships with their closest female friends where, as Ashley said, 'those questions ... come up' in safety, about 'the role of women, female identity' and 'about ourselves as women and ... how that's changed'. This becoming was especially apparent beyond the women's first year at university as they became increasingly confident and felt more at home in their new environment. Yet feminism was often experienced as a tentative awakening, rather than as the adoption of a complete or total system.

Female friends and family

This chapter has sounded largely negative, focused on the challenging post-feminist norms the women faced. I now turn to a primary source of the women's joy and comfort as they crafted a home for themselves at university: the vital importance of their closest relationships with other women.

The importance of relationality in identity development is well documented. Elias argues that identities can, in fact, only be understood in relationship. Identity is produced through social relations that people utilize to gain greater self-understanding.[44] Many theorists argue that relational development is a particular characteristic in women's growth. While some such studies have been critiqued for essentialism,[45] they provide a significant counterpoint to theories of identity and faith development emphasizing detachment, based largely on research with men. Gilligan argues that women's moral processes are characteristically relational, based upon an ethic of care, where attachment knits human relationships together. For Gilligan, the central metaphor for identity formation is that of dialogue – for women, the self is known through connection and interaction.[46]

Female friends were a consistent source of support and safety as the women negotiated their new surroundings and shifting identities, creating comfortable spaces where they could be themselves. Most of the students' friends, especially their closest friends, were female, perhaps ironically given the repeated stereotype of women as mean and dishonest reported above. Stephanie said, 'in my main friendship group it is predominately girls ... I'd want to ensure that I always had at least one close female friend'. These friendships often became chosen-families. The women used remarkably similar words to one another in describing their 'close' female friendships, including: 'comfortable', 'relaxed', 'less pressurized', 'more empowering', and 'just being myself more'. These terms echoed those used when describing feeling at home at university or finding a new church.[47] For some, the best thing about being female was the 'bonds ... with other women', while several, like Courtney, wondered whether 'boys ... have anyone to actually talk to'. Amber found other women 'easier to talk to' about 'difficult issues', while Sarah reflected that they were 'the ones I go to with a problem'. While some women resisted the prevalence of female friendships, such as Nicole who wished that she had 'a more rounded mixture' of genders in her friendship group, close female friendships came most easily.

Female friendships provided crucial support for these students during their traumatic transitions, serving as the primary context where they engaged in significant meaning-making conversations. Female friends discussed gendered life together, feeling safe enough to acknowledge the impact of being women on how they experienced the world. For example, Ashley discussed definitions of womanhood with her friends, while Kimberly and Courtney shared safety fears and experiences of harassment with their friends.

Alexis, Melissa and Stephanie, in their facilitated gathering, embodied many of these reflections on female friendship. The friends were dressed similarly with matching hairstyles, and joked about owning the same clothes. As Kate Massey finds, in their conversation they worked together to create a 'group voice' where 'their shared experience and communal discovery was key'.[48] Opinions were reached through mutual encouragement rather than individual self-reflection, and even in disagreement their words were couched in relationship. In one example, the women discussed their university highlights so far:

Melissa: We just go [shopping for] fancy ball gowns [all laugh] ... That's one of my favourite things cos you [Stephanie] were talking about being able to be a bit more childish and I think it's just the friendship group here has been so wonderful ... exemplified by trying on ball gowns!

Stephanie: With you guys I feel really comfortable ... you're not judging me for it, you may laugh but not in, the, sort of, a bad way [laughs].
Melissa: My friends at home think I've got a lot weirder, and what it is is, I've just stopped holding it back!
Alexis: Yeah, I think the best moments were just like when we're all just hanging out as friends so like dress shopping and when we, so [laughs] like, we had this box [all laugh].
Stephanie: Yes! That was amazing!
Alexis: This is gonna sound like so weird ...

Here, Melissa begins by remembering a highlight (dress shopping), comparing it with an earlier story Stephanie told (about 'childish things'). For Melissa, these outings 'exemplify' their friendship. In agreement, Stephanie expands on her original point. Melissa adds further encouragement, including other friends' similar opinions. Alexis then shares Melissa's highlight. She expands Stephanie's understanding of 'childish' to include Melissa's 'weird', by beginning another story (about hiding something in a box). Stephanie offers affirmation in her brief interjection when realizing the story that Alexis is about to tell. There is much laughter as the layers of the conversation develop. For these women, their friendship was not just one of the most significant aspects of their university experience so far, it was the lens through which they made meaning of that experience, and of their identities in that place. This played out as they explored together what it meant to be gendered, embodied women at university.

Janice G. Raymond argues that female friendship must begin with 'companionship of the Self', otherwise women can lose themselves in others' company.[49] This is perhaps particularly true for adolescents, who can over-identify with peers[50] or find themselves lost in what Parks calls 'the tyranny of the they'.[51] For Alexis, Melissa and Stephanie, however, this important friendship provided much-needed safety in the processes of crafting home.

As well as with friends, as noted in Chapter 2 the students often had close, significant relationships with their mothers. The women in Belenky and colleagues' study valued 'two-way talk', in which both mothers and daughters 'had an equal say'. They took inspiration when 'mothers developed strong, clear voices of their own'.[52] Gilligan finds that adolescent girls observe when other women speak or when they are silent, learning appropriate gendered behaviour but also sometimes challenging it. She advocates for the importance of mothers who are also friends, reflecting that 'girls themselves say clearly, they will speak only when they feel that someone will listen'.[53] In this book, mothers offered a range of emotional and practical *gendered* support to the women. Many students involved their mothers in making daily decisions, regularly couching the relationship in *gendered* terms. For example, the women asked their mothers about what are commonly thought of as women's concerns, including cooking, washing, personal safety and appearance. Kat noticed that she was especially 'cuddly' with her mum since leaving home, while Courtney and Stephanie enjoyed 'mother–daughter time' like going shopping or for afternoon tea. Amber thought that 'gender does matter' with her mother, and Kimberly recognized that 'it allows us to bond over shared life experiences specific to our gender'. Briana appreciated that her mother was 'a very good listener … she will let me just ramble on', and Haley was glad that her mother listened rather than telling her, 'This is what you need to do.' Several women, like Melissa, rang their mothers when 'feeling particularly down or particularly happy' to share the moment or seek comfort. Many women spoke to their mothers 'most days', or found that they were closer than before starting university.

Other female family members were important to the women. Briana wrote regular letters to her aunt, because 'She's like my second mum.' Ashley's aunt was always 'supportive' and one of Stephanie's friend's mothers had 'been a mentor for me'. Abigail called a family friend 'aunty' because 'she's been pretty influential in my life'. Olivia and Danielle missed their elder sisters, referring to them often. Mary exchanged letters with her older sister and regularly messaged her younger sister. Amber considered her 'mum and grandmas' to be role models.

Caitlin named several reasons why she found relationships with other women to be safer than with men. Because of 'an abusive father', she had 'trust issues with men', so she 'gravitate[d] more towards women and trusting women more'. Moreover, she struggled with 'the lad culture of straight men'. While Caitlin was self-aware about trying to break these patterns of trust in therapy, her childhood trauma had been triggered by lad culture, meaning that these trust issues became reinforced at university. She acknowledged this as an ongoing struggle, repeating, 'I don't find it easy to trust men.' The fact that Caitlin was pursuing therapy indicates both a desire to heal and the significant impact these trust issues have on her life.

Thanks to a variety of close, affirming relationships with other women, the students were able to feel confident in their psychological safety, and began to craft a new home for themselves at university.

Conclusion

For these Christian women students, personal safety dominated their gender-related concerns, reflecting the constant threats to both their emotional and physical well-being. These threats undermined not only their security but also their ability to feel they truly belonged as women at university. In response, and typical of post-feminist cultural norms, they often sought safety through avoidance rather than engaging with these challenges directly. The exception emerged in relationships with new female friends and trusted older women. These safe women-families provided a transformative space where students could explore and challenge their gendered experiences. Those who had survived prior personal ruptures and explored their gendered identities often awakened to feminist perspectives. Fundamentally, these women were initially not at home in their own skin, constrained by external and internalized threats. However, through supportive female relationships, they found pathways to understanding, resistance and self-discovery.

The book now explores how faith intersects with the students' multiple identities at university, examining the complex interplay of race, class, sexuality and gender within their lived experiences of Christian student life.

Notes

1 The Parable of the Prodigal can be found in Luke 15.11–32. Marilynne Robinson, *Home* (London: Virago Press, 2009).

2 Nicola Slee and Helen D. Cameron, 'Peering into the Shadows or Foregrounding the Feminine? Feminist Rewritings of the Parable of the Prodigal', *Practical Theology* 7, no. 1 (2014), p. 55.

3 Annemarie Vaccaro, 'Third Wave Feminist Undergraduates: Transforming Identities and Redirecting Activism in Response to Institutional Sexism', *NASPA Journal About Women in Higher Education* 2, no. 1 (30 January 2009), p. 3.

4 Patricia Lewis, Yvonne Benschop and Ruth Simpson, 'Postfeminism, Gender and Organisation', *Gender, Work and Organisation* 24, no. 3 (2017), p. 214.

5 Catherine Redfern and Kristin Aune, *Reclaiming the F Word: Feminism Today* (London: Zed Books, 2013), pp. 183, 181.

6 Marcella Althaus-Reid, *From Feminist Theology to Indecent Theology: Readings on Poverty, Sexual Identity and God* (London: SCM Press, 2004), p. 41.

7 Lyn Mikel Brown and Carol Gilligan, *Meeting at the Crossroads: Women's Psychology and Girls' Development* (Cambridge, MA: Harvard University Press, 1992), pp. 5–6, 16, 20, 216–17.

8 Christina Scharff, *Repudiating Feminism* (Farnham: Ashgate, 2012), p. 10.

9 Angela McRobbie, *The Aftermath of Feminism: Gender, Culture and Social Change* (London: Sage, 2009), p. 5.

10 Lewis, Benschop and Simpson, 'Postfeminism', pp. 214, 219.

11 John Hull, *What Prevents Christian Adults from Learning?* (London: SCM Press, 1985), p. 123.

12 Judith Butler, 'Performative Acts and Gender Constitution: An Essay in Phenomenology and Feminist Theory', *Theatre Journal* 4, no. 40 (1988), pp. 520–1, 531.

13 Rosalind Gill, 'Postfeminism Media Culture: Elements of a Sensibility', *European Journal of Cultural Studies* 10, no. 2 (2007), pp. 149–51, 154, 162.

14 Lauren's words are also reported by Girlguiding itself. See Girlguiding, 'Girls' Attitudes Survey', 2015, https://www.girlguiding.org.uk/globalassets/docs-and-resources/research-and-campaigns/girls-attitudes-survey-2015.pdf, accessed 8.10.2019.

15 Elisa S. Abes, 'Constructivist and Intersectional Interpretations of a Lesbian College Student's Multiple Social Identities', *Journal of Higher Education* 83, no. 2 (2012), p. 201.

16 Redfern and Aune, *Reclaiming the F Word*, p. 20.

17 Gill, 'Postfeminism Media Culture', p. 155, italics author's own.

18 Yvonne Tasker and Diane Negra, 'Introduction' in *Interrogating Postfeminism: Gender and the Politics of Popular Culture*, ed. Yvonne Tasker and Diane Negra (Durham, NC: Duke University Press, 2007), p. 18.

19 Gill, 'Postfeminism Media Culture', p. 151.

20 Philip H. Miller and Ellin Kofsky Scholnick, eds, *Toward a Feminist Developmental Psychology* (London: Routledge, 2000), p. 5.

21 Jennifer Baumgardner and Amy Richards, 'Feminism and Femininity: Or How We Learned to Stop Worrying and Love the Thong' in *All About the Girl: Culture, Power and Identity*, ed. Anita Harris (New York: Routledge, 2004), pp. 60–1.

22 Anne Phillips, *The Faith of Girls: Children's Spirituality and Transition to Adulthood* (Farnham: Ashgate, 2011).

23 I have published parts of this section elsewhere; see Jenny Morgans, 'Emerging Christian Women at Uni: Intersection of Gender and Faith Identities on Campus', *Research in the Social Scientific Study of Religion* 32, Lesser Heard Voices in Studies of Religion (2022), pp. 147–63.

24 Carolyn Jackson and Vanita Sundaram, *Lad Culture in Higher Education: Sexism, Sexual Harassment and Violence* (Abingdon: Routledge, 2020).

25 See, for example, Rhiannon Graybill, Meredith Minister and Beatrice Lawrence, 'Introduction: Engaging Rape Culture, Reimagining Religious Studies' in *Rape Culture and Religious Studies: Critical and Pedagogical Engagements*, ed. Rhiannon Graybill, Meredith Minister and Beatrice Lawrence (London: Lexington Books, 2019), pp. 1–20.

26 Jackson and Sundaram, *Lad Culture*, pp. 131–3, 136.

27 National Union of Students, 'Hidden Marks: A Study of Women Students' Experiences of Harassment, Stalking, Violence and Sexual Assault', 2010.

28 Alison Phipps and Geraldine Smith, 'Violence Against Women Students in the UK: Time to Take Action', *Gender and Education* 24, no. 4 (2012), pp. 357–73.

29 Deborah Jones, 'Gossip: Notes on Women's Oral Culture' in *The Feminist Critique of Language: A Reader*, ed. Deborah Cameron (London: Routledge, 1990), p. 247.

30 Gill, 'Postfeminism Media Culture', p. 152.

31 Alyssa N. Bryant, 'Assessing the Gender Climate of an Evangelical Student Subculture in the United States', *Gender and Education* 18, no. 6 (2006), pp. 613–34.

32 Vaccaro, 'Third Wave Feminist Undergraduates', p. 17.

33 Donna Freitas, *The End of Sex: How Hookup Culture Is Leaving a Generation Unhappy, Sexually Unfulfilled, and Confused About Intimacy* (Philadelphia, PA: Basic Books, 2013).

34 Linda R. Hirshman, *Get to Work: A Manifesto for Women of the World* (New York: Viking, 2006).

35 Lewis, Benschop and Simpson, 'Postfeminism', p. 219.

36 Michaele L. Ferguson, 'Choice Feminism and the Fear of Politics', *Perspectives on Politics* 8, no. 1 (2010), pp. 247–53.

37 Jonathan Dean, 'Feminism in the Papers: Contested Feminisms in the British Quality Press', *Feminist Media Studies* 10, no. 4 (2010), p. 361.

38 Scharff, *Repudiating Feminism*, pp. 7, 2.

39 Fran Porter, *It Will Not Be Taken Away from Her: A Feminist Engagement with Women's Christian Experience* (London: Darton, Longman and Todd, 2004), p. 20.

40 Rosalind Gill, 'Post-Postfeminism? New Feminist Visibilities in Postfeminist Times', *Feminist Media Studies* 16, no. 4 (2016), p. 617.

41 Maria Harris, *Dance of the Spirit: The Seven Steps of Women's Spirituality* (New York: Bantam, 1989), pp. 2–3, italics author's own.

42 Nicola Slee, *Women's Faith Development: Patterns and Processes* (Aldershot: Ashgate, 2004), pp. 112–13, 39.

43 Hull, *What Prevents?*, pp. 98–9.

44 Norbert Elias, *The Civilising Process*, ed. Edmund Jephcott (Oxford: Blackwell, 1994).

45 See, for example, Cressida J. Heyes, 'AntiÐEssentialism in Practice: Carol Gilligan and Feminist Philosophy', *Hypatia* 12, no. 3 (1997), pp. 142–63.

46 Carol Gilligan, *In a Different Voice: Psychological Theory and Women's Development* (Cambridge, MA: Harvard University Press, 1982).

47 See Chapters 3 and 5.

48 Kate Massey, 'Listening for the "I": Adapting a Voice-Centred, Relational Method of Data Analysis in a Group Interview to Examine Women's Faith Lives' in *Researching Female Faith: Qualitative Research Methods*, ed. Nicola Slee, Fran Porter and Anne Phillips (Abingdon: Routledge, 2018), p. 151.

49 Janice G. Raymond, *A Passion for Friends: Toward a Philosophy of Female Affection* (London: The Women's Press, 1986), p. 6, author's own capitalization.

50 See, for example, Erik H. Erikson, *Identity: Youth and Crisis* (London: Faber, 1968), p. 132.

51 Sharon Parks, *Big Questions, Worthy Dreams: Mentoring Young Adults in Their Search for Meaning, Purpose, and Faith* (San Francisco, CA: Jossey-Bass, 2000), p. 83.

52 Mary F. Belenky et al., *Women's Ways of Knowing: The Development of Self, Voice and Mind*, 10th Anniversary ed. (New York: Basic Books, 1986), p. 176.

53 Carol Gilligan, 'Preface: Teaching Shakespeare's Sister' in *Making Connections: The Relational Worlds of Adolescent Girls at Emma Willard School*, ed. Carol Gilligan, Nona P. Lyons and Trudy J. Hanmer (Cambridge, MA: Harvard University Press, 1990), pp. 14, 25.

7

Intersectionality and Faith

The previous chapter demonstrated the importance of the students' gender at university, exploring how they negotiated being women in their everyday lives. It argued that the women lived and studied in a context saturated with normalized post-feminist narratives which impacted their everyday experiences. This chapter continues exploring identity at university, providing an account of the women's experiences of intersectionality as their multiple identities overlapped or diverged, including their gendered, sexual, class, racial and religious identities. First, gender and faith are presented in several sections dedicated to how the women experienced these identities as connected. I examine the women's complex navigation of femininity and faith regarding relationships and reproduction, their views on female church leadership, and how Christian feminists use faith to advocate for gender equality. I then discuss the women's sexuality, including experiences of heterosexism and faith, before examining the students' economic backgrounds, highlighting the experiences of those who felt on the margins of student subcultures due to class. I explore the women's experiences of racism, including in Christian contexts, and highlight how the women used Black theology to critique racist discrimination. Lastly, this chapter indicates how the women's gender, race and faith are experienced in their learning environment, demonstrating the challenges of these intersecting identities in university settings.

The term 'intersectionality' was coined by Kimberlé Crenshaw in 1989[1] and continues to resonate with the experiences of those who face multiple discriminations. Intersectional feminism names the connecting structures of oppression that women experience due to their ethnicity, sexuality and socioeconomic status as well as gender. This chapter emphasizes the significance of intersectional experiences, in contrast to previous chapters that highlight what Clydesdale calls an 'identity lockbox'.[2] While I have organized this chapter by different identity categories, these divisions are sometimes arbitrary due to overlapping concerns. Lisa Bowleg argues that each person's intersecting identities create a 'unique social space', which approaching each identity separately cannot explain since 'multiple factors uniquely combine to define an individual's experience'. The separation of different identities becomes impossible as each identity is impacted by another.[3] As Audre Lorde explains, ignoring intersectionality involves 'constantly being encouraged to pluck out some aspect of myself and present this as the meaningful whole, eclipsing and denying the other parts of the self'.[4]

With Sharma and Guest, I find that the 'structures of class, gender and ethnicity continue to frame the perceived limitations of personal experience and self-reinvention among university students'.[5] Some of the women themselves clearly articulated these structures and limitations. For example, Alexandra 'recognized that I'm in a lot of minority groups in life, so, I think, I would consider myself a woman, a person of colour, queer.' Similarly, Chloe ascribed to 'intersectional feminism' because 'there's a lot of issues and difficulties we have just as women existing, and especially as a woman of colour and an LGBT woman ... there's so many issues, there's so many challenges that women face.' Both Alexandra and Chloe struggled to isolate their gendered identities from their other marginalized identities, and feminism only made sense to them when amplified through an intersectional lens. This chapter demonstrates how experiences of intersecting identities shaped the women's lived realities at university, and acted as spaces of both restriction and exploration, contributing to the challenge of feeling at home.

Christian femininity: A double-bind?

'Really nice', 'conservative', 'prim and proper', 'oh so perfect', 'reserved', 'not do[ing] anything wrong', 'really boring', 'kind and motherly', and 'good little Christian girl' – these are some of the expectations that the women faced, as Mary said, 'as soon as you tell people you're a Christian.' She explained these as 'stereotypes' of Christian behaviour, yet they are also quintessential so-called *feminine* attributes, especially among white middle classes. Several women felt these expectations from others, particularly 'in how I dress and how I act', yet tried 'not to live up to them'. Many noticed 'misconstrued' ideas among their peers about their attitude to alcohol, assuming that Christians were more conservative than in reality. Vicky mentioned 'really ridiculous' assumptions that she encountered as a Christian woman, such as 'not having any other friends that aren't Christians' and that 'the only book we ever read is the Bible'. Christian women were expected to be respectable and conservative, even by other students, in an idealized version of femininity that, Page and Heather Shipley argue, 'was predicated on Christian piety'. In their foundational text, *Religion and Sexualities*, these authors argue that, historically, Black women and working-class women 'did not epitomize idealized domestic femininity and were not representatives of sexual purity', and ideal women represented 'domesticated, privatized white middle class femininity'. While femininities have changed over time, these traits were still expected by other students when meeting *Christian* women.[6] Assumed Christian attributes placed alongside ideal femininities presented a double-bind for the women, restricting them to passivity and caring roles in what Riet Bons-Storm calls 'a narrow space in which they can develop their identity and self-narrative.'[7]

However, it was not only among their non-Christian peers that the women faced such expectations; these were also expressed by other Christians and in church contexts. In her first year, Ashley was beginning to think about her gendered experience in church. She thought, 'People in [church] don't expect that I would feel this pressure, but I think I do ... we're expected to act in a certain way', adding, 'I feel confused about how I'm supposed to feel about being a woman in church.' These were new considerations for Ashley, who had not previously given attention to these thoughts and lacked the resources and language to interpret them. In contrast, Lauren had given much thought to her experience as a woman in church, and discussed it with other Christian women. She gave examples of typecasting that she faced, from being asked to bake cakes to being told not to study medicine because 'you shouldn't be bossy, or, you know, ambitious'. She believed that the church had a narrow and 'patriarchal' view of women. Similarly, Kimberly encountered the expectation that women should volunteer 'with the kids' in church. These roles ascribed to women, including baking, children's work, and not being ambitious, resulted in the students feeling confused and limited. Resonating with Zoë Bennett Moore's research, they were under pressure in church to do 'the less honourable routine tasks',[8] and to be *nice* about it. It is unsurprising that the women's non-Christian peers had these expectations of the women when churches have themselves perpetuated these stereotypes.

Althaus-Reid highlights the legacy of colonial Christianity's exaggeration of gendered formulations, denouncing women's bodies as 'problematic' and 'essentialized' due to 'the faulty biological construction of female identities from previous centuries, [including] racial conceptualizations' and 'contributing to heteronormative ideologies'.[9] The double-bind of femininity and faith contributed to the women feeling unhome at both university and at church. They faced stereotypes and expectations due to the intersection of faith and gender, including pressure to conform to a limiting pre-feminist ideal of femininity.

Dating, sex, marriage and motherhood

Page and Shipley demonstrate how religions theologize Western gendered essentialism and heterosexuality, prizing women's virginity, modesty and purity. They argue that heteronormativity assumes a 'standard form of sexual attraction', from which, 'assumptions have been made that women's proper sexual role is in terms of the private sphere – childbearing and child rearing. Religious discourses have done much to support and embed these constructions.'[10]

The most common examples of the double-bind of faith and femininity were expressed in the women's thoughts on dating, sex, marriage and motherhood. About a third of the women discussed sex, most of whom expected to confine sex to their married life. Students who were having sex still wanted to be married someday, including queer women and those from liberal traditions. Interestingly, no students critiqued sexual promiscuity or casual sex at university, reflecting the credence paid to others' individualized choices.

Courtney was single. She wanted her first boyfriend to be the person she would marry, hoping to be married with children by her mid-twenties. This desire was common among evangelical students who, Perrin finds, consider heterosexual marriage a 'biblical mandate for relationships'.[11] Several women experienced pressure or expectation to marry and reproduce, particularly in evangelical contexts. Ashley felt such pressure was 'invasive', and Amber noticed it was 'something girls struggle with ... it's a thing you do'. Kimberly and Danielle saw new Christian couples being quickly encouraged to marry. Discussing dating, Ola said she would prefer to go out with someone who was not from her church because 'there is a lot of pressure'. While talking with a young man at church, she 'kept it a secret' because 'we're not even dating yet, but we were trying to figure out if we actually liked each other' while 'if people knew ... they'll pressure you to actually start dating'. Perrin continues that among evangelical emerging women, 'Going out with someone is a serious commitment, rather than an exploratory friendship ... This illustrates the seriousness with which devout Active Affirmers take romantic relationships and their desire for approval – both from God and their religious community.'[12]

Danielle certainly felt this desire for approval. She was not having sex with her girlfriend in her first year at university because of her theological belief that same-sex relationships should be celibate. However, in her second year, Danielle said that she 'cannot wait!' to be married to a woman. It is possible that her theological position on lesbian sex had changed, and perhaps this was a factor in her decision to stop attending church. Her prioritization of marriage above her church's insistence on celibacy was perhaps a means of claiming some sexual and religious autonomy.

Other queer participants also spoke positively about marriage, including Caitlin who would 'definitely' like to marry her girlfriend. Alexandra would only want to marry her girlfriend if they could settle in the UK since her home country did not recognize same-sex marriage and so would not afford them the 'rights' of having 'a family or insurance'. If they stayed in the Caribbean, they considered having a ceremony with friends demonstrating their 'commitment before God and before people who affirm [us]', without being legally married. Page and Shipley state that 'the blanket adoption of marriage by queer individuals has been critiqued for not disrupting heteronormative systems'.[13] Yet these queer women seemed to be asserting their right to 'equal marriage' and to celebrate their relationships as loving and legitimate, rather than conforming to external pressures. However, none of the women critiqued the idea of marriage per se, despite its patriarchal history and its narrow interpretation of sexual morality.

In her first two interviews, Ashley did not want to have sex until she was married, nor did she want to 'be rushed into a decision to marry'. She reflected that conservative Christians' confinement of sex within marriage 'makes it [a] quite pressured environment at uni'. For this reason, some friends 'get married straight away, just because it's hard not to have sex with someone if you want to.' However, in her third interview in her mid-twenties, Ashley had experienced a sexual relationship with a boyfriend which was 'significant in my life, my sexuality, but also in my life in general ... I felt able to express myself and felt really cared for.' She continued, 'I don't have fear anymore of myself, or decisions that I make, or dating, or even of having sex.' She reflected upon the culture of fear at her university church: '"Sex is the be all and end all", which made me feel afraid of dating cos it made me uncertain that I could trust myself ... why would I want to put myself in that context where I'm afraid?'

This shift in Ashley's theology was part of her journey of 'deconstructing' her previous conservative evangelicalism, discussed in Chapter 4. The process of deconstruction could not be kept separate from her sexuality and her embodied self as she attempted to find a faith that enabled her to feel more comfortable and less afraid.

Stephanie, a liberal Anglican, was in a relationship with a conservative Christian with whom she often disagreed theologically. They had not had sex and avoided discussing it. Stephanie remained passive, 'not bringing it up if he doesn't'. She felt under-resourced in her own sexual identity, so conformed to stereotypical gender roles whereby decisions about women's (sex) lives rest with men. Melissa reported that the only Christian teaching she had received about sex was 'why homosexuality is wrong, and why you have to wait till you're married to have sex', feeling similarly under-resourced in navigating Christian ethics for herself. Freitas argues that the only alternative such Christian teaching offers to 'hook-up culture' is to label sex as 'dangerous' and call for total abstinence,[14] which fails to empower students to make positive decisions for their bodies. Melissa responded to these teachings by disengaging, thinking 'that's just wrong' without having the language to engage theologically.

Tumi was the only student attending a conservative church who discussed having sex while at university. She described it as 'difficult … because it's something that I never intended to happen'. Partly, she attributed having sex to the Covid-19 pandemic since 'When I met [my boyfriend], I had zero expectations of anything happening in my life back in 2020, so, like, things just happened.' While the relationship was mostly positive, Tumi described herself as going into it 'so naïve', finding that having sex 'does affect me spiritually … which again is difficult.' She repeated several times that 'it's not something that I ever intended to happen'. She felt scared to tell Christian peers and 'older women' from church about her boyfriend, fearing judgement as well as not wanting to 'hurt them'. Tumi's conservative stance influenced her refusal to use contraception, which made navigating her sex life stressful. She could not accept anything other than a conservative theology, and distanced herself from any positive decision-making in her relationship. While she enjoyed having sex with her boyfriend, she did not find these feelings easy to accept. The pandemic, as well as feeling 'naïve' and under-resourced, meant that Tumi began a sexual relationship partly due to feeling hopeless and passive in her sexual decisions. Patricia Beattie Jung points to the impact of Christian teaching on sexual experiences, arguing that the limitation and moralization of 'good sex' has resulted in 'the absence of sexual joy' in women's lives.[15] This limitation reinforces gender inequalities, emphasizes heterosexual vaginal sex while denying other sexual encounters, and privileges male pleasure. As with Stephanie and Tumi, it takes sexual autonomy away from women, leaving them silent and passive in the bedroom.

Yip and Page find that university can offer Christians a space to critique the sexually permissive student culture without being sex-negative, and to be open to sexual activity within any loving context.[16] However, with the exception of Ashley, such exploration was not evident among the women in this book, whose discussion of sex demonstrated the double-bind of faith and femininity, and the women felt powerless to shape their sexual narratives. Moreover, Perrin argues that while getting married young has long-term benefits for many evangelical Christians, it can be detrimental to others' faith and well-being.[17] Sharma's research with previous members of conservative churches demonstrates the internal conflict that women experience. Their sexual, gendered and religious selves were found to be irreconcilable, and many had to leave their community before they could feel positive about their sexual selves.[18]

For many women in this book, discussing marriage led to expressing the expectation that they would also have children. Page and Shipley note that in some traditions 'womanhood is referenced through motherhood, denying a place for women who either choose not to have children or who cannot have children'.[19] Womanhood's correlation with motherhood, they argue, reinforces what Tom Boellstorff refers to as 'straight time', reflecting a linear, heteronormative understanding of the life course,[20] although they indicate that these narratives 'also underpin many secular discourses'. Religious emerging women, they argue, actively construct their future maternal identities, demonstrating how motherhood interacts with religion in shaping women's sense of self.[21]

Nicole had thought 'a great deal, probably too much' about having children, discussing motherhood as 'fantastic' and a 'joy'. Mary 'definitely' wanted children; Megan hoped 'sooner rather than later'; and Abigail wanted to adopt. Samantha discussed having children as vocational: 'It's what I'm called to do, and, I feel like it's how I can best serve God.' Lauren was the only student to express not wanting children, and could not see herself being a mother. As with women in research by Dawn Llewellyn on chosen childlessness,[22] Lauren faced disapproval from some who argued that motherhood was her 'Christian vocation' as a woman. Lauren was instead 'more passionate about career', revealing assumptions requiring women to prioritize children at the expense of their occupation.

Two of the queer women were excited about having children. Danielle said, 'I can't wait to be a mother', believing that motherhood was the best thing about being a woman. Caitlin wanted children in her 'twenties' and hoped for 'a relatively large family'. Taylor, an asexual student, was more ambiguous than other students about motherhood. She said, 'If I don't have children that will be fine, I'm also open to the idea of having children.' She asked, 'What kind of mother would I be? Should you have children if you're not 100 per cent [sure]?'

Like Lauren, other women saw a tension between children and future employment. Kimberly was unsure about wanting children, 'But I wouldn't want to have to give up my career for them.' Nicole would not want to be 'a working mum' but would stay home with her children. For Megan, 'having to choose between a career and having a family' was the worst thing about being a woman, while Courtney said she would take a 'job' rather than a 'career' so that she could dedicate more time to children. While becoming a mother was one of Courtney's 'main goals', she worried this would put pressure on a relationship and 'scare' men. These women presumed that male peers were less interested in parenthood than they, and recognized that motherhood came with greater responsibility than fatherhood. In choosing children over career, these women subscribed to wider social understandings of women as unproductive and reproductive, while men are productive.[23] They also conformed to what Sharon Hays refers to as the prevalent parenting model in the West: 'intensive mothering'.[24]

Many women experienced their faith as narrowing their options concerning dating, marriage, sex and parenthood. While post-feminist femininity has shifted from motherhood and domesticity towards bodily appearance, this is not the case within churches. Christian femininity is largely constrained to pre-feminist domestic ideals resonant with theologies of women's self-sacrifice, which feminists have widely critiqued.[25] The students already experienced these challenges, yet felt that their future selves were compelled to conform, and many actively chose this. Those that articulated autonomy in their sexual, married or parenting selves did so tentatively and referenced encountering opposition.

Women's leadership or submission

The students held diverse and sometimes ambiguous views about women's leadership roles in church and submission within heterosexual marriage. Mostly, these diversities were not clearly split by theological tradition, as might be expected. Some women were grappling with these topics in mature or creative ways, resisting prescriptive theologies or overt sexism in the process. The students deliberated women's roles while considering the intersection between their faith and gendered identities, their relationships with authority (including the Bible and church teaching), and their important friendships. Some women had heard a considerable amount of Christian teaching on women's roles in churches and within marriage, while others had received none. This section begins by exploring the students' thoughts about women's roles in church, then on women's marital submission.

Discussing women in church leadership, some students, like Mary and Olivia, told me that they 'don't think about it', or simply accepted their received teaching. Other women 'completely support women in ministry', and were 'passionate' about all roles being available to women because they were 'just as good' as men. Some were 'surprised' when they realized this was not the case. Melissa thought this was 'medieval' and 'ridiculous'. Alexis preferred worship led by her female university chaplain compared to that of her 'misogynistic' male vicar at home. At her church, which denied leadership roles to women, Tumi attended a talk on 'relationships' hosted by two men. She thought, 'It would have been nice to have a female there, I think the place of females for girls is really important ... because I feel more comfortable with a female.' Support for female church leadership stemmed from the recognition that women preachers fostered an environment of respect, empowerment and authentic humanity, echoing research by Perrin.[26] Other women were mixed or, as Nicole said, 'split' in their responses. Samantha thought that in the Catholic tradition, a priest and a nun were 'equal', although 'obviously they don't do the same things'. Nicole ascribed to essentialist thought: she had a 'difficult' experience with a woman vicar causing 'disruption' by being 'the worse side of females'; she preferred her female university chaplain who took on 'some male characteristics' like 'leadership'.

Several women discussed debate in the Church of England taking place at the time about admitting women to the episcopacy. Despite being an Anglican who considered female priests 'normal', Megan preferred Catholicism's consistency in barring women from ordination completely, believing not ordaining women bishops to be 'illogical'. Other women were 'confused' about the 'old-fashioned' reasons against ordaining women as bishops, arguing for 'equality'. Alexis thought that female bishops would 'improve quality' and mean more 'respect for women' and 'for the church'.

Demonstrating post-feminist individualism, several women thought that in choosing a church, its theology of women's leadership would only matter if they themselves were pursuing ministry. Perhaps surprisingly, this opinion was shared by Megan who had previously wondered whether she might herself be called to the priesthood, and Sarah whose mother was a minister. Several women attended churches barring women's access to leadership positions despite not holding that theological view. In keeping with Perrin's conclusion that often only a church's leadership are aware of its beliefs,[27] Kat and Taylor both attended the same church without knowing that women were excluded from being elders. Kat had thought it 'was coincidence' that all the preachers were male before realizing the church's position. Although she felt that male-only leadership 'isn't equality', she did not consider this a reason to change church.

Three women were particularly wrestling with the theology of women's leadership: Ashley, Briana and Ola. Ashley attended an independent evangelical church where women were not permitted to lead, and in her second year was the president of an evangelical student society. It was a 'struggle' for Ashley to 'understand why' women could not lead, 'or if it should change'. She discussed the issue with others, read and prayed about it, as she was 'discovering what I think ... and what I think God thinks'. At her church, 'you have to pretend you agree with it' even though there was 'no explanation', and resented not being resourced to 'form your own opinions'. She was 'confused' as she tried to balance 'what I want to believe' alongside 'what the Bible says' and with 'respectful ... relationships with other[s]'. She questioned if Paul's letters were for 'one particular church' or if they were intended for 'the flourishing of the [whole] church' and wondered how to interpret them in 'a modern-day setting'. She was considering 'leadership and headship', since in the student society, 'I'm leading them ... to where God wants them to be.' Ashley reflected upon the evangelical position of 'headship', the conservative evangelical belief that men have a divinely ordained leadership role with martial and church contexts. She did not 'know what that means' or 'why I would want to believe like that'. She concluded that 'there is more scope for female leadership ... but it's not allowed and that really frustrates me.'

Briana attended an evangelical Anglican church which had a female curate but had never had a female vicar, and was on the committee for the CU. Although she believed women should hold leadership roles, she 'struggled' with the issue because while one of her female housemates was exploring her vocation, another disagreed with women's leadership and felt 'victimized'. Briana wanted 'to talk about it', and was reading books to help her understand 'why I believe what I believe'.

Maintaining an essentialist stance, in both her interviews Briana discussed voting for the next president of the CU. In her first year, she felt that 'it should be a boy' in keeping with the 'expectation that it will'. She thought this because 'guys are the more in-charge people', which was simply 'how boys and girls work' and 'how we're wired'. She added, 'that's just a generalization obviously ... it would be great if there was a girl'. She also wondered if she was being influenced in this belief by the fact that 'all my lecturers are men', demonstrating the position of Christian subcultures amid broader social inequality. In her second year, however, while maintaining that women and men were 'different ... but ... equal', she thought that there would be 'a woman president', which would be 'quite a step' for the CU and for 'the boys in the committee'. Briana had gained awareness of the inner workings of the CU, realizing that its umbrella organization UCCF was 'very conservative' compared with the society.

There are parallels between Briana's experience and Bryant's research in the US, highlighting how conservative Christian subcultures often default to masculine leadership paradigms. This default determines who holds power to shape fundamental aspects of religious practice, including how God is conceptualized. Bryant reports that female rather than male students are 'often the most adamant about maintaining their "proper" roles in the community as the most submissive sex', yet she concludes that 'an emerging evangelical minority that support gender equality is gaining visibility'.[28]

Ola had grown up in an evangelical church in Nigeria where her parents were 'both pastors'. Her gradual realization about gender inequity in church leadership suggested an awakening consciousness. She said, 'I have seen my mum still be submissive to my dad ... they're both equal, they both give each other respect ... they're the same, we're all doing God's work.' Ola felt that since God was 'speaking ... through us', God can use everyone. However, her dad was still 'The general overseer of the church, he's the one that, um, God placed [the church] on his heart.' Despite her mother not being permitted to preach sermons, as a child Ola had created 'this book with, like, sermons ... I'd pick a topic, and I'd think "OK, let's think of all the passages related to this topic and see how I can make a sermon."' While she did not express a specific sense of vocation, Ola felt that as an adult 'if God asked me to [preach], it would be nice to', demonstrating an openness to her involvement in church leadership in the future.

At university, Ola attended an independent church with women pastors, but they were not permitted to preach. She said, 'I don't know why, to be honest.' She thought, 'It'd be nice to see a woman preach, to hear what she would have to say from her perspective.' When she first arrived at university, Ola attended a church where a woman preached, which she found to be 'nice' and 'encouraging', yet she did not stay. At the end of her interview, Ola said that she would 'go to my church and ask, "How come none of the female pastors have actually preached?!" because I've never actually thought about that.'

During the pandemic, Ola attended an online church with a Black female pastor who 'preaches a lot'. Ola described the woman's 'encouraging' preaching as convincing her to continue attending, saying,

> I love how ... [I] really understand what she's trying to say ... and I'm like, 'That was so helpful!', I actually want to be like her ... I'd say [she] was sort of my mentor, someone I look up to ... cos I could relate to a lot of things she was saying.

Ola's journey with women in church leadership reflects early mixed messages. Her mother helped lead while her father was the head pastor. Though she wrote sermons as a child, she rarely saw women preach and later chose a church without questioning its male-only leadership. A transformative moment came when she joined an online community specifically for its female pastor, again sparking Ola's own vocational pondering, perhaps due to their shared race as well as gender.

Women's submission within marriage was discussed less often than their leadership, and was only referenced by women who had attended conservative evangelical churches. This lesser focus on marital submission suggests this doctrine may be less prevalent or acceptable among emerging women. It may also reflect Generation Zers' belief in gender equality, making marital submission increasingly out of step with their values. It is possible that this was not the case for women in church leadership because societal norms still favour male leaders.

Melissa saw a generational shift in her evangelical home church where, although older women fulfilled 'stereotypical gender roles', they did not prevent younger women pursuing 'whatever they wanted'. Other women discussed sermons or biblical texts. Taylor heard 'that women are equal but not the same as men, that they … should voluntarily submit to their husbands'. She did not agree but felt unable to 'refute something from the Bible'. Danielle thought this view was 'old-fashioned'. She argued that biblically, 'Men are meant to submit to women as well, but a lot of people tend to leave that out.' Olivia thought that although there were 'biblical examples' of women's submission, they were 'contextual'. She wanted clearer teaching on gender, believing that Christianity should never 'be about suppressing women'. Unlike other women above, she did not agree with her church's claim that 'we have equal roles but just different'. Ola was the only student to not critique the teaching that women should submit at home. She thought that in marriage husbands 'are superior … biblically, as women you are just supposed to submit'. Yet she argued that this superiority was confined to their domestic sphere, and was not for men to 'misuse' or 'make you a slave'. She clarified that even though husbands are superior to their wives, they are not 'superior to everyone, to all females'.

Both Olivia and Ashley emphasized the need to 'be willing to listen' to 'both sides of the Christian argument' so that they could 'learn about' the 'different interpretations' including those 'that make me uncomfortable', rather than 'react immediately to something that I'm not comfortable hearing'. Ashley was a mixed-race woman who wanted to treat people with whom she disagreed about gender roles with the same respect that she wanted herself concerning her race. This was a mature response to embracing different opinions that she had developed due to her own intersectional experience. She said, 'I don't want people to run away from conversation cos it's uncomfortable, so I'm willing to make myself uncomfortable in certain situations.' Sara Ahmed argues that 'discomfort' is important in offering 'a different viewing point' and 'disorientat[ing] how things are arranged'. Discomfort 'allows things to move by bringing what is in the background ... back to life.'[29] Ashley was open to dialogue that might both challenge her and enhance her understanding, even amid a time of insecurity as a university student.

Research regularly finds discrepancies between the actual lived practice of those who attend conservative churches and teachings about submission, which are considered the ideal rather than a necessity.[30] However, survey data in the UK and US demonstrates that religious women are more likely to be wives and mothers rather than in full-time employment, while women employed full-time are less likely to be religious.[31] Taylor noted that her church's teaching 'goes against society'; however, Carolyn Heilbrun argues that similar restrictions on women's lives are found in secular culture, whereby women's 'desires and quests are always secondary' to men's.[32] Marion Maddox argues that conservative evangelical teaching about submission and leadership plays into wider societal fears about women's authority, as well as into post-feminist gendered norms, giving them 'a theological gloss'.[33]

Some words above were used repeatedly: *equal but different* (six women); *struggle* or *confusion* (three women); *medieval* or *old-fashioned* (three women); and *listening, learning* from *difference* (two women). These words demonstrate the women's resilience in exploring their faith through a gendered lens, questioning church instruction while eager to maintain relationships. They did this within a society and a church that failed to offer feminist resources for engaging in conversation. Yet they saw themselves as able to make decisions for themselves and to influence policy about outdated teaching. Aune argues that churches benefit from feminist engagement, arguing that 'recent victories' for women would not have occurred 'if feminists had not fought from within their religions for these changes'.[34] Emerging Christian women need further resourcing if churches are to fully include and represent women's realities.

Christian female friendships and mentors

Slee's faith development theory holds relationality as a 'fundamental epistemology which underlies and undergirds the whole of a woman's spiritual journey'. In contrast to Fowler,[35] she demonstrates women's achievement of a 'grounded self-in-relation via embeddedness in the demands of relationship'.[36] While Slee theorizes connectedness between women, God, creation and the other, in my own work the women's interdependence, explored in Chapter 3, was primarily expressed in their immediate relationships with other women. This discrepancy could be due to the students' younger age compared with the women in Slee's research, or perhaps to the transitional nature of the university experience narrowing the women's focus. The previous chapter details the importance of female friends in the women's university life. Here, I explore the significance that the women placed on their *Christian* female relationships: particularly friends, and then also with women mentors. Liz Carmichael reflects that friendship 'sets people free to be and to become ... invit[ing] reciprocal love and the joy of fulfilment in mutual relationship'.[37] As Ashley said, 'the closest relationships I have are with women, and those have been the places where I've learned the most about God, and most about myself.'

Amber and Briana attended church and CU together. In their first year they recognized the 'formative' nature of making 'really good friends here that I can have for a very long time'. The following year they lived together with other Christian women, all 'best friends'. Amber described the household as feeling 'more like family than friends' due to it feeling 'real' and them offering 'support'. Briana agreed that it was 'good to have that support' where they 'really understand each other' and 'I can talk to them about pretty much anything'. Briana found that shared prayer practices made these friendships 'more deep'.

Briana valued that when they are together, 'Girls are more inclined to talk about emotional things, gossip more, well not gossip more but like, um, talk about other people, kind of, in that way, um, probably more pastoral.' Briana's tentative reflection demonstrates the importance of gossip in naming the everyday truths that, as Jones argues, 'give the comfort of validation'[38] and help in showing care for others. Belenky and her colleagues argue that gossip is not 'a trivial activity ... Gossipers tell each other about themselves by showing how they interpret the information they share.'[39] Briana rephrased her sentence to withdraw the term 'gossip', presumably resisting its negative (gendered) connotations, but saw it as an emotionally intelligent and caring method of deepening friendships. Amber and Briana's faith and their friendship (as with that of Alexis, Melissa and Stephanie; see Chapter 5) enabled them to develop a connection through which they could feel at home at university, in their Christian contexts, and in themselves, and increased their confidence in their faith lives.

Similar to the need for Christian female friendships, the women reported reliance on female mentors or role models that acted as *intentional friends* in the women's faith journey. These included older women in their family or church, and Christians closer to them in age. The desire for intentional friendships with Christian women was another area of the women's lives in which they recognized the importance of gender.

The significance of Christian mentors for young people is noted elsewhere. Clydesdale argues that students need supportive adults while exploring their identities.[40] For Parks, young adults require help navigating the 'wilderness' of their formation.[41] Girls transitioning into adolescence in Anne Phillips's research were 'both birthing and being birthed into a new identity', aided by supportive Christian 'midwives'.[42] Brown and Gilligan write, 'Relationships between girls and women are crucial for girls' development, for women's psychological health, and also for bringing women's voices fully into the world.'[43]

For Slee, 'teachers, ministers [and] spiritual guides' provide 'guidance, direction and encouragement' and model 'a quality of faithfulness which mediated hope, healing and acceptance'. These mentors are mostly men, 'reflecting the unequal gender distribution of leadership roles within the church'.[44] However, like Perrin, I find that for these emerging women, mentors were almost exclusively female.[45]

Many students spoke of a Christian woman in their family or home church that had a mentoring role, but were yet to find intentional friends at university. Nicole had a 'choir family' at her home church 'that sort of check on me' and whom she could 'ask questions', including one woman who was 'like a godmother'. Similarly, Kimberly's intentional friends included a 'chosen godparent', and she could 'envision myself following in their footsteps'. Amber recognized how her role model 'has lived out her life as a woman of God', and Mary had several 'strong women to look up to in the church'.

The women also had intentional friendships with, as Briana said, 'slightly older Christians ... girls from my church', including young women in church leadership, who understood the specificity of Christian women's transitionings at university. The children's worker at Vicky's home church was 'like an elder figure, but not that much older' because of her 'immense faith in God' and because she related to 'what I was talking about'. Olivia asked a slightly older woman at church for advice about being a Christian at university. Haley appreciated female youth workers because 'as a role model ... I know I ... connect better with a woman'. Ashley was being 'discipled' by a woman at church who was a few years older than her. Together they reflected on what they wanted to 'act like and be like' as women, and Ashley sought 'guidance' from the relationship when she was 'struggling'. She explained that the friendship had 'intentionality ... in that she is purposefully supporting me' and was 'lead[ing] me forward in my relationship' with God.

Apart from older and peer women, Ashley and Samantha discussed Christian female role models in different contexts. Ashley had been 'inspired' by an online blog written by a woman 'about feminism and her faith, how ... they're coming together', and Ashley hoped to be 'kinda like' the author. Samantha found a 'female role model' in Mary, the mother of Jesus, 'Because she said "yes" to God when she ... must have been really, really scared, and I've felt like that.'

According to Dorothy Lee, redemption in feminist theology is 'relational', centred on 'mutuality' rather than individual salvation. She writes, 'Abiding in the love of God is never an abiding in isolation ... to abide in love with others is to live together in a community that works to overcome alienation and isolation.' While community is crucial, for Lee, developing a personal identity is equally important, particularly for women who have been encouraged to sacrifice their needs for others by patriarchal demands, making it hard for women to have 'a strong interior awareness of dwelling place or homecoming'. True spiritual 'abiding' requires both personal growth and deep relationships, combining authentic selfhood with meaningful connections to others and God.[46]

Many women were developing close Christian friendships with other women that they had not long known but were quickly becoming their new family. These women had been encouraged and nurtured in their faith by slightly older female peers and mature women who acted as intentional friends. While none of the women had yet met a similar Christian woman-mentor in their student life, the emotional safety and stability that these two support networks provided were instrumental in the women's feeling at home at university.

Christian feminists

Christian women have spoken truth to the patriarchal powers of both church and society for centuries, from Sojourner Truth's anti-slavery message in 1851, to Elizabeth Cady Stanton's biblical exegesis published in 1895, and Maude Royden's critique of World War One.[47] Bowleg argues that, 'Black women pioneers such as Sojourner Truth used their own lives to illustrate the experience of intersectionality ... Indeed, Truth's speech provides an invaluable lesson for the conceptual and methodological advancement of future research on intersectionality.'[48]

Llewellyn and Marta Trzebiatowska argue that secular feminism was 'spearheaded by religious women and Christian organizations in the nineteenth century'.[49] Yet feminism and Christianity have been sceptical, even derisive, of one another. For Aune, churches reject feminism partly because it 'challenged traditional religion [and] helped lead women away from it'.[50] While some women in this book struggled to see the intersection between their gendered and faith lives, many were beginning to do this work, and some had given their lived experience as Christian women considerable thought.

First, several women were using their faith to transgress post-feminist rules for bodily femininity. They did not necessarily name this as feminism, yet they demonstrated a collective challenge to the essentialist roles determining women's lives. Some were reflecting theologically on post-feminist culture, while others made simple, yet counter-cultural, bodily choices informed by their faith. One example included resisting consumerist fast-fashion. Olivia reflected that fashion 'could become a form of idolatry'. She was beginning to think ethically about how she spent her money, and wanted her 'security' to be in God not her clothing. Inspired by her faith, Vicky resisted buying an excess of clothes and steered clear of brands known for using sweatshops. Other examples included women who felt less pressure to fit in by being 'cool', 'normal', or 'to dress in certain ways' required 'because I'm a woman'. Instead, they were 'happy not doing that' because 'we've got God'.

The women's faith also allowed them to opt out of wearing uncomfortably revealing clothing. Some women described this decision as *modesty*. Samantha, a Catholic student, had given modesty much thought. Manifestations of femininity in the media made her 'cringe' and feel 'sad', including advertising that demands women show 'either legs or cleavage'. Samantha argued that bodies are 'special' and 'reserved for the Holy Spirit'. She felt that her Catholicism required her to be modest, and at first she found this difficult amid post-feminist norms: 'I did dress, I suppose, fairly immodestly a few years ago, I was just trying to make myself feel better cos ... self-esteem was a big problem for me.' In navigating the seemingly dual territories of modesty and femininity, Samantha tried to find a way of being modest 'without looking like we're 80' and 'frumpy'. Eventually, she confidently negotiated a way that felt right: 'Modesty is my kind of femininity.' Samantha added a further level of theological reflection to her clothing choices. She associated 'showing how beautiful you are by being modest' with 'chastity', having decided not to have sex outside of marriage. She cited Matthew 5.28, saying, 'It always makes me think of when Jesus says, "If you've looked at a woman with lust then you've committed adultery with her in your heart."' Samantha felt a Christian male gaze on her choice of clothing, saying, 'We should help them out a bit' by not 'leading people into temptation'. Yet Samantha also added that men had the same responsibility to not 'go around topless', and was one of the few students to name female sexual desire, saying, 'We can still look at people with lust.'

Samantha experienced modesty as empowering, and the responsibility of Christians of all genders. However, the requirement to dress modestly is often applied uncritically, and, as Rachel Joy Welcher argues, places 'pressure on women to guard the purity of both genders'. She continues, 'modesty begins to feel less about being wise and selfless and more about the sin of having a female body', which is a sentiment Samantha would have rejected outright, although it is possible that she had internalized it.

Welcher argues that the oversexualization of women of colour in the West means that they experience intersectional pressure to maintain modesty.[51] Tumi, a Black British student, felt this acutely. She expressed frustration with church dress codes and body-shaming culture, saying, 'I love wearing short tops ... and I feel like I can't wear that around, like, in church ... and when I sit down my skirt rides up ... above my knees and I'm like, "You know what, I'm not gonna not wear this."' She highlighted her discomfort at narrow clothing expectations, feeling judged for her body shape and clothing choices, and the burden on women to manage men's sexual morality. She simply wanted to wear 'comfy' clothing that suited her body and the weather, and that she 'loves'. Her tone was a mix of defiance, humour and exasperation, using rhetorical questions and personal anecdotes to challenge these restrictive social norms. She rejected the notion that she was somehow responsible for men's behaviour, critiquing the double standards that disproportionately police women's bodies, saying, 'People do tell you, like, "You don't want the guys to stumble" and you're like, "Then they shouldn't walk around topless!" [laughs].' She said:

> It's harder for girls, isn't it, because you've got the whole bra strap, you've got the whole cleavage, you've got the whole stomach, and, like, sorry I've got a big bum, I'm sorry that's not my fault, it's genetics, leave me alone ... I can't change that.

Her reference to 'genetics' and a 'big bum' was potentially a reference to her Blackness, which she also felt was being policed. While Tumi wanted to 'just ignore it', she also wanted 'to respect other people'.

Tumi found the expectation to be modest a problem when 'growing up especially ... I was brought up in a ... certain way ... and never really had honest conversations about it', suggesting that she lacked the resources to challenge the issue. She also thought that the pressure on women to protect men gave contradictory messages in a pressurized dating environment: 'That makes it harder to get to know Christian guys because they're like, "Don't speak to Christian guys cos you'll make them stumble", but you've got to marry a Christian! ... It just doesn't make must sense!'

While dressing in less revealing ways than their peers, Ashley and Lauren, an evangelical and a Methodist student respectively, critiqued modesty altogether. Lauren had once been told in church that her skirt was too short. She responded, asking 'Why were you looking there?! [laughs].' Ashley thought that even though modesty was in 'the Bible and also in church ... I'm quite sceptical about the whole thing [laughs].' Instead, she spoke about body-positivity as a Christian virtue, citing Colossians 2.20–3. She said,

> 'Humans will say do not taste, do not smell, but they are merely human rules and they have ... no power and, like, constraining sensual indulgence', but whereas actually, we're not taught to do that as Christians, like, we're told that was condemned.

Ashley believed that Christians have a responsibility to speak up against a culture of women 'starving themselves' which is 'bad' and 'not what we're supposed to do'. Lisa Isherwood critiques Christian subcultures that reject food as excessively sensual, needing restriction so that 'the female body will ... shrink publicly'.[52] Hannah Bacon advocates for 'feminist theologies of fat liberation' that:

> interrogate the roots of fat phobia in interlocking systems of power, including misogyny, patriarchy, neoliberal capitalism and racism ... [and] offer a critique of the church and how Christian systems ... [support] ideological systems of violence against fat people, and fat women in particular.[53]

While Isherwood and Bacon uncover Christian femininities that require women to 'Slim for Him', Ashley rejects restricting food and sizeism outright, applying her biblical knowledge to construct a feminist theology that embraces the body's senses.

Strong social-cultural codes were at work, from which the women could not withdraw, and their self-consciousness belied the power of the male gaze. However, the women quoted above recognized that gender was performed through their clothing and appearance. They utilized the Bible and Christian ethics to resist post-feminist bodily demands and transgress cultural norms. Some drew attention to the discriminatory nature of conservative demands placed on women's bodies, while others found 'modesty' empowering in rejecting the sexualization of their bodies. They demonstrated the need for feminist resourcing, enabling Christian women to reject both Christian and post-feminist definitions of femininity. In the meantime, these tentative explorations enabled them to feel more confident and comfortable in their own skin as Christian women.

Second, and less subtly, many women were explicit about being feminists, and about the relationship between their faith and their feminism. Connecting their feminist and Christian identities proved to be a powerful experience, contributing to their 'labour of integration'[54] involving both identity work and theological reflection. Several women saw their faith influence their feminism in that 'God loves everyone equally', 'it says in the Bible that we're equal', and 'God ... sees men and women to be equal in his eyes and of equal worth'. Briana saw feminism as imperative 'especially for Christians'. According to Althaus-Reid and Isherwood, feminist theology's emphasis on *equality* tends to downplay important differences between people's experiences, failing to challenge deeply embedded heteronormative assumptions at theology's core.[55] However, for these women, post-feminism's emphasis on equality had reinforced this as the primary aim, and it was language that the women already had in talking about gender. That they were using faith rather than secular norms to call for equality demonstrated their intersectional integration between the two identities. For example, Alexandra was a feminist because 'God is *for* women.' Vicky said, 'If Jesus was walking about at the minute ... it would be an issue that he was trying to change people's thinking about.' Caitlin said, 'We need feminism more than ever in Christianity.'

Ashley and Melissa were especially interested in theologically reflecting on feminism. In her first year, Ashley was beginning to 'think about how being a woman and feminism and femininity fits within faith'. In her second year, she thought that 'the solution' to gender inequality 'is Jesus ... and his act of, reconciling the whole earth'. Ashley reflected upon being created in God's image, which 'affects how I expect to be treated ... [and] the world just doesn't meet that'. She understood that her fundamental identity shaped her expectations of dignity and respect, since being made in God's image confers inherent worth that demands compassion and equality for all, yet this was not the case. Melissa saw her feminism as being 'based on what Christ said' and on female leaders in the early Church, as opposed to 'St Augustine [and] Constantine' who 'messed a lot of it up'. She interpreted Christianity as 'having been impacted by very misogynistic society' and was assessing 'what parts of our faith do we believe actually come from Christ', not from patriarchal interpretations.

Other women engaged with feminism's fourth wave, believing that Christians need to fight gender injustice both outside and within church. Aune argues that this repositions 'religious women as agents whose faith is part and parcel of modernity (rather than ... [a] reaction against it)'.[56] For example, Vicky campaigned with the Everyday Sexism Project,[57] and Lauren engaged with the No More Page 3 Campaign and Girlguiding's work for 'gender and youth equality'.

These women, in integrating their Christian and gendered identities, found that this strengthened both their feminism and their faith. Such integration counteracted the challenges discussed in Chapter 6, and was significant in their feeling at home at university and in their own bodies, transforming both their university experience and their self-understanding.

Sexuality and heterosexism

This chapter has focused on the intersections between the women's gendered and faith identities. This section and the next now consider sexuality, first discussing the women's words unrelated to Christianity, then considering the intersection between their sexuality and faith.

Emily Falconer and Yvette Taylor argue that university is generally considered a time for encountering new, diverse and – in particular – liberal attitudes to a range of different topics, including sexuality. University, they write, is assumed to be 'progressive', placed in 'a distorted and polarised binary' with 'traditional, backwards' religion. However, they find that 'despite expectations of universities as inclusive ... those who inhabit multiple diversities do not always fit into place within academic spaces'.[58] Similarly, research with queer students in New Zealand, conducted by Claudia Garcia and colleagues, suggests that queer students are not always welcome in universities where 'queer people are exposed to ... heteronormativity and cisnormativity that can lead to the development of negative core beliefs ... [and] mental health difficulties'. They give examples of queer students feeling unsafe or excluded, including aggressively heteronormative party cultures and cisnormative ideologies of clothing. Many queer students 'conceal their identities on campus to avoid intimidation', even 'fearing for their physical safety'.[59] The researchers argue that queer university students lack 'adequate support' with their 'unique challenges'. They write, 'ongoing mental health disparities of queer students highlight the need to understand the experiences of this group'.[60]

Four of the women included in this book identified as queer, lesbian or bisexual: Alexandra, Caitlin, Chloe and Danielle. The remaining 22 women were heterosexual, although Taylor also identified as asexual, 'if I have to give myself a label.' All were cisgender. Only two straight women discussed their sexuality, demonstrating heteronormativity and less need to negotiate heterosexual identities.

Research into sexuality and religion is predominantly white-led and white-focused,[61] so the inclusion of two queer women of colour is valuable. Chloe experienced her sexuality as being alongside, rather than integrated with, her East Asian heritage:

> [Sexuality is] a thing you keep separate from the race ... it's not something I'd tell my extended family because I know they'd react badly to it and I'm, like, I'm not going to make my life more difficult than it is!

However, Chloe was beginning to realize, 'You know what, I can be all of it.' She described her friends with 'obvious' queer appearance facing family rejection and 'abuse', while those who could hide their sexuality had different experiences. Chloe said,

> I am lucky in that – like, this is a controversial phrase – but I am 'straight-passing' (in inverted commas, because it's like, what does a bisexual person look like anyway?). But I am, as it is, straight-passing ... so I can hide it ... compared to my friends, I feel like I've had it quite easy.

Page and Shipley note that while bisexuality can be viewed as a '"safer" designation' than other queer identities, bisexuals face discrimination from both straight and gay communities, often being dismissed as 'confused' about their attraction.[62] Perhaps due to both her (racial and straight-passing) appearance and her bisexuality (rather than being a lesbian), Chloe was relaxed about her involvement in LGBTQIA+ causes. While she did not necessarily campaign for equality, she attended Pride events and appreciated how 'LGBT people of colour, like, we really understand each other.'

Alexandra also understood her queer identity through the lens of her race. She felt more drawn to joining the Caribbean Society than the LGBTQIA+ Society, prioritizing her cultural identity, 'because I could find queer people in the Caribbean Society, but not necessarily the other way around.' Alexandra recognized that how she performed her queerness might be different from white lesbians, highlighting the exclusionary whiteness of many queer spaces. She also struggled with being open about her sexuality with her family, especially her father, who she described as 'pretty homophobic' and had 'the tendency to get violent'. Her younger brother had recently confided in Alexandra that he was gay. She worried about him 'because I think it's a bit more difficult for gay men who, um, express themselves in a more effeminate way', recognizing toxic masculinity in her Caribbean culture. She looked forward to her brother becoming old enough to move out of the family home so he would not have to negotiate his sexuality around their parents. Page and Shipley reflect that, 'Home is often considered as a place of safety; it is often the underpinning reference point within people's lives. But homes can be volatile and even dangerous spaces for queer people.'[63]

Alexandra's fear of violence, and the abuse suffered by Chloe's visibly queer friends, demonstrate the dangerous consequences of queer as a contested identity. These two women also reveal sexuality and race as integrated minority identities needing constant negotiation.

As an undergraduate, Taylor had identified as heterosexual. Seven years later she was living with her boyfriend but had never had sex. While she said, 'I don't think that label is useful for me', she thought she was 'probably asexual'. Since she did not have a 'noticeable sex drive', she thought, 'Even if I wasn't Christian I probably wouldn't have had sex.' She wondered if this might be 'nervousness of something I've never done before', but then added, 'Eurgh! I don't want to!' Page and Shipley demonstrate the 'huge emphasis on sexual lives in contemporary culture', so it is perhaps unsurprising that Taylor was reluctant to label herself asexual. They argue that 'giving greater legitimacy to asexual identities may disrupt and challenge such normative understandings'.[64]

Sexuality and faith

Discussing sexuality and faith, this section begins by presenting theological journeys that some of the women navigated, before describing encounters with queerphobia. I then show the women navigating their sexual and religious identities in a 'labour of integration',[65] before sharing the women's reflections on queer Christian justice.

Several women navigated a theological journey as they considered homosexuality. At university, Ashley's church preached the need for all to accept a conservative theology of sexuality because 'that's what God believes'; however, she thought this was 'completely inappropriate' and said, 'I really don't know if I can stand for that.' Noticing the assumed dichotomy between conservative religions and liberal secular spaces critiqued by Falconer and Taylor in the previous section,[66] Ashley struggled to find a balance between her church's teachings and being 'at a uni where everyone is so open and accepting'. She longed for 'space where I'm allowed to say that and no one's gonna tell me I'm not a Christian for it', a space to understand 'what God wants' that was 'respectful and humble'. Her evangelical church did not provide alternative theological interpretations, and Ashley could not find a safe community in which such respect was modelled so found herself lacking the resources to come to her own conclusions about what to believe. She felt angry, frustrated and sad about this.

Alexandra had previously struggled with her queer identity because her family had 'interpreted Scripture ... antagonistically'. However, unlike Ashley, Alexandra met friends with a liberal theology, introducing her to different biblical understandings. She thought, 'Scripture is created by a kyriarchical approach ... And we have to understand what is prescriptive and what is descriptive within it ... It's helped [me] to grapple with the antagonism that I'm facing at home.'

Drawing on her studies in feminist and queer theologies, Alexandra drew on the theory of kyriarchy coined by Elisabeth Schüssler Fiorenza to understand both the Bible and her own life. Schüssler Fiorenza describes kyriarchy as 'a different understanding of patriarchy, one which does not limit it to the sex/gender system but conceptualizes it in terms of interlocking structures of domination'.[67] She continues,

> Kyriarchal power operates not only along the axis of gender but also along those of race, class, culture, and religion ... One can map not only how these systems of oppression form the kyriarchal social pyramid, but also how they criss-cross the subject-positions that the politics of domination offers to individuals.[68]

Recent intersectional feminism could be said to borrow Schüssler Fiorenza's theory as marginalized people, including queer folk, must navigate layers of structural oppression. As Falconer and Taylor observe, 'academia can work as therapy for those making sense of their lives',[69] and this was true for Alexandra. Alexandra took comfort and strength from both this theory and from having a community where she could share her experiences of marginalization, explore her faith, and be herself.

In contrast, Chloe was not involved with church or theological study, so lacked this sense of belonging. She said, 'I don't feel like there's any problems with me being bisexual and being Christian. But I think when I was younger there definitely was, and I think that's what stopped me from finding out more about Christianity.'

As a bisexual teenager, she had thought conservative Christians 'hate us', and had actively resisted exploring her faith due to these teachings. At university, she found peace between these two different identities, but still was not ready to find a Christian community.

Both queer and straight women challenged queerphobic exclusion within Christian communities. In their survey of Christian students published in 2013, Guest and his colleagues find that 65 per cent of Active Affirmers (consistent church attenders) viewed same-sex relationships as 'always wrong'. This is contrasted with the views of those who attended church irregularly: for example, only 4 per cent of Unchurched Christians believed this.[70] These percentages may well be lower now, given the more widespread acceptance of same-sex relationships, including the legalization of same-sex marriage that same year. However, this is speculation, and many Christian spaces are still hostile, even dangerous, to those identifying as queer. Page and Shipley argue that there are 'highly negative consequences' for queer Christians, including being disowned by churches and family members, mental ill-health, and attempted and actual violence. Naming the emotional labour that queer Christians undertake, they write, 'Such constraining cultures can have an enormous impact on young religious people who are trying to work out their identity.'[71]

Haley's home church was not 'open to ... being gay'. Being at university, her own theology had become 'more accepting of [queer] people'. Lauren felt that 'being straight is quite a big expectation, I don't envy anybody who has to come out in church.' Lauren felt that being queer was 'a bigger issue' for lesbians than gay men because of the pressure on women to have children within heterosexual marriage. While single, Lauren had faced 'awkward' assumptions from other Christians that she might be queer.

The intersection between Danielle's evangelical faith and her sexuality was present in her everyday life. She had never encountered queer-inclusive theology, but had attended churches enforcing celibacy upon queer people. When other Christians were critical of her sexuality, she said it 'doesn't really matter to me, cos it's a personal thing with God', yet it was clear that it did affect her, perhaps as the number of breaks (represented by commas) in this sentence suggests. She reflected that because of the 'arguments and debates we had over it, I don't really tell people [about my sexuality] ... it's just kind of, like, that thing of being judged.' In church, she felt that 'every time that I say that I'm gay, people automatically assume that I'm not a Christian.' Being queer forced Danielle into a defensive position – she anticipated needing to justify her identity and found it emotionally draining to have it become a subject for debate. Despite trying different churches and Christian societies upon arriving at university, by her second year she had decided not to join a Christian community, but rather to practise her faith in ways that were 'personal to me' because she did not want to be 'asked about my sexuality'. Danielle faced a double burden of concealment and judgement in navigating a painful disconnect between her sexual identity and her religious community, requiring a huge amount of emotional and spiritual labour. Withdrawing from Christian contexts altogether was seen as her safest means of self-protection.

Caitlin was a member of the CU before she realized their conservative stance on homosexuality through 'homophobic things ... said by speakers and by other members'. Despite having made some close friends, when they discovered her queer identity, 'there was definitely a distancing that occurred', and some members 'would not really talk to me or wouldn't want to sit next to me'. Caitlin described leaving the CU as difficult: 'I think I felt sort of guilty about it but at the same time it was hard to put myself in a position where I knew I was continually getting hurt.' She was frustrated that while many members did not ascribe to conservative views, 'They are led by people who hold the beliefs, and they don't necessarily want to rock the boat by arguing.'

Alexandra's mother had described her queer friends as 'heretic[s] and betraying what God wants, and pushing society's standard onto the Word'. Alexandra's girlfriend had previously been taken 'to a reverend to remove the gay from her'. As Page and Shipley argue, 'one's queer identity is seen as rectifiable' with so-called 'therapies'.[72] After this experience, 'rumours spread' and Alexandra was warned 'to stay away from her'. In hiding their relationship, Alexandra and her girlfriend found themselves being hypervigilant in church contexts, fearful of discovery. She said, 'Interactions matter, even the way that you approach somebody, like, if I give her my water bottle ... people could speculate.' Just as a straight friend 'almost wasn't ordained' due to rumours about being queer, Alexandra recognized her sexuality might become a 'barrier' in her own vocation to ordained ministry. Her limited options and hypervigilance meant that Alexandra was forced to constantly focus on her sexual orientation in the multiple spaces of home and church.

Some of the women were undertaking a 'labour of integration' as they negotiated their intersectional sexual and Christian identities in multiple contexts.[73] These lived experiences were named particularly by one heterosexual woman, Ashley, and two queer students, Caitlin and Danielle. After university, Ashley attended a talk about 'a theology of sexuality', which taught that 'sexuality is our attempt to connect'. This included 'having physical sex with someone', but was 'holistic' and 'imbued into all of your life and relationships, so, in your creativity, in your connection with God, your connection with other[s]'. She found this talk 'really influential, because I always had this point of really wanting to flourish in all areas of my life'. Althaus-Reid observes 'a deep link between doing theology and our sexual identity as women'.[74] Ashley was beginning to understand this as she encountered new theologies of sex. For Ashley, sexuality became a source of holistic inspiration and connection, not merely something reserved for a future husband.

Both Caitlin and Danielle were working-class queer women, and all three of these marginalized identities were prominent in diverse ways in their lived experience. Abes argues that sexism, heterosexism and classism are 'embedded in society and create dominant-subordinate binaries that privilege some identities at the expense of others, defining what is "normal"'.[75] Elizabeth McDermott finds that working-class religious lesbians can be more open about their sexuality at university, being both geographically and symbolically 'away from the home' and its 'surveillance'.[76] At university, Caitlin and Danielle recognized the freedom that having left home afforded them, yet both spoke about needing to keep their queer and religious identities secret in different spaces. Caitlin thought,

> Being a queer Christian ... is sometimes a burden because [of] inhabiting a space which is made for straight people ... hav[ing] to continually justify your existence ... [But] it's also a blessing because ... the more diversity we have in a church, in whatever form it comes ... the better, and it's up to my generation ... to speak out.

Caitlin described walking 'a tightrope of spaces ... you're too queer for a Christian space but too Christian for a queer space'. She now 'intentionally' only chose affirming Christian spaces and struggled to share her faith with queer friends 'who've had harm done to them by the church'. She found some queer spaces 'unnecessarily cruel towards religious people ... and hurtful'. She concluded, 'sometimes in solely queer communities I am restricting my religious identity more than I am in religious communities restricting my queer identity.' In resisting religious heterosexist attitudes and queer anti-religious narratives, Caitlin was marginalized by both queer and Christian subcultures, balancing precariously on this 'tightrope'.

When discussing homosexuality and religion, many women spoke about the need for justice in churches, and (following on from Chapter 4) in their understanding of who God is. It is not only *Christian* queer students that emphasize this need for justice and advocacy.[77] However, faith gave the women in my research a framework and a language for countering heterosexism.

Continuing her reflection on kyriarchy above, Alexandra thought that 'the system of the world and society' was structured around 'abuse' of 'power and wealth'. She argued that *everybody* would benefit from a hermeneutic of liberation, yet saw how 'by not being a man and by not being straight, it has opened my eyes to just the way othering affects people'. Alexandra reminded herself that she is 'a beloved child of God and that [my sexuality] is how God made me ... part of who God created me to be'. Her faith was an avenue to combat injustice due to 'who God is'.

Other students discussed how their relationship with God affected their theological position about sexuality. For Ashley, this meant 'knowing that he is *for* and he loves everyone unconditionally'. Chloe thought of God as 'all-loving and all about equality, it really solidifies my feelings about how I think real Christianity is about love.' She joked, 'What God is not going to let you into heaven because you kissed a girl!'

Some women were passionate about challenging queerphobia in churches, and their feminism involved solidarity with queer people. Melissa campaigned for churches to allow same-sex marriage, 'because otherwise you just see the Christians with terrible banners'. Lauren spoke at a Methodist debate about conducting same-sex marriages: 'This is what we need to do ... we need to be bold, we need to be strong, we need to say, we need to do this, we need to say that we're going to do gay marriage.' Alexandra felt ambiguous that her denomination 'doesn't have a stance on LGBT'. While it prevented her from 'advocat[ing] for LGBT people', yet 'if we don't have a stance then you can't prevent me from going into ministry'. Debating whether to move to the UK permanently or stay in the Caribbean after her studies, Alexandra and her girlfriend began to lean towards the latter, 'not just for queers, but for gender justice ... We think it's important ... to stay and do something.'

For these women, both queer and straight, the inclusion of LGBTQIA+ people in the church was necessary for their own faith to flourish. They needed to believe that churches would become more progressive in their lifetimes, and that this was something that they could influence, to participate in them at all. They campaigned for this, unafraid to educate others both inside and outside of the church, and to speak truth to church powers. The women took this vocation upon themselves in response to their relationship with the God of justice. Cornwall argues that 'universities and churches' need to be 'homes' for queer theology, in order that they are 'veritably the "homes" of queer people just as much as of others'.[78] In seeking justice, the women found safe communities with other queer (or queer-allied) Christians to craft home, including their chaplaincy, student society and affirming church. Chaplaincies in particular, as I explore in Chapter 5, were unexpected spaces where all students could find welcome, including non-religious queer students as Garcia and colleagues find. These authors argue that queer students create strategies for negotiating university life, including 'relying on social connections, advocating for themselves and others, and creating a sense of agency'.[79] For the women in my research, Christian communities could be hostile and isolating spaces of queerphobia and enforced heteronormativity, yet for those who found themselves in affirming and inclusive environments, they found support, safety, and the courage to challenge narratives of heterosexism.

Class and classism

Beck and Beck-Gernsheim refer to class as a 'zombie category' because it is simultaneously 'dead and still alive'.[80] In discussing their intersectional identities, social class was often left unmentioned, hidden or unexamined by the women, and it is also overlooked in literature on student life.[81] With some exceptions, most women considered their class to be 'average' or 'middle', while some struggled to articulate their class at all when first asked. For example, Ola thought, 'I don't know, maybe middle?', and Tumi said, 'I think middle.' Guest and colleagues argue that 'former divisions between working and middle classes have fragmented, and class is no longer easily understood in collective terms'.[82]

Seven of the women identified as working or working-middle class, two as middle-upper class, and the remaining 17 as middle class. Despite its hidden nature, social class impacted many women's sense of belonging and identity work at university. Bourdieu emphasizes that class is not merely an economic descriptor, but encompasses a number of capital resources, including social and cultural, influenced by a person's 'habitus' typically learned through their upbringing.[83] How this looks for university students is not simple. Social class is communicated through dress and accent, and intersects with gender, ethnicity and sexuality. Class correlates with students' choice of university, with so-called 'traditional students' coming from middle- or upper-middle-class backgrounds and attending elite universities away from home. Guest and Aune argue that 'working class students at elite universities are preoccupied by the challenges of fitting in socially' while 'the ideals of young adulthood are especially difficult to maintain during periods of economic constraint.'[84]

Holdsworth seeks to identify how students adapt to their new environment. She finds that leaving home has a significant impact upon their university experience, as moving away involves a less disrupted habitus between home and university than for students who commute. This is especially true for working-class students, who typically find less continuity upon attending university, and thus have to adjust more than their middle-class peers. She finds that working-class students are 'in a better position to adapt to student life away from the pressure of having to negotiate between two distinct worlds' if they 'leave behind' parts of their class identity and compartmentalize these worlds.[85]

Class was most often discussed by working- or working-middle-class students. Classism rendered these women's social status abnormal, and their class acted as a distinguishing feature that set them apart from other students. McDermott argues that individualism presents the middle classes as normal, where the self is produced 'through choice and self-management'. In contrast, 'working class habitus is characterised by necessity and limited choices', and thus is lacking and inferior.[86] She differentiates between working-class women and women who are 'working class educated'. A significant difference between the two is geography, as moving away from home to university affords 'working class educated' women social mobility and greater opportunity to self-explore and self-define through the creation of 'geographical boundaries'.[87]

Four of the working-class women were white, while two were mixed race and one was British-East Asian. Mixed-race Samantha was struck by the different lives of students that she met from middle-class backgrounds. She felt an *otherness*, 'a bit like I don't belong' and 'I'm very different from people'. Being 'white-passing', Samantha was unusual for students of colour in that her class was more relevant to her everyday experiences than her race, which was only apparent when discussing East Asian food with her flatmates. Demonstrating her 'unique social space',[88] she said,

> I don't really think about my race ... But about being working class ... I've had such different childhood experiences to people, so I'll meet people that have chickens at home [pause] and, yeah, we probably couldn't even afford to *eat* chicken when we were younger.

Samantha was struck by the difference of her experiences compared with students from a middle-class background. Her class identity significantly shaped her sense of difference, particularly evident in childhood economic constraints including never owning a computer or affording to eat chicken. Her reflection highlights how socioeconomic background profoundly influences students' sense of self, creating an otherness when encountering students from more privileged backgrounds at her redbrick university.

Chloe was British-East Asian with immigrant parents, and although she considered herself to be working class, felt that 'We don't really fit into the traditional white-people working class, at the same time we're definitely not middle class.' Race also made it difficult for Alexandra, a middle-class international student from the Caribbean, to relate to the British class system. Although she was 'well off' at home, studying in the UK she felt 'excluded in terms of like not having certain things, like, my friends and stuff, they have iPads and I feel like I need to get one because I see how it's helped them, but it's just not something affordable.'

Mixed-race Ashley recognized how being working class impacted her university experience; for example, her first trip abroad was on a 'mission trip' with her Christian student society. Her parents had encouraged her to attend university because they considered it the best way 'to make money', perhaps demonstrating immediate financial pressures, a stronger focus on tangible career outcomes, or a mindset of economic survival. In contrast, middle-class students often have more space to consider education's intrinsic intellectual and personal development benefits, having greater economic cushioning. She discussed the intersection between her race and class differently from Samantha, experiencing these two identities as similarly marginalizing since her mixed-race status was more visible:

> I've always been very conscious of [these identities], even from a young age, but ... I haven't always had the language to articulate ... why I was confused and why certain things would upset me ... and I see that other people don't have them.

Being from a working-class background inspired two of the students to help others who were from similar backgrounds, including Ashley. She had 'always wanted to ... support creative development within young people in a context that is more marginalized ... because there's a lot of lack of funding.' White student Vicky wanted to become a secondary school teacher back in her home city which has 'the worst secondary school education system, like, ever, and so that comes from a desire to help people ... because of socioeconomic factors'. Both students said that this desire to advocate for working-class people was influencing their work ethic at university.

Class was a way for working-class women to locate themselves within a student habitus, while white middle-class Briana lamented the fact that, at her redbrick university, most students were like her. In her first year, she was disappointed to notice that 'everyone in my [accommodation] block seems to have come from a white middle-class background ... I haven't got any [friends from] ethnic or from disadvantaged backgrounds.' By her second year, she had encountered more diversity, and reflected that 'I understand more about other people ... I have a bit more of an awareness of [different] people.' Meeting people of diverse racial and class backgrounds was an important part of Briana's university experience, yet she was the only white middle-class student to discuss class, demonstrating its assumed norm.

Guest and colleagues argue that 'subtle differences within the middle-class' are often noticeable among students.[89] For the two women identifying as middle-upper class, their socioeconomic background was significant for their self-understanding and their navigation of university life. Kimberly had attended an all-girls private school in the countryside, and at first felt disorientated attending a redbrick university in a multicultural city. She had hoped to attend an elite university which would have felt 'like private school, it's like going to boarding school'. However, she was glad to be somewhere with 'a bit more going on, and also a bit more diversity [than] white and middle class'.

Nicole felt that her middle-upper-class 'background [and] childhood' was having a significant impact upon her time at university, and she sometimes recognized that she could be 'a bit of a snob ... picking people that are similar to me ... and maybe that makes me very judgmental'. Growing up in a village that always voted for a Conservative MP, Nicole campaigned with the Conservative Future Society at university. Her socioeconomic status enabled her 'to actually understand where my principles come from'. Nicole struggled to make friends when first arriving, and in her second year she lived with two friends from school, saying 'we all get on and the house is great'. Although she had faced criticism, she explained that being with people who were 'not so worldly-wise about inner cities', including not locking their front doors, helped her to feel a sense of belonging:

> Everyone always says, 'Oh you shouldn't really go for people that come from a, sort of, similar schooling to yourself', but it just generally happens ... I tend to go for people who have sort of been brought up in a similar kind of bubble.

Despite feeling isolated by her middle-upper-class status, Nicole was intentional about choosing friends who felt safe and familiar. She was self-aware about potentially limiting her own experience but felt that this was the best means of feeling at home at university.

Unlike other studies finding that Christian spaces are class-specific,[90] none of the students specifically mentioned their class in relation to their faith. Guest and colleagues argue that 'class is not significant in determining Christians' patterns of religious involvement'. With these authors, I find that class impacts 'Christian students' negotiation of the university environment ... with exclusionary as well as inclusionary outcomes'.[91]

To conclude, students' social experiences and comfort at university were influenced by working-class and upper-middle-class statuses, shaping their choice of social circles and how they navigated different spaces. Being middle class was experienced as the norm and often unmentioned. University was, for many although not all students, an opportunity to encounter others with different socioeconomic circumstances. For students of colour, especially those with darker skin, the experience of class was also influenced by its intersection with race. It is to race and experiences of racism that I now turn.

Race and racism

This section focuses on the women's experiences of 'race', highlighting experiences of being Black, Asian or minority ethnic (BAME), including racism. The next section explores race and faith together. Finally, experiences of racism at university are explored at the end of this chapter, alongside gender and faith. 'Race' is a social construct based particularly on skin colour and other biological characteristics, as well as ethnicity and culture, although its boundaries are blurred. It is ambiguous and shifting, not fixed or static. Alana Lentin describes how the origins of 'race' were neutral, not intended as a means to differentiate between superior and inferior, yet it has since been used to distinguish and marginalize groups of people across the world.[92] In the West, people have problematically been categorized as Black or white, with the latter considered dominant and thus afforded power simply by the accident of 'race'. Yet 'race' is neither a biological nor a scientific term, but rather cultural and political. Reddie defines Black in two ways: first, people of African descent; second, those 'who have come together in order to fight the central and dominating power that is White Euro-American normality'.[93] Willie James Jennings describes whiteness as 'a way of being in the world and seeing the world that forms cognitive and affective structures able to seduce people into its habitation and its meaning'.[94] For Ahmed:

> Whiteness is invisible and unmarked, as the absent centre against which others appear only as deviants ... Spaces are orientated 'around' whiteness ... If whiteness allows bodies to move with comfort through space, and to inhabit the world as if it were home, then those bodies take up more space.[95]

While recognizing the complex concept of 'race', to be BAME, or indeed to be white, has a significant impact upon a person's experiences.

In the early twenty-first century, record numbers of BAME students attended British universities, making up 24 per cent of the student population,[96] with traditional elite universities the most ethnically diverse institutions.[97] The six women of colour included in this book spoke more about race than other students. Ashley and Samantha defined themselves as mixed-race and were born in the UK (British-Caribbean and British-Chinese respectively). The other two women born in the UK were Chloe, who was British-East Asian, and Tumi, Zimbabwean-British. Alexandra and Ola were international students, defining themselves as Indo-Caribbean and Nigerian respectively. Even in this small sample, there was much diversity in experience and outlook, demonstrating the clumsiness of the monolithic label of BAME. While four of the six students were born in the UK, British BAME students had much in common with Black international students, and the experiences of international students in this respect were not that different from home students of colour. Whiteness was very much experienced as the norm by all the students, and whiteness was associated with Englishness. For example, Chloe, born in the Midlands, experienced racism when 'people look at you and think you're not British'.

George M. Fredrickson argues that racism validates 'a sense of deep difference' in 'practices, institutions and structures', establishing '*a racial order*, a permanent group hierarchy that is believed to reflect the laws of nature or the decrees of God'. But this is 'neither a given of human social existence ... nor simply a modern theory'.[98] Reddie asserts that while white people are influenced by and may participate in white privilege and racist systems, they are not destined to perpetuate these harmful patterns, but can choose to resist racism.[99]

The fragile nature of racial categories was demonstrated in the two mixed-race women's experiences of colourism. Nadia Craddock and her colleagues define colourism as:

> discrimination based on skin shade penalizing those with dark skin ... both within and between racialized/ethnic groups ... whereby people of colour with dark skin experience greater disadvantage compared

with their peers belonging to the same racialized/ethnic group with light skin.[100]

Samantha passed as white, and so her marginalized race did not factor as significantly as her class identity, mentioned in the previous section. Ashley felt Black while she was in England but was assumed to be white while on a year abroad in Jamaica, and consequently felt that she did not belong fully in either country.

Black Lives Matter (BLM) is a campaigning organization originating in the US in 2013, which grew significantly in the UK following George Floyd's murder in May 2020. Several women spoke about their experiences of BLM in different contexts, demonstrating the shocking nature of Floyd's murder and its widespread impact. Despite finding support among her Black friends at the time, Ashley experienced frustration with:

> white people being really annoying ... asking for advice, what they could do, and I was like, 'Honestly, I don't care, this is not new to me, this is like the everyday reality ... figure this out on your own.'

Chloe, of Asian descent, described being unable to 'understand Black experiences, which can be pretty horrible'. Yet as a person of colour, BLM inspired her to be 'an ally', including 'speaking out if I hear anything slightly off'. Demonstrating the intersectionality between race and class, Chloe described 'the model minority myth' whereby she received comments such as 'You're Chinese, you don't really seem to suffer ... you're smarter, you're richer', yet, being working class, she knew this to be false. She critiqued racism from the Asian community towards Black people, recognizing a racial hierarchy among minority ethnicities, arguing that 'We're all people of colour ... [we're] all in it together.'

Chloe experienced racial harassment during the Covid-19 pandemic, since the virus's Chinese origin led to misinformation and blame of East Asian communities. She described people saying 'slurs' and avoiding her on public transport. Her family's Chinese restaurant suffered 'racist abuse' and reduced takings. Again referencing her intersecting marginalized identities, Chloe discussed experiencing 'racist misogyny ... a lot of sexual harassment I would face on the streets and stuff are also racist abuse'.

Despite these negative experiences, the students discussed how their racial identity facilitated their feeling at home, including appreciating diversity in their communities and friendships which, Chloe said, 'helped me fit in'. At the Chinese Society, she appreciated being able to speak her language and share experiences specific to her racial identity and culture 'that I never got to speak to anyone about'. Similarly, Alexandra planned to join the Caribbean Society. She wanted others with whom to share an 'understanding of the strict parents, and the struggle with money, and the coming from a colony to the colonizer place'.

Many of the women encountered greater diversity at university than in their school or home environments and were able to find friends of the same race for the first time. Ashley had 'more mixed-race friends' at university than previously. In the future, she would be sure to 'intentionally seek it out' because 'it's something that I actually really need'. These friendships were safe spaces where she could 'dig a little deeper' into her experiences.

Most of Ola's closest friends were Black women, 'cos it's so much easier to relate to them, cos they would understand about like racism or microaggressions'. She appreciated that her friends understood the same references and jokes as her, meaning that she did not need to downplay her Nigerian identity and could be fully herself. The friends could 'bond over like, "Oh, *we all* don't know what's going on!" [laughs].' With her Black UK-born friend Tumi, she explained, 'We just clicked, it was just so easy [and] effortless', including shopping for ingredients for 'home food' together. She said, 'It does help, I sort of have a piece of home.'

Tumi described her friendship with Ola too. It was important that they shared the same gender and faith, and that 'we look very similar'. While Nigeria and Zimbabwe were 'completely different', the friends 'integrated each other's cultures, like, they say things that I say, and it's just great fun … it's just so freeing … [and] easier.' For Tumi, friendship with other Black women was something that she'd never had before. She described an intimacy between them, including putting out her friend's laundry or cleaning her bedroom, saying, 'It just makes sense, it's nothing we've spoken about, it just happens.' The similarities between them felt like 'home', 'family' and 'relaxed and safe'.

Having friends the same race as well as gender made a huge difference to the women. 'Race', particularly skin colour, was more significant than nationality, class or other identity markers.[101] Racial and cultural similarity created a sense of comfort, ease of communication and shared cultural knowledge, including familiarity with food from home, mentioned by Alexandra, Ola and Samantha. Sometimes, this comfort particularly resonated because of shared challenges, including microaggressions or colonial history. Racial and cultural, as well as gendered, familiarity created a sense of belonging, safety and feeling at home.

Race and faith

Frederickson traces the 'invention of racism' to Christian accounts of religious difference, especially anti-Semitism.[102] In the last two decades, church denominations have attempted to accept and repair some of the racist harm that has been caused in the UK and globally, not least in their legacy of slavery. For the students, church and Christian activities were sites of racial awareness and sometimes tension. For example, Chloe explained that it was difficult to find a church at university after attending a Cantonese church in the Midlands, pointing to the racial segregation of UK church life.[103] Christianity was 'directly linked to my [racial] identity' because her church was '*no* denomination ... an independent church' meaning that she 'didn't really feel like I fit into Christianity ... in Britain'.

Two students discussed their race influencing their understanding of God. Briefly, when Alexandra was younger, God 'was always a *man* in the clouds, an *old* man, an old *white* man in the clouds'. Ashley, in her three interviews, discussed her race and faith in depth. In the first interview, aged 19 and in her first year, she thought that although God is 'both male and female, and he's of every race and creed', and 'we are all made in the image of God', 'racism and colonialism and then also – what's the term – patriarchy, still makes the image a white man.' When I interviewed her again a year later, she was thinking more about how her racial identity was positioned in Christian communities. She recognized the protection of whiteness as some people ignored her experiences of racism or interpreted her naming these experiences as 'criticism of them'. She felt that 'any conversation I have is, sort of, blocked because they feel uncomfortable with it'.

In her third interview, Ashley was 27 and described many experiences involving racism in the evangelical churches she had attended over the years. In particular, she reported 'a racial tone towards or behind the evangelism' in the organization where she worked, demonstrating deeply problematic historical and colonial overtones. When she tried to understand what was being said, she was told that the organization was '*so* not racist, they just ... wanted people with, like, lighter skin to join the organization'. She said:

> I'm the only person of colour on this team, so I stand *alone*. And ... it's gonna all fall on me to enact the change, and I was like, 'I don't really know if I can take that responsibility and do this alone.'

Ashley's deliberation over how to respond to situations of racism recognizes the dilemma that students of colour face. Her repetition of the word 'alone' highlights the isolated position that racial discrimination placed her in, and the difficult decision of whether to challenge instances of racism or to focus on 'self-preservation' by staying silent. She was a solitary observer of this behaviour, considered normal and unproblematic by her white peers. As Reddie observes, 'The majority of White people … have rarely taken the trouble to understand their Whiteness.' Rather, 'The normative Whiteness of the Church blinded them to the realities of racism within the church and the wider city.' Chloe, Alexandra and Ashley were recognizing what Reddie describes as 'the contested nature of what it means to be a Black human being'.[104]

There were, however, some positive racial experiences of church. Four women spoke about the importance of diversity in their congregations, including one white woman. None of the other white students mentioned race or diversity in their churches, suggesting with Guest and colleagues that, 'Attending white-majority churches or student groups also functions as an expression of ethnic identity, in this case as an expression of a whiteness that is often "unmarked".'[105] Ola and Tumi attended international-majority churches. Ola said that she felt comfortable in her church, whereas 'if you go to a … mostly-white church … I might just feel a bit left out.' The number of Zimbabweans at the church helped her to feel 'the love of God'. She said, 'Because I'm Zimbabwean, they reach out to me, and that's really special cos growing up in the UK and being born here, it's very difficult to connect with my parents' roots.' This connection to her family's ethnic heritage provided a space where her Black identity was accepted and normalized. This cultural grounding not only deepened her spiritual experience but also helped her navigate life in a predominantly white university town, helping her to feel at home.

Alexandra found home in her diverse university chaplaincy, reflecting research by Guest and colleagues suggesting that 'chaplaincies play an especially important role in easing international students' transitions into university life'.[106] Alexandra referenced an Indian member of staff who attended some of the same events, experiencing 'a sense of belonging [there] … it feels like we're in this together, you know, and I think [he] helps because … [of] him being a person of colour.'

An article that Ashley read about Jesus' heritage as both divine and human spoke to her experience as being mixed race. She found it easier to understand this dual nature of Jesus because she saw 'how that is true in myself':

> Both [identities] existed within him, and in the same way being both Black and white exist within me, and there's no point where someone can categorize that one aspect is more Black or more white than another, and it's the same with Christ.

Ashley saw something of her own experience reflected in God, and felt that she understood an aspect of God's being that other people might struggle to see. By associating herself with the dual nature of Christ, Ashley was beginning to develop what Reddie refers to as 'a Black hermeneutic: ... the art or science of interpreting biblical texts in light of Black African concerns, which can include Black cultures, experiences, ideas [and] histories.'[107]

Black theology, for Reddie, is grounded in the belief that God sides with the oppressed, exemplified by God's decisive intervention in the Exodus narrative. There, 'God is neither neutral nor distant ... God in Black theology is the active force that overthrows injustice and releases the captors from their oppression.'[108] Alexandra also reflected on Exodus, and found that it 'helped me to recognize the God of liberation' during the BLM movement, 'when things were really bad with people at home'. BLM also impacted upon how Alexandra felt about the person of Jesus: 'Where would Jesus be in that moment? And Jesus would be walking with everybody on the street, Jesus would be protesting ... [and] Jesus is also like a man of liberation and justice.'

For other students, BLM prompted a shift to thinking about the central place of justice and prophetic witness in Christianity. Caitlin, a white woman, went to a number of protests in London because, 'As a Christian, we have to be looking at these issues of equality more and fighting for them harder.' When thinking back to the eruption of BLM in 2020, Ola's main memory was of how angry and upset it made her, and how she presented this anger to God:

> Why is it that some people think ... some people don't deserve to be whatever they are, just because of the colour of their skin? ... God, *you* can change that with a snap of your finger! ... Why is God letting this happen, or letting these people die?

Ola called out to the God of the oppressed to liberate her people. Her questions escalate from challenging racism itself to questioning God's apparent passivity in allowing racism's deadly consequences. Ola's words reflect a common spiritual struggle to reconcile belief in an all-powerful, loving God with the continued existence of human suffering and injustice. The progression from human-focused to divine-focused questioning suggests that witnessing racism in the world prompted an intense spiritual wrestling.

This section has demonstrated how race interacted with the women's faith identities, highlighting Christianity as a space for racial discrimination, while also offering a context for liberation and challenging injustice. The next section moves to consider the intersection of gender, race and faith in the women's academic studies.

Gender, faith, race and academic study

This section examines how the women integrated their intersectional identities of race, gender and faith with their academic study, including students' experiences of racial discrimination and attempts to diversify their course. I highlight exclusion and challenges in male-dominated fields, and discuss how some women integrated their academic studies with their faith, transforming their educational journey.

Women encountered racial discrimination in their university context more than in other spaces, yet, as Solomon Zewolde argues, there is a 'deafening silence around the centrality of race in the lived experiences of Black students'.[109] The gap between lived experiences and institutional awareness is evident – while all women of colour in the research identified 'race' as significant in their studies, their universities remained racially silent. The lack of UK-specific research into students' racial experiences is problematic, making them easier for institutions to dismiss. When students collectively identify structural racial ignorance, microaggressions or thoughtless exclusion but find their institutions unresponsive, they must bear the double burden of navigating both racial inequality and institutional denial. In this book, there was no discernible difference in racial experience between the elite, redbrick or post-1990s universities, except that some students noted the importance of geographical location: Chloe felt at home in her multicultural city, while Ola wondered if it 'might have been easier' for her to study in a more diverse place than her white university town.

Manuel Madriaga and Colin McCaig note that while research into the BAME attainment gap considers home students of colour, it fails to consider racism experienced by international students. They argue that while 'whiteness impacts upon our daily lives particularly in education' there is a 'lack of honesty about racism'. Instead, international students are often blamed for failing to 'integrate'.[110] Zewolde highlights the significant presence of Black Africans, as one in every 16 international students. He writes that these students find 'being questioned, doubted and unwelcome to be insidious and hard to dismantle'. However, Black Africans are often invisible in research and institutional awareness, creating knowledge gaps and structural marginalization in UK universities.[111]

There are two international students in this book: Ola from Nigeria, and Alexandra from the Caribbean. Both described feeling excluded when references were made by lecturers to British norms that they did not understand. Something that Alexandra 'wasn't familiar with' was discussed in a class, and she felt that 'how it was addressed could have been better'. Instead, she 'felt othered and I felt like I was at a disadvantage'. Ola said, 'I wasn't here ... my childhood was somewhere else, it's like, "I don't understand what's going on!"' She felt that these references made it 'even harder to understand what they're talking about'. These experiences suggest clear systemic failings in supporting international students' integration and academic participation.

UK students of colour also felt othered. Chloe experienced microaggression from a member of staff who regularly called her the name of a Filipino student. Although the university invited reports of 'complaints about racism', they had a policy where complaints could not directly name individuals. Although Chloe 'sent a complaint', the staff member 'laughed it off, and she never apologized or said anything', and the university 'just ignored it'. Since the university would not 'hold anyone responsible', Chloe thought, 'what's the point then?!' While none of the women mentioned experiencing racism from their peers, other students were named as silent witnesses, unable or unwilling to speak up. In this case, Chloe reported that her peers never 'said anything, and they thought it was funny because they're all white students'.

Chloe felt 'offended', 'isolated', 'out of place' and 'like in class I didn't fit in'. Azariah D.A. France-Williams refers to microaggressions as 'micro-racisms', necessitating emotional labour through the adoption of a 'neutral or friendly mask ... in spite of the discomfort, displeasure, or even distress one may feel ... to keep smiling when one is internally suffering.' In a vivid metaphor, he argues that 'these mini assaults on one's personhood are death by a thousand paper cuts.'[112] Similarly, Nosayaba Idehen refers to microaggressions as 'an everyday obstacle ... like slow poison', preventing people of colour from feeling welcome.[113] Chloe said that when her university wonders, 'Why don't people of colour wanna stay?', the answer, for her, was that she did not want to be 'somewhere where I feel uncomfortable'.

Chloe being confused with another Asian student assumes students of the same racial background are interchangeable rather than individuals, communicating a profound message about belonging and value. Race and ethnicity are themselves seen as the problem while racism itself is never acknowledged, and the subtle nature of structural racism makes it particularly challenging to address through formal channels. Like Chloe, without clear evidence of explicit discrimination, students struggled to articulate their experiences in ways that institutions recognized as actionable, even when complaints were made. This left them feeling doubly marginalized – first by the original experiences, and then by the inability to seek meaningful redress. As Ahmed writes, complaining 'is exhausting, especially given that what you complain about is already exhausting'.[114] Ashley, Chloe and Ola all expressed feeling silenced or excluded when discussing their race at university. While Chloe actively engaged with racial equality, many others felt unable to voice their experiences due to institutional barriers, fear of consequences or lack of support.

Research suggests that international students seek social comfort with peers from similar backgrounds while struggling with anxiety-provoking experiences of learning.[115] Ola would sit with the only other two Black students in her class, both men. When racist things were said, it was 'hard to speak up because you feel looked down on', and she worried that 'people will look at me differently if I make comments in my lectures'. Instead, when things 'don't feel right, we all just keep quiet' and 'just go with it' because there is a 'majority of white people'. Gender also played a part in Ola's friendship with these two students. When Ola felt that some comments needed calling out, she relied on the men to do so. She described a time when she reacted by saying, 'You know what, it's fine,' while they responded, 'No, that's not fine!' She said, 'They do speak out more than I do ... I don't know how to fight, I don't know *how* to, so I would just rather not, like, just say [anything], but they could.' Ola did not feel resourced to call out discrimination or ask what she felt were important questions. The requirement to 'go with it' rather than 'speak out' took a huge amount of Ola's energy and contributed to her feeling isolated at university. Her experience reflected the requirement for women, especially Black women, to be passive and silent rather than 'fight' or stand up for themselves in the face of exclusion.

Because of their racial experiences, Ashley and Chloe saw decolonizing and diversifying their universities as important. Ashley said that this included being able to 'not just accept everything that I'm told' and 'challenging what you learn'. She thought that her course was 'inherently racist', and was 'passionate' about 'the fact that that isn't addressed'. In sharing this realization with friends, Ashley found it 'frustrating ... not being listened to' by her white peers or 'closed-off' lecturers. Ashley saw that university was providing her with a language with which to challenge assumed norms and bring her own experiences into the classroom. Dave S. P. Thomas and Kathleen M. Quinlan's research into university curricula finds that teaching is consistently culturally ignorant, while diversifying teaching could have transformative results for all students. They argue that 'BAME students notice the Whiteness of this curriculum and ... it erodes their engagement – specifically their interest in the subject and their interactions with teachers.'[116]

Chloe was studying the 'very white and very upper class' subject of Classics, and was concerned with the lack of diversity on her course. She was involved in a project 'trying to work on diversity for people of colour in arts and humanities'. Although her department asked for feedback during a university-wide BLM campaign, she said that the students' feedback was ignored: 'I was like, "You should get black lecturers in" and stuff like that. And my department doesn't have any black lecturers, we don't have any people of colour lecturing us.'

Milagros Castillo-Montoya and her colleagues have created a 'racially liberated pedagogy' based on BLM principles – relational, emotional, transformative, justice-oriented and intersectional. They argue that despite higher education's diversification, Black student advancement stagnates as institutions maintain policies protecting whiteness and heteronormative patriarchy.[117] While Chloe and Ashley attempted to address racial inequity through course diversification and decolonization efforts, their universities failed to reciprocate with meaningful institutional changes. The disconnect between student advocacy and institutional inaction compounded feelings of isolation and alienation. Despite their engagement and hopes for positive change, the lack of university support reinforced the very exclusion these students were trying to combat.

Many of the women similarly found their gender to be exclusionary at university. Several felt stress and discord between their subject of study and their gender, or kept silent as a means of protecting themselves. While some students were integrating their study into their lives and engaging with their education, when seen through the lens of gender they were struggling with their academic experience.

Research in both US and UK universities highlights how higher education institutions perpetuate gender discrimination through multiple mechanisms, including masculine-centric language, teaching staff's exclusion of female students, and gender stereotyping. These systemic barriers actively work against women's full participation and recognition in academic spaces. For example, Gilligan finds that young women in education are under pressure to ask 'good' or 'important' questions, rather than those that are real or relevant to them.[118] Frances Ward argues that women choose to steer clear of arguments in classrooms rather than damage interpersonal relationships, since 'women who argue are regarded as disagreeable'.[119] Belenky and her colleagues find that women are often reluctant to speak in higher education seminars, advocating for feminist pedagogies that emphasize personal experience and relational learning. Their 'connected teaching' model values student perspectives and collaborative learning over hierarchical methods, challenging the conventional academic focus on detached, objective knowledge.[120] Michelle Webber explores the possibility of feminist pedagogy, including intersectional awareness, critical engagement with experience, and participatory classes. However, she finds that feminist teaching is prevented by: formal lecture spaces and large classes; fear of negative evaluations from students; and academic requirements for individual assessment over relational learning.[121] Abes calls for 'critical pedagogy' at university, writing that marginalized women find 'little success in a place where they do not feel at home. To help students feel at home in college, their upbringing and values, or habitus should be considered when creating educational contexts.'[122]

The women recognized many gendered challenges in their learning. Lauren noticed that she often kept quiet in a weekly seminar because she worried about the opinions of 'two lads' that she found 'intimidating'. As a strategy, she planned to change where she sat in the class. This physical repositioning demonstrated a solution to her problem, but it is an example of a woman needing to alter her own behaviour rather than being able to challenge others. Lauren questioned the 'male-dominated' nature of the academy, reflecting that her course involved 'reading articles by men who used very patriarchal language', or what Adrienne Rich refers to as 'He-Man' language.[123] This recognition influenced reflection upon how she was herself 'perceived' in a negative essentialist light due to her gender. Lauren highlights the often-ignored, highly gendered power dynamics within study spaces, reflecting what Rhiannon Graybill and colleagues name 'the non-neutrality of the classroom'; rather, they continue, 'the classroom is political'. The authors argue that without naming these dynamics it is impossible to challenge a culture that normalizes sexual harassment.[124]

Women need listening others to enable them to feel at home at university. Danielle named the importance of having supportive women as role models in academia. She felt insignificant on her course, believing that 'No one really cared and so I couldn't motivate myself.' She eventually found a lecturer she could speak to when she was in difficulty. Having a woman to talk to who was both an 'expert' and 'easy going' not only meant that Danielle felt cared for, but it also inspired her learning.

Students reported missing the close relationships with school teachers who really 'know you' from spending significant time together, while struggling to form supportive connections with university academic staff.

Amber articulated feelings of impostership,[125] limiting her learning and becoming. She wanted 'to become a bit more of a scientist ... [to] be able to think like that' but worried that 'I'm not good enough.' Women will feel like imposters in higher education without structural and emotional support that enables university to become home for them.

Several women reflected on studying male-dominated subjects. Stephanie had been told, 'You shouldn't do engineering, you're a girl', and lamented not having 'female engineers' to 'look up to'. When in charge of an academic project, she navigated a gendered dilemma: 'Where is too bossy and where is actually what you need to do to get the job done? And I don't think guys worry about this as much.' Alexis wanted to specialize in a 'male-dominated' area of music. She repeated the phrase 'I don't know' four times, demonstrating uncertainty about studying something that seemingly only men excelled at. Olivia, a medical student, saw that some specialisms were considered 'more of a female role'. Sarah had a friend studying (male-dominated) physics who was 'judged purely on the fact that [she's] a girl', while in contrast Sarah thought women studying (female-dominated) biology did not 'judge the boys' in the same way.

Despite the challenges of bringing their race and gender into their seminars and lectures, some women were becoming more confident and inner-dependent through engagement with their studies. Arnett writes that emerging adulthood often includes 'educational exploration' while 'waiting for something to click ... when they know they have found their true calling'.[126] For Parks, education that resonates with the student's truth results in breakthrough and moments of intellectual 'aha!'[127] Such moments are not only significant for the students' formal education, but are also synonymous 'with a reordering of feelings and relationships' and a 'recomposing [in] our sense of what is ultimately dependable (or our sense of "God")'.[128] For Abigail, helping families in need through studying social work was influencing her growth 'as a woman, which I quite like!'. Samantha engaged with 'feminist criticism' in her English literature degree, and was asking questions about 'women being submissive ... [and] power dynamics'. Thoroughly enjoying her demanding engineering course, Stephanie said: 'education is sort of at the heart of everything I do at the moment'. Use of the term 'heart' suggested that it was the centre around which everything else revolved and to which everything was connected – including her social life, faith and futurity.

It also suggested an emotional, deep connection between her study and her very sense of self, calling or God.

Many women's experiences were contrary to other research in which academic study was to be survived merely for the sake of achieving good grades.[129] Some of the women, at least to a partial extent, were able to make *home* in their academic studies through explicitly integrating their faith with their learning. Some students, especially those studying science, spoke directly about how they saw God in their work. Amber was keen to integrate her faith and study, saying, 'I wanna be a Christian biologist.' Even though for Amber this integration was sometimes 'hard' and 'challenging', she could 'definitely see God in the biology ... then I phone my mum and I'm like, "Look what I found out!"' Her studies impacted upon 'how I think' and had 'changed me'. Kimberly explained to her course-mates, 'God created this amazing world, why wouldn't I wanna discover more of it ... I wanna find out what he's done.' Both women said that seeing God in their studies was 'cool', enabling them to make connections between God, their study and their own sense of purpose.

Several women spoke about their course shaping who they were. Sarah said that studying biology had 'challenged' her faith, and was 'overawed by the beauty and complexity of what we get to study'. For Lauren, studying Islam had 'strengthened my faith in that I know now that this is what I believe ... [it] has really made me reflect a lot more on my faith.' Having to explain her beliefs in the face of different perspectives led Lauren to consider 'how my faith affects my political views'. Mary and Olivia wanted to 'take opportunities where you can get them at university while you're here to learn'; to 'enjoy your course ... and get the most out of it'; and 'to be involved'. As Rich advocates, these women were assertively 'claiming' their study, taking responsibility for their education as its rightful owners, rather than passively receiving it.[130] The students were not content with what Belenky and colleagues refer to as the 'separate knowing' of indifferently rehearsing 'the way They want you to think',[131] but rather demanded more of themselves, their peers and their tutors. Nicole saw that her study was influencing both her current outlook and her idea of who she wanted to be as she matured: 'It gives me a better understanding of the society I live in and will hopefully make me a better person for understanding other people.'

While Clydesdale finds that most higher education students do not engage deeply in their studies, for those that felt fully welcome on their course and were able to involve their creative energies the impact 'is substantial and sustained'.[132] This was certainly the case for the women in my study who, along with students in Arnett's work, 'develop clearer aesthetic and intellectual values, ... gain a more distinct identity and become more confident socially' through their academic engagement.[133]

The women's studies were a primary area in which their different identities were challenged and enacted, with scope for growth, formation and discovery. However, they often felt unwelcome and unhome in their higher education institutions, and there were too many examples of feeling othered, excluded and discriminated against due to their intersecting marginalizations. Women must feel at home in their academic environment if they are to thrive in their learning and becoming.

Conclusion

By her third interview, in her late twenties, Ashley had given much thought to the intersection of her identities. She exhibited a level of reflexivity that few of the women had achieved, likely in part because she was older, with more life experience. She described the intersection as 'natural' and something that 'influences how I see the world, the places that I feel more comfortable, and the people who I want to spend more time with', while the experiences of her white middle-class friends had 'been limited'. She continued:

> Being on the edge of all of these intersections has given me access to understanding ... that other people don't have ... I'm very thankful, in a way, that I get to live life with these lenses, and these experiences, because for all of the difficulties ... [they] have enhanced my capacity to love and connect.

For Ashley, being triply on the margins provided her with 'lenses' that offered her a nuanced worldview; an enhanced understanding of difference; the ability to challenge others' limitations; and increased capacity for connection and empathy. She viewed her 'unique social space'[134] as a source of insight and compassion, not as a burden, and was grateful for the broader perspective it offered.

This chapter has explored the intersectionality between the women's identities, and how this intersection is negotiated in everyday life. Some women described moments of awakening in realizing how cultural and religious structures shaped their identities. These women felt confident in this growth, and in turn took greater responsibility for the world around them. Zygmunt Bauman writes that 'individualization' involves 'the emancipation of the individual from the ascribed, inherited and inborn determination of his or her social character'.[135] While full 'emancipation' is neither possible nor desirable, university allowed some women to distance themselves from their habitus, at least enough to examine and critique it to an extent.

Christianity has, in this chapter, been found at times to be inherently misogynist, racist and queerphobic. Sharma and Guest find that 'where students' expressions of Christianity may ostensibly seek and promote universal fellowship, they can simultaneously reinforce social norms based on race, gender, sexuality or class.'[136] In particular, religiously sanctioned sexism was common, requiring emotional labour and identity work to navigate. However, an important thread that repeatedly emerged for the women is that of Christian justice and advocacy. As both Alexandra and Ashley observed, God is *for*: for women, for people of colour, for all on the margins. Christianity provided a framework for the women to challenge the oppression they experienced and witnessed, and to fight for equality and inclusion for all. Several women made explicit their desire to advocate for those who, like them, had experienced discrimination, and saw their faith in the God of liberation as the means to facilitate this.

The women's intersectional experiences had a significant impact on whether, where or how they felt at home at university. Ahmed argues that 'to be comfortable is to be so at ease with one's environment that it is hard to distinguish where one's body ends and the world begins ... Those spaces are lived as comfortable as they allow bodies to fit in'.[137] However, at times, the women all experienced their bodies to be, as Nirmal Puwar describes, 'space invaders',[138] neither fitting in nor feeling comfortable. Yet, through relationality, community, inner-dependence and self-confidence, they interpreted faith through a justice lens, finding resources to feel at home and discovering 'strength and solidarity through the intersection of value-laden identity and belonging', as Katz and colleagues note.[139]

As intersectional women, the students were critical of Christianity's exclusionary traits, and faith still needed navigating. Yet, through encounters with other Christian women with similar experiences, beliefs and practices, they were able to find their home, navigate the world, and encounter the God who is *for*.

Notes

1 Kimberlé Crenshaw, 'Demarginalizing the Intersection of Race and Sex: A Black Feminist Critique of Antidiscrimination Doctrine, Feminist Theory, and Antiracist Politics', *University of Chicago Legal Forum* 139 (1989), pp. 139–67.

2 Tim Clydesdale, *The First Year Out: Understanding American Teens after High School* (Chicago, IL: University of Chicago Press, 2007).

3 Lisa Bowleg, 'When Black + Lesbian + Woman ≠ Black Lesbian Woman: The Methodological Challenges of Qualitative and Quantitative Intersectionality Research', *Sex Roles* 59 (2008), pp. 313, 319. Bowleg borrows the term 'unique social space' from H. Edward Ransford, 'The Prediction of Social Behavior and Attitudes' in *Social Stratification: A Multiple Hierarchy Approach*, ed. Vincent Jeffries and H. Edward Ransford (Boston, MA: Allyn & Bacon, 1980), p. 277.

4 Audre Lorde, *Sister Outsider: Essays and Speeches* (Freedom, CA: Crossing Press, 1984), p. 120.

5 Sonya Sharma and Mathew Guest, 'Navigating Religion Between University and Home: Christian Students' Experiences in English Universities', *Social and Cultural Geography* 14, no. 1 (2013), p. 72.

6 Sarah-Jane Page and Heather Shipley, *Religion and Sexualities: Theories, Themes and Methodologies* (London, New York: Routledge/Taylor & Francis Group, 2020), pp. 131–2.

7 Riet Bons-Storm, *The Incredible Woman: Listening to Women's Silences in Pastoral Care and Counselling* (Nashville, TN: Abingdon Press, 1996), pp. 134–5.

8 Zoë Bennett Moore, *Introducing Feminist Perspectives on Pastoral Theology* (London: Sheffield University Press, 2002), p. 34.

9 Marcella Althaus-Reid, *From Feminist Theology to Indecent Theology: Readings on Poverty, Sexual Identity and God* (London: SCM Press, 2004), pp. 98–9.

10 Page and Shipley, *Religion and Sexualities*, p. 129.

11 Ruth H. Perrin, *The Bible Reading of Young Evangelicals: An Exploration of the Ordinary Hermeneutics and Faith of Generation Y* (Eugene, OR: Pickwick Publications, 2016), p. 201.

12 Ruth H. Perrin, *Changing Shape: The Faith Lives of Millennials* (London: SCM Press, 2020), p. 88.

13 Page and Shipley, *Religion and Sexualities*, p. 163.

14 Donna Freitas, *The End of Sex: How Hookup Culture Is Leaving a Generation Unhappy, Sexually Unfulfilled, and Confused About Intimacy* (Philadelphia, PA: Basic Books, 2013).

15 Patricia Beattie Jung, ed., *Good Sex: Feminist Perspectives from the World's Religions* (New Brunswick: Rutgers University Press, 2005), p. 83.

16 Andrew Kam-Tuck Yip and Sarah-Jane Page, *Religious and Sexual Identities: A Multi-Faith Exploration of Young Adults* (Farnham: Ashgate, 2013); Sarah-Jane Page, Andrew Kam-Tuck Yip and Michael Keenan, 'Risk and the Imagined Future: Young Adults Negotiating Religious and Sexual Identities' in *The Ashgate Research Companion to Contemporary Religion and Sexuality*, ed. Stephen J. Hunt and Andrew Kam-Tuck Yip (Farnham: Ashgate, 2012), pp. 255–74.

17 Perrin, *Changing Shape*, p. 98.

18 Sonya Sharma, 'When Young Women Say "Yes:" Exploring the Sexual Selves of Young Canadian Women in Protestant Churches' in *Women and Religion in the West: Challenging Secularisation*, ed. Kristin Aune, Sonya Sharma and Giselle Vincett (Aldershot: Ashgate, 2008), pp. 71–82.

19 Page and Shipley, *Religion and Sexualities*, p. 166.

20 Tom Boellstorff, 'When Marriage Fails: Queer Coincidences in Straight Time', *A Journal of Lesbian and Gay Studies* 13, no. 2–3 (2007), pp. 227–48.

21 Page and Shipley, *Religion and Sexualities*, p. 17.
22 Dawn Llewellyn, 'Voluntary Childlessness and Christianity: Rejecting the Selfish Other', *Modern Believing* 6, no. 2 (2019), pp. 147–56.
23 Helen Colley, 'Understanding Time in Learning Transitions Through the Lifecourse', *International Studies in Sociology of Education* 17, no. 4 (2007), p. 433.
24 Sharon Hays, *The Cultural Contradictions of Motherhood* (London: Yale University Press, 1996), p. 8.
25 See, for example, Valerie Saiving, 'The Human Situation: A Feminine View', *Journal of Religion* 40 (1960), pp. 100–12; Rita Nakashima Brock and Rebecca Ann Parker, *Proverbs of Ashes: Violence, Redemptive Suffering and the Search for What Saves Us* (Boston, MA: Beacon Press, 2001).
26 Perrin, *Bible Reading of Young Evangelicals*, p. 197.
27 Perrin, *Bible Reading of Young Evangelicals*, p. 5.
28 Alyssa N. Bryant, 'Assessing the Gender Climate of an Evangelical Student Subculture in the United States', *Gender and Education* 18, no. 6 (2006), pp. 630, 632.
29 Sara Ahmed, 'A Phenomenology of Whiteness', *Feminist Theory* 8, no. 2 (August 2007), p. 163.
30 See, for example, Bryant, 'Assessing the Gender Climate'.
31 Penny Long Marler, 'Religious Change in the West: Watch the Women', in *Women and Religion in the West: Challenging Secularisation*, ed. Kristin Aune, Sonya Sharma and Giselle Vincett (Aldershot: Ashgate, 2008), pp. 23–56; Linda Woodhead, 'Gendering Secularisation Theory', *Women, Gender and Research (Kvinder, Køn Og Forskning)* 1–2 (2005), pp. 24–35.
32 Carolyn Heilbrun, *Writing a Woman's Life* (New York: Ballantine Books, 1988).
33 Marion Maddox, '"Rise Up Warrior Princess Daughters": Is Evangelical Women's Submission a Mere Fairy Tale?', *Journal of Feminist Studies in Religion* 29, no. 1 (2013), p. 25.
34 Kristin Aune, 'Much Less Religious, a Little More Spiritual: The Religious and Spiritual Views of Third-Wave Feminists in the UK', *Feminist Review* 97 (2011), p. 52.
35 James W. Fowler, *Stages of Faith: The Psychology of Human Development and the Quest for Meaning* (New York: Harper Collins, 1981).
36 Nicola Slee, *Women's Faith Development: Patterns and Processes* (Aldershot: Ashgate, 2004), pp. 159–60.
37 Liz Carmichael, *Friendship: Interpreting Christian Love* (London: T. & T. Clark, 2007), p. 200.
38 Deborah Jones, 'Gossip: Notes on Women's Oral Culture' in *The Feminist Critique of Language: A Reader*, ed. Deborah Cameron (London: Routledge, 1990), p. 243.
39 Mary F. Belenky et al., *Women's Ways of Knowing: The Development of Self, Voice and Mind*, 10th Anniversary ed. (New York: Basic Books, 1986), p. 116.
40 Clydesdale, *The First Year Out*.
41 Sharon Parks, *The Critical Years: The Young Adult Search for a Faith to Live By* (New York: Harper & Row, 1986).
42 Anne Phillips, *The Faith of Girls: Children's Spirituality and Transition to Adulthood* (Farnham: Ashgate, 2011), p. 166.

43 Lyn Mikel Brown and Carol Gilligan, *Meeting at the Crossroads: Women's Psychology and Girls' Development* (Cambridge, MA: Harvard University Press, 1992), p. 7.

44 Slee, *Women's Faith Development*, p. 72.

45 Ruth H. Perrin, 'Searching for Sisters: The Influence of Biblical Role Models on Young Women from Mainstream and Charismatic Evangelical Traditions' in *The Faith Lives of Women and Girls*, ed. Nicola Slee, Fran Porter and Anne Phillips (Farnham: Ashgate, 2013), p. 113.

46 Dorothy Lee, 'Abiding in the Fourth Gospel: A Case Study in Feminist Biblical Theology' in *Feminist Companion to John*, ed. Amy-Jill Levine, vol. 2 (London: Bloomsbury Publishing/Sheffield Academic Press, 2003), pp. 74–7.

47 See bell hooks, *Ain't I A Woman: Black Women and Feminism* (London: Pluto, 1982); Elizabeth Cady Stanton, *The Woman's Bible* (Boston, MA: Northeastern University Press, 1993); Sheila Fletcher, *Maude Royden: A Life* (Oxford: Blackwell, 1989).

48 Bowleg, 'When Black + Lesbian + Woman', p. 323.

49 Dawn Llewellyn and Marta Trzebiatowska, 'Secular and Religious Feminisms: A Future of Disconnection?', *Feminist Theology* 21, no. 3 (2013), p. 245.

50 Aune, 'Much Less Religious', p. 48.

51 Rachel Joy Welcher, *Talking Back to Purity Culture: Rediscovering Faithful Christian Sexuality* (Westmont, IL: InterVarsity Press, 2020), pp. 42, 44.

52 Lisa Isherwood, *The Fat Jesus: Feminist Explorations in Boundaries and Transgressions* (London: Darton, Longman and Todd, 2007), p. 20.

53 Hannah Bacon, 'Embodying a Different Word about Fat: The Need for Critical Feminist Theologies of Fat Liberation', *Religions* 14, no. 696 (25 May 2023), p. 11.

54 Slee, *Women's Faith Development*, p. 157.

55 Marcella Althaus-Reid and Lisa Isherwood, 'Thinking Theology and Queer Theory', *Feminist Theology* 15, no. 3 (May 2007), p. 306.

56 Aune, 'Much Less Religious', p. 34.

57 See Laura Bates, *Everyday Sexism* (London: Simon & Schuster, 2014).

58 Emily Falconer and Yvette Taylor, 'Negotiating Queer and Religious Identities in Higher Education: Queering "Progression" in the "University Experience"', *British Journal of Sociology of Education* 38, no. 6 (2017), pp. 787, 789.

59 Claudia Garcia et al., '"We'll Be Okay Together": Navigating Challenges as Queer University Students in Aotearoa New Zealand', *KÐtuitui: New Zealand Journal of Social Sciences Online* 19, no. 2 (2 April 2024), pp. 191, 197.

60 Garcia et al., '"We'll Be Okay Together"', p. 203.

61 Page and Shipley, *Religion and Sexualities*, p. 6.

62 Page and Shipley, *Religion and Sexualities*, pp. 120–1.

63 Page and Shipley, *Religion and Sexualities*, p. 115.

64 Page and Shipley, *Religion and Sexualities*, pp. 124–5.

65 Slee, *Women's Faith Development*, p. 157.

66 Falconer and Taylor, 'Negotiating Queer and Religious Identities', p. 787.

67 Elisabeth Schüssler Fiorenza, *But She Said: Feminist Practices of Biblical Interpretation* (Boston, MA: Beacon Press, 1992), pp. 18–19.

68 Schüssler Fiorenza, *But She Said*, p. 134.

69 Falconer and Taylor, 'Negotiating Queer and Religious Identities', p. 792, citing Heidi Safia Mirza.

70 Mathew Guest et al., *Christianity and the University Experience: Understanding Student Faith* (London: Bloomsbury, 2013), p. 50.
71 Page and Shipley, *Religion and Sexualities*, p. 113.
72 Page and Shipley, *Religion and Sexualities*, p. 113.
73 See Chapter 4 for some of the other ways that the women were undergoing the labour of integration, and for Slee's definition.
74 Marcella Althaus-Reid, *From Feminist Theology to Indecent Theology: Readings on Poverty, Sexual Identity and God* (London: SCM Press, 2004), p. 43.
75 Elisa S. Abes, 'Constructivist and Intersectional Interpretations of a Lesbian College Student's Multiple Social Identities', *Journal of Higher Education* 83, no. 2 (2012), p. 194.
76 Elizabeth McDermott, '"I Wanted to Be Totally True to Myself": Class and the Making of the Sexual Self' in *Classed Intersections: Spaces, Selves, Knowledges*, ed. Yvette Taylor (Farnham: Ashgate, 2010), p. 203.
77 See Garcia et al., '"We'll Be Okay Together"', p. 200.
78 Susannah Cornwall, 'Home and Hiddenness: Queer Theology, Domestication and Institutions', *Theology & Sexuality* 23, no. 1–2 (4 May 2017), p. 42.
79 Garcia et al., '"We'll Be Okay Together"', pp. 201–2.
80 Ulrich Beck and Elisabeth Beck-Gernsheim, *Individualization: Institutionalized Individualism and Its Social and Political Consequences* (London: Sage, 2001), p. 203.
81 Abes, 'Constructivist and Intersectional Interpretations'.
82 Guest et al., *Christianity and the University Experience*, pp. 171–2.
83 Pierre Bourdieu, *Distinction: A Social Critique of the Judgement of Taste* (Cambridge, MA: Harvard University Press, 1984).
84 Mathew Guest and Kristin Aune, 'Students' Constructions of a Christian Future: Faith, Class and Aspiration in University Contexts', *Sociological Research Online* 22, no. 1 (February 2017), para. 4.4.
85 Clare Holdsworth, 'Don't You Think You're Missing Out, Living at Home? Student Experiences and Residential Transitions', *Sociological Review* 54, no. 3 (2006), p. 510.
86 McDermott, '"I Wanted to Be Totally True"', p. 212.
87 McDermott, '"I Wanted to Be Totally True"'; citing Gill Valentine, 'Negotiating and Managing Multiple Sexual Identities: Lesbian Time-Space Strategies', *Institute of British Geographers* 18 (1993), p. 243.
88 Bowleg, 'When Black + Lesbian + Woman', p. 313.
89 Guest et al., *Christianity and the University Experience*, p. 171.
90 See Sharma and Guest, 'Navigating Religion'.
91 Guest et al., *Christianity and the University Experience*, p. 170.
92 Alana Lentin, *Racism: A Beginner's Guide* (New York: Oneworld Publications, 2012), Chapter 1.
93 Anthony Reddie, *Is God Colour-Blind? Insights from Black Theology for Christian Faith and Ministry*, 2nd ed. (London: SPCK, 2020), p. xii.
94 Willie James Jennings, *After Whiteness: An Education in Belonging*, Theological Education between the Times (Grand Rapids, MI: W.B. Eerdmans, 2020), p. 9.
95 Ahmed, 'A Phenomenology of Whiteness', pp. 157, 160.
96 Kristin Aune, Simon Perfect and Ben Ryan, 'Building Bridges or Holy Huddles? Student Religious Organizations in British Universities', *Journal of Diversity in Higher Education* (27 June 2024), p. 2.

97 Guest et al., *Christianity and the University Experience*, p. 170.

98 George M. Fredrickson, *Racism: A Short History*, Princeton Classics (Princeton: Princeton University Press, 2015), p. 6, italics author's own.

99 Reddie, *Is God Colour-Blind?*, p. 51.

100 Nadia Craddock et al., 'Understanding Colourism in the UK: Development and Assessment of the Everyday Colourism Scale', *Ethnic and Racial Studies* 46, no. 10 (27 July 2023), pp. 2242–3.

101 See also Solomon Zewolde, '"Race" and Academic Performance in International Higher Education: Black Africans in the UK', *Journal of Comparative & International Higher Education* 14, no. 3a (11 July 2022), p. 221.

102 Fredrickson, *Racism*, Chapter 1.

103 Guest et al., *Christianity and the University Experience*, p. 173.

104 Reddie, *Is God Colour-Blind?*, pp. 49, 107, 38.

105 Guest et al., *Christianity and the University Experience*, p. 178; citing Ruth Frankenberg, *White Women, Race Matters: The Social Construction of Whiteness* (Minneapolis, MN: University of Minnesota Press, 2005).

106 Guest et al., *Christianity and the University Experience*, p. 173.

107 Reddie, *Is God Colour-Blind?*, p. 50, 53.

108 Reddie, *Is God Colour-Blind?*, pp. 57–8.

109 Zewolde, '"Race" and Academic Performance', p. 222.

110 Manuel Madriaga and Colin McCaig, 'How International Students of Colour Become Black: A Story of Whiteness in English Higher Education', *Teaching in Higher Education* 27, no. 1 (2 January 2022), pp. 85, 87.

111 Zewolde, '"Race" and Academic Performance', p. 216.

112 Azariah D.A. France-Williams, *Ghost Ship: Institutional Racism and the Church of England* (London: SCM Press, 2020), pp. 5–6.

113 Nosayaba Idehen, 'Racial Inclusion: Guidelines to Being a More Racially Inclusive Church' in *Young, Woke and Christian: Words from a Missing Generation*, ed. Victoria Turner (London: SCM Press, 2022), pp. 35–6.

114 Sara Ahmed, *Complaint!* (Durham, NC: Duke University Press, 2021), p. 5.

115 Michele Schweisfurth and Qing Gu, 'Exploring the Experiences of International Students in UK Higher Education: Possibilities and Limits of Interculturality in University Life', *Intercultural Education* 20, no. 5 (October 2009), pp. 463–73.

116 Dave S. P. Thomas and Kathleen M. Quinlan, 'Why We Need to Reimagine the Curricula in Higher Education to Make It More Culturally Sensitive', *Widening Participation and Lifelong Learning* 23, no. 3 (9 December 2021), p. 39.

117 Milagros Castillo-Montoya, Joshua Abreu and Abdul Abad, 'Racially Liberatory Pedagogy: A Black Lives Matter Approach to Education', *International Journal of Qualitative Studies in Education* 32, no. 9 (21 October 2019), pp. 1140, 1125.

118 Carol Gilligan, 'Preface: Teaching Shakespeare's Sister' in *Making Connections: The Relational Worlds of Adolescent Girls at Emma Willard School*, ed. Carol Gilligan, Nona P. Lyons and Trudy J. Hanmer (Cambridge, MA: Harvard University Press, 1990), p. 8. See also Alexandrina Scarbrough and Carolyn Hicks, 'Student Gender and the Probability of Referral for Counselling in a College of Further Education', *British Journal of Guidance and Counselling* 26, no. 2 (2007), p. 235.

119 Frances Ward, *Lifelong Learning: Theological Education and Supervision* (London: SCM Press, 2009), pp. 159–60.

120 Belenky et al., *Women's Ways of Knowing*, p. 219.

121 Michelle Webber, 'Transgressive Pedagogies? Exploring the Difficult Realities of Enacting Feminist Pedagogies in Undergraduate Classrooms in a Canadian University', *Studies in Higher Education* 31, no. 4 (August 2006), pp. 453–67.

122 Abes, 'Constructivist and Intersectional Interpretations', pp. 210–11.

123 Adrienne Rich, 'Taking Women Students Seriously', *The Radical Teacher* 11 (1979), p. 41.

124 Rhiannon Graybill, Meredith Minister and Beatrice Lawrence, 'Sexual Violence in and around the Classroom', *Teaching Theology & Religion* 20, no. 1 (2017), p. 71.

125 See Stephen Brookfield, *The Skillful Teacher: On Technique, Trust, and Responsiveness in the Classroom*, 2nd ed. (San Francisco, CA: Jossey-Bass, 2006).

126 Jeffrey Jensen Arnett, *Emerging Adulthood: The Winding Road from the Late Teens Through the Twenties* (Oxford: Oxford University Press, 2004), pp. 122, 124.

127 Sharon Parks, *Big Questions, Worthy Dreams: Mentoring Young Adults in Their Search for Meaning, Purpose, and Faith* (San Francisco, CA: Jossey-Bass, 2000), p. 150; Parks, *The Critical Years*, pp. 147–50.

128 Parks, *The Critical Years*, p. 53.

129 See, for example, Clydesdale, *The First Year Out*; Arnett, *Emerging Adulthood*.

130 Adrienne Rich, 'Claiming an Education: Speech Delivered at the Convocation of Douglass College', 1977.

131 Belenky et al., *Women's Ways of Knowing*, pp. 103, 108, authors' own capitalization.

132 Clydesdale, *The First Year Out*, p. 66.

133 Arnett, *Emerging Adulthood*, p. 139.

134 Bowleg, 'When Black + Lesbian + Woman', p. 313.

135 Zygmunt Bauman, *The Individualized Society* (Cambridge: Polity Press, 2001), p. 114.

136 Sharma and Guest, 'Navigating Religion', p. 72.

137 Ahmed, 'A Phenomenology of Whiteness', p. 158.

138 Nirmal Puwar, *Space Invaders: Race, Gender and Bodies Out of Place* (Oxford, New York: Berg, 2004).

139 Roberta Katz et al., *Gen Z, Explained: The Art of Living in a Digital Age* (Chicago, IL: University of Chicago Press, 2022), p. 118.

PART IV

Crafting Home and Looking Forward

8

A Model of Homing

This chapter presents a model of Homing, detailing emerging women's crafting of home at university, developed from the everyday transitionings of the 26 women interviewed for this book. The model incorporates their experiences and has emerged from their narratives. It crystallizes what I have presented so far, and offers a visual map of the women's becomings that illuminates this research. By insightfully retelling the women's experiences, this chapter offers a model which may be relevant and useful to others amid transitionings.

Introducing the model

Emerging Christian women's crafting of home involved five patterns of homing, each with different processes of constructing their gender, faith and intersectional identities and praxis. These patterns make a home of five 'rooms', named: Trauma and Unhome, Uncertainty and Ambiguity, Safety and Comfort, Exploration and Resistance, and Integration and Becoming. The language of 'rooms' is borrowed especially from Teresa of Ávila's account of spiritual development, describing the soul as a mansion of many rooms into which the self must enter to commune with God; and Virginia Woolf's insistence that women writers must have 'a room of one's own'.[1] The model evolved through creative analysis of the women's interviews and surveys. Placing their words and experiences alongside one another, similarities across different patterns of 'homing' became clear. Here they are enriched by being drawn together.

'Homing' is a metaphor that I have developed into a sustained model. Metaphors use figurative language to suggest correlations and, for Paul Ricoeur, involve '"thinking more" at a conceptual level' with a 'spark of imagination'.[2] McFague describes theological models as metaphors 'with staying power', explaining unfamiliar phenomena in familiar language and 'envision[ing] ways of talking' about human–divine relationships. Models 'redescribe reality' with 'stability and scope'.[3]

Home, in this model, is a creative space where the women dwell with themselves, others and God, with varying levels of awareness. The model does not narrowly define reality, but images and imagines the multiple transitionings at university. Rather than generalizing, it tentatively and creatively offers a rich understanding of university transitions through 'thick' descriptions, committed to the women's diverse narratives. It communicates the women's experiences visually to other emerging Christian women, and their allies.

In keeping with feminist practical theology, the model is most of all 'pragmatic ... [and] bringing about fulfilment for living beings',[4] as McFague advocates. So far in this book, the women are discussed in the past tense, recognizing that their interviews were just a snapshot in their lives, which inevitably have moved on. The model, however, shifts to the present tense, offering general patterns in the women's narratives rather than the prior specificities of each individual woman, and allowing for its relevance in lives and contexts beyond these 26 women, looking onwards.

The model borrows from Taylor and Harris-Evans's description of students' becoming at university. They offer the verb *transitioning* over the more static *transition to*, arguing that transitions are not simple, linear movements from one state to another, but are complex processes that often occur simultaneously across multiple spheres. For students, transitionings are fluid and unpredictable, taking place within and throughout different identities, and often intuitive rather than the result of deliberate decision-making.[5]

I first provide an overview of the five rooms of the model. I then explore it in detail, examining the movement between rooms and the key themes that emerge.

The Homing model

Room 1: Trauma and unhome

Starting university is a *traumatic* transition. Students in room 1 experience various 'sicknesses' of separation from the familiar: they are homesick, friendsick,[6] churchsick and, as Kimberly said, oldlifesick. They feel vulnerable and overwhelmed. Under-resourced and under-supported, Balk argues, 'loss, often unresolved, simply form[s] the story of the students' lives'.[7] University can be a hostile environment for emerging women, and they are unhome; unable to create safety; and unable to interpret or to step back from their experiences. Brueggemann argues that the home-*less* feel like outsiders and abandoned orphans.

A MODEL OF HOMING

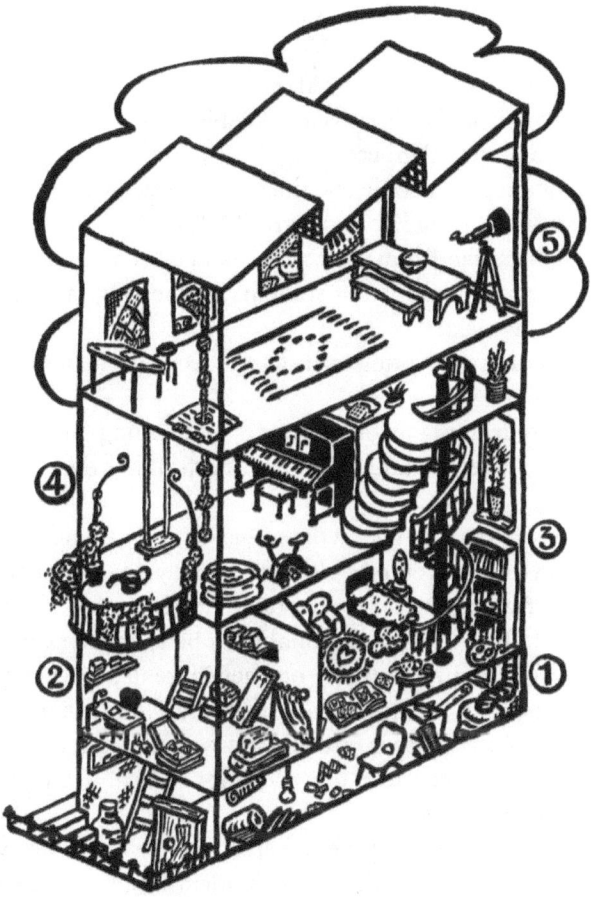

Without place, belonging or advocacy, they are 'everywhere at risk'.[8] In the first term at university, loneliness is common as the students feel orphaned from their families, their previous communities, and their previous selves. Laura Smit writes,

> We are not where we ought to be ... we are exiles here. Even if we should find a community that accepts and welcomes us ... we still know ourselves to be displaced ... We are stranded far from home, unable, in fact, to remember where home is – yet knowing that, wherever it is, it is not here.[9]

Words commonly used to describe this room include 'nervous', 'hard', 'scary/scared', 'struggle/ing', 'overwhelmed', 'panic', 'emotional', 'lonely', 'daunting', 'unsettled', 'terrified', 'shock', 'confused', 'horrible', 'stressful' and 'exhausted'. 'Hard' experiences include:

- not getting on with new housemates and leaving her parents behind (Abigail)
- the death of her grandmother (Alexis)
- being far away from her best friend, keeping in touch with old friends, and being homesick (Amber)
- being surrounded by people she does not know (Ashley)
- not going home during her first term (Haley)
- negotiating old friendships that have changed (Lauren)
- trying to meet other Christian students, witnessing racism, and making new friends (Ola)
- listening to God and making faith-based decisions in her new environment (Olivia)
- saying 'no' to drinking alcohol and going clubbing (Stephanie)
- settling in at university and claiming a faith of her own (Tumi).

Relationships are hard. The women need new friends, but this is scary, and they think everyone else has already found friends. Despite constantly meeting new people, new relationships do not facilitate playfulness or trust. They are lonely, unable to be themselves or to confide in others. In this room, many rely on their parents, especially mothers, even though they are geographically distant. They either travel home most weekends because they are unable to settle, or they do not go home at all because they fear they will not return. They feel sad and bewildered, like imposters.

The women navigate multiple spheres: the 'two distinct worlds' of home and university that Holdsworth identifies;[10] but also between student life and Christian faith, as their religious practice struggles to adapt to their environment. Caitlin describes this navigation as walking a 'tightrope', with the ever-present risk of falling. God is not mentioned in room 1, since God is not a cause of trauma, nor are relationships with God sites of unhome. Rather, the relationship with God contributes to women being able to leave this room. As Danielle says, 'It's a big change', a 'lot to take in ... you are so busy trying to do so much' and so 'It's easy to lose God in all of that.'

They are in shock: at their academic work, at encountering people so different from them, at being at university at all. This room includes women at their second choice of university, adjusting to being in an unexpected city, studying an unexpected subject. Kat says, 'It's hard at the moment, cos I had it planned out in my head for so long ... and I'm not doing that.' It also includes women studying during the Covid-19 pandemic, feeling hopeless, isolated and uncertain.

In their intersectional identities, the women experience racism on their course, queerphobia in church, and misogyny everywhere. Post-feminism, especially gender essentialism and bodily femininity, means that they are not home in their own skin. Lad culture and avoiding alcohol consumption induces fear. There is no map for how to become women in this new environment.

This room is a dark, enclosed and messy cellar, with bare furnishings. Climbing a rickety ladder is the only route to the next room. Inside, the women feel uncomfortable, claustrophobic, overwhelmed and alone, which negatively impacts their mental health. Debra Phillips, during a period of depression, painted 'dark interiors with rambling corridors ... empty of people ... in which the Self could be dissolved', in 'a graphic representation of a non-explainable reality'. Within this room, she 'did not want to escape it. It had formed a protective cocoon that prevented me from talking to another person. I refused to speak for I was ashamed.'[11]

Bridges argues that,

> Before you can begin something new, you have to end what used to be. Before you can learn a new way of doing things, you have to unlearn the old way. Before you can become a different kind of person, you must let go of your old identity. So beginnings depend on endings. The problem is, people don't like endings.[12]

This whole room is a difficult ending, with too much to say goodbye to.

Room 2: Uncertainty and ambiguity

In room 2, women participate in tentative and ambiguous homing. They negotiate each day as it comes, and focus on the 'daily life management' of time, money and relationships. For Clydesdale, the task is all-encompassing and 'leaves little time for anything else',[13] including engaging with core identities of faith, gender and race, thus placing them into 'identity lockboxes', resisting self-understanding. Holdsworth observes certain students better adapting to university life by leaving some parts of themselves behind, 'away from the pressure of having to negotiate between two distinct worlds on a daily basis', whether intentionally or otherwise.[14]

Unintentionality is a sensible and reasonable response to unsafety in room 2. Parks names the need to pause, to consolidate current experiences. She writes that this time is integral to the process of faithing in a time of 'incubation' and 'lingering'.[15] Students live in ambiguity, and common words in room 2 are 'yet', 'middle', 'between' and 'limbo'. They are no longer children at school but not yet adults in the workplace. Aware of their liminality, they are not yet ready for the challenge of venturing further, particularly in their first year. Experiences and transitions that they describe not 'yet' having or doing include:

- not volunteering yet (Abigail)
- not exploring church or faith yet (Alexis, Danielle, Mary, Sarah)
- not evangelizing new friends yet (Amber, Briana, Olivia)
- not meeting many people or making 'close friends' yet (Briana, Kimberly, Nicole)
- understanding of God not yet changing (Haley)
- not yet feeling at home at university or in church (Lauren, Tumi)
- not feeling like or looking like a woman yet (Megan, Samantha).

These reflections capture the women's potential. The temporary uncertainty reflects the fluid nature of identity and belonging at university. 'Pause' is experienced in personal, faith and identity development. These things *will* change at some undisclosed point in the future, at university or afterwards, but they are not yet easy to access, and not yet the priority. Faith and their relationship with God is stable and on hold. The women join replica Christian communities that remind them of previous 'homes', beginning new relationships with other Christian women who feel similar and familiar, which facilitate initial attempts to feel safe.

This room is temporary in appearance, with makeshift, uncomfortable furniture. Having more light than the cellar brings potential, although not actual growth. It is a small room, offering an illusion of safety while still quite stifling, and the door onwards is obscured. Challenge can easily result in 'regressing' down the ladder. It is as if the women have not quite unpacked their bags at university. Being both Christian and women makes this room difficult, along with other marginalized identities that require negotiating, bringing dissonance and narrow options.

This room is, in many ways, just as scary as the first. Students use techniques to delay change, separate identities and delegate responsibility. They assert their threatened identity through othering, focused on, as Smith and Snell argue, 'knowing, confirming and protecting' who they are.[16] They leave decision-making to God; blame others for injustice; and refer to themselves as children or 'girls'. They remain fixed in essentialist understandings of identity, emphasizing their individual 'choice' over structural change, denying any responsibility for others.

Mary says, 'I know who I want to be and who I am, and I'm not gonna change that because of other people.' Yet in new friendships, they are tentative, watching what they say, feeling unable to be fully themselves, navigating complex social dynamics of self-presentation and identity. Melissa says it 'depends ... whether or not I feel entirely comfortable around that person yet.' Comfort is contextual, and self-expression is conditional. Mary and Melissa experience tension between personal authenticity and navigating new social spaces, balancing self-protection with a desire for genuine connection. They suggest a careful, strategic approach to self-presentation, knowing who they are, but being selective about how fully they express that identity. They tentatively try out provisional selves, trying on different postures to see if they fit, but in room 2 this is never comfortable. Change is resisted as the students feel uncertain in their identities and in their own skin.

Room 3: Safety and comfort

Room 3 is vital in the women's recovery from trauma and unhome. Relationships are at the heart of students' safety, including friends, family, mentors and 'intentional friends'. Here, the women are no longer orphans away from everyone they know and love. New relationships at university, predominantly with other women, are growing deeper. Being women is hard, but relationships with other women enable feeling at home. New friends become chosen-families, secure foundations from which life can be negotiated and understood. They retreat into these relationships when threatened by the unhome nature of university and society. Fowler critiques 'sororities' that 'substitute one family group for another'.[17] But for Parks, everyone needs a home 'where we are comfortable; know that we belong; can be who we are and can honour, protect and create what we truly love'.[18] Webster argues that this kind of safety is found most often with 'those whom we assume to be like us'.[19] Pohl and Wright agree separately that a secure communal environment, and meaningful connections within it, are essential for personal and spiritual transformation.[20]

Being comfortable is the primary expression of feeling at home in room 3, including positive experiences of housemates and 'comfy' accommodation (especially in their second year); deepening new friendships; and finding a 'cosy' church. 'Comfortable', 'confident', 'relaxed' and 'settled' are the key terms for this room, with the women describing a wide range of things as 'comfortable':

- her new church is 'homely ... like a family', she feels 'more relaxed' around her female friends, and is 'more comfortable' with her housemates (Amber)
- moving out of student halls of residence into a house in her second year was 'much cosier', and she is 'learning to be more comfortable' with herself there (Ashley)
- becoming 'more comfortable ... knowing I'm in God's presence' without 'need[ing] to know every Scripture' (Chloe)
- feeling 'really comfortable in myself' around new people (Courtney)
- new flatmates feeling 'like a little family' (Danielle)
- Christian societies feel 'comfortable' and 'part of your family' (Olivia)
- becoming 'more comfortable ... being away from home' (Sarah)
- second year feels 'more relaxed, because I know what to expect' (Taylor)
- 'church has made [university] feel more homely', she feels 'relaxed and safe' around female friends (Tumi).

Several of these examples demonstrate growth in inner-dependence. Parks refers to this shift as moving from 'wilderness' to the 'Spirit within' as students value their inner authority.[21] Tumi describes her move to Christian inner-dependence as walking on grass after being in mud. In mud, the women's lives are messy, they get stuck, they can slip backwards. The move to grass feels new, fresh, comfortable. It is much less work.

New, close friendships are transformational. Sarah says that since 'start[ing] to meet people who were on my level', and 'having met some people that I get on with a bit better and finding where I fit in', she has 'continued feeling more and more comfortable as I made a niche for myself'. This niche means that she has 'settled in now' and 'it's more like home'. She continues, 'I can be more relaxed around my really close friends ... As I have gained confidence and got to know my friends, I have relaxed into my normal character around them.'

As for many women, Sarah's niche includes her faith community. Faith facilitates safety, as other Christians and safe, familiar Christian spaces become a refuge, where, Sharma and Guest write, 'students' imaginaries of family extend, where they experience and cultivate intimate ties that become "home"'.[22] This home includes a relationship with a safe, undemanding God who provides reassurance and comfort, and wants the women simply to be happy and nice. Smith critiques a passive faith that reduces religion to therapeutic benefits and a transactional relationship with God.[23] But this safe community and safe God help the women feel more secure in themselves and connected to others. Stephanie attends

AngSoc where she likes the chaplain and 'just felt comfortable there', and so does not attend a church as well. At AngSoc, she makes friends with Alexis and Melissa, and they are all 'very happy there'. She says,

> It's the community feel, and it does feel like home, and when you're saying the words of the service and they're the same as at home ... it's very familiar and comfortable [pause]. And then, it is the society where I've probably made friends, like better friends, with the people.

Room 3 is warm, cosy and safe. It is the heart of the home, with comfortable furniture and room to lie down and rest, offering reassurance and refreshment. It is a family room with space to gather, with no need to worry about those not included. Liminality and deferral can continue from room 2, yet it is viewed more positively here, as a freedom in which to relax. Room 3 has a clear exit, but it is a spiral staircase, and there is a temptation to stay.

Room 4: Exploration and resistance

In time, safety enables exploration, as the women move beyond their comfort zones into room 4. They develop greater confidence and self reliance, becoming aware, to some extent, of their own growth and maturation. Relationships remain important, yet students in room 4 are more comfortable with difference. Carmichael emphasizes the need for friendship to guard 'against group selfishness and fear of other groups'. Instead, 'friendship is love between diverse people in dynamic interaction'.[24] The women recognize the importance of encountering strangers and embracing friends with whom they disagree. The insights of Belenky and her colleagues reveal how direct exposure to difference transforms otherness into familiarity. Fear and alienation give way to understanding, making the world feel more comprehensible and less threatening.[25] Partly through learning from difference, the women in room 4 are, as Michael D. Berzonsky and Linda S. Kuk find, 'willing to test and revise aspects of their self-identity.'[26]

Commonly used words in room 4 are 'confident', 'grown', 'aware', 'explore' and 'mature'. The women notice increased confidence or growth in a variety of spheres:

- feeling more secure in who she is (Amber)
- 'exploring ... what to commit to and what to explore', for example, learning about Black and feminist theology (Ashley)

- engaging with therapy, putting clearer boundaries in friendships, and having 'great friends who love me' (Chloe)
- having 'really put down roots here' (Kimberly)
- being 'a lot more in control' (Mary)
- having a job and being president of a student society (Nicole)
- thinking about and discussing 'the meaning of things' (Samantha)
- studying, feeling more professional and speaking up in front of classmates (Stephanie).

Room 4 is a creative playroom, with new opportunities to embrace. Here, the women attempt new things and can be playful in their relationships. There is space to run around and test boundaries, like small children mischievously running from a parent. It is a room for dreaming, with a greenery-filled balcony for looking outwards. The women are playful with their faith and gender identities, resisting harmful practices, including 'modesty', women's submission, and 'cold contact' evangelism. Courtney T. Goto advocates for religious play, for to 'be truly at home in the external world [and] ... understand what we like to call "reality", we have to live poetically.' Creativity and 'aliveness ... leads to a sense of feeling real ... which means having a sense of self and of being.' Reflecting earlier rooms, without this creative aliveness, people feel 'that they are not themselves, they are in limbo, they are nothing, or they are detached from their bodies'. For Goto, a person can only play where it is 'safe', that is, where 'freedom and authenticity' mean that the 'true self' feels 'home'.[27]

Women in room 4 recognize that university is impacting their faith, and they are on a journey with God. For Astin and colleagues, students become 'more actively engaged in a spiritual quest' at university. Engaging with diverse people and experiences at university is transformative, and 'students become more caring, more tolerant, more connected with others'.[28] Briana discusses growing and becoming more aware 'of people who are more different' at university. Through attending the CU and her 'amazing' and 'deep' friendships with her female Christian housemates, she has 'grown a lot in my relationship with God' and 'grown more as person', both in 'knowledge' and in 'confidence', including on 'my course' but also in 'Christian matters'. Her faith has grown through trying 'things like prophecy', 'understanding worship a bit more', 'having quiet times', 'talk[ing] about God' and 'spending time with Christians'.

In their spiritual quest, Harris argues, women experience an *awakening* in the midst of transitions, making room for change: 'people awaken *to* and *toward* something', beginning 'when people awaken to ... their deepest inner selves'. Awakening involves connection and integration between different aspects of experience, leading to a new dawning and the hope for wholeness.²⁹ In room 4, there are initial moves towards integration, particularly through engaging with studying. Alexis says, if 'I want something' she is 'more likely to ask for it now, or [to] tell them ... what I want to happen, rather than being just ridiculously polite.' She is also 'more confident in seminars ... I'm much more likely to speak up.' Alexis ended a relationship with her first-year boyfriend that 'wasn't very good', where she was 'insulted sometimes, and other things I didn't want.' This gave her confidence to think, 'Now, instead of just going through [it] and being sad ... if I don't want that to happen I can make it not happen, and be more, not *forceful* ... more assertive about it. It's better for me.'

Moving on from room 4 is fun and even exciting, but nonetheless challenging.

Room 5: Integration and becoming

In room 5, becoming involves increasing intentionality, changes in identity, integrating different identities and experiences, and broadening awareness about oneself and the world. The shift is profound. Becoming happens in the women's second year and beyond, once they are less consumed by their traumatic transitions and daily life management. For students, Taylor and Harris-Evans argue, 'Becoming is about change as ongoing flux and dynamic flow, as emergence and unfolding in micro-moments and instants. Becoming is the endless play of difference ... Becoming is the working of self-differentiation.'³⁰

These elements are present in the women's narratives. However, self-differentiation involves both widening and narrowing as they move to interdependence while relationships deepen. Their relationships are essential in their faith and becoming. Slee observes that relationality is expressed in 'strong empathic connection to others, an incarnational sense of the sacredness of the ordinary, and through the prizing of integration as the ideal of faith'.³¹ Together with integrating aspects of their own identities, the women's connection with others and with God is part of their differentiation, not in opposition to it. In room 5, women react against the idea of total independence, of being completely free to shape their own world.

Room 5 involves embracing multiple and intersecting identities, seeing diversity as strength. Recognition of their intersectional marginalized identities includes advocating for others who are marginalized, volunteering and campaigning, encouraged by faith in the God of liberation. Students integrate their experiences as women with their faith, and some see themselves as intersectional Christian feminists. As awareness grows, the women understand God as working with them in shaping their futures. Theological reimagining includes viewing God or Jesus as liberator or protestor; centring justice, inclusion and empowerment; and using faith as a framework for challenging oppression. The women see themselves as agents of transformation, committed to creating inclusive religious communities and challenging inherited patriarchal and exclusionary structures. Common words in room 5 include 'advocate', 'injustice', 'involved', 'diversity/difference' and 'feminism':

- recognizing 'injustice against women worldwide, which I don't want to ignore', and volunteering with refugees because 'that's where Jesus wants to be, he wants us to go to the people who are in difficult situations' (Abigail).
- seeing her generation as agents of change, wanting 'to make the world a better place', being involved with a political party, multifaith work, queer justice and 'racial injustice', and advocating for inclusion in church (Caitlin).
- embracing 'intersectional feminism', integrating her sexuality and faith, recognizing with God that her negative experiences have been 'injustice', and committing to 'work[ing] on diversity for people of colour' (Chloe).
- studying 'power and how people are treated' which is 'about my faith and its relation to social action', campaigning against poverty and discrimination in church (Lauren).
- rooting her feminism in 'what Christ said', critically distinguishing Christ's teachings from patriarchal interpretations, and volunteering because 'one of the best ways to practise your faith is through helping other people' (Melissa).
- 'charity work and volunteering' because 'Christianity has influenced me in ... wanting to help others' (Nicole).
- becoming vegetarian as 'being responsible for everything we do, and about the environment' and because 'it's not fair to just keep doing things we love just because they're easy' (Samantha).
- engaging with 'social justice and equality' in church, volunteering with Girls' Brigade and conservation projects 'because I care about the planet and want to do something myself to help' (Sarah).

As Astin and colleagues write, 'one of the surest ways to enhance the spiritual development of undergraduate students is to encourage them to engage in almost any form of charitable or altruistic activity'.[32] Vicky finds this to be the case. Not only is she becoming 'aware of all kinds of different people and ... [the] experiences that they have', this is helping her see that, 'God really does love everybody and you can either choose to see the good in the person that God can see, or you can choose to write people off.' Thus, her 'understanding of God has strengthened and made me want to try and have that approach.' Vicky recognizes that, in part, this 'passion' and advocacy comes from her own working-class background in a city that people 'slag off, even though they've never been there, and like the government forgets about it, and it's filled with all those kinds of stereotypes of people that, like, are [pause] "scroungers" and "poor" and, like, "rubbish".' She wanted to 'champion' her city by becoming a secondary school teacher there. This was a 'conscious decision' impacting both her time at university and her future plans.

Similarly, working-class and mixed-race Ashley is engaged with 'social justice things', sharing with others that 'God sees it's not right'. She sees 'brokenness in the world':

> and [when] people agree on the brokenness, there's an opportunity ... to speak truth ... about God and the fact that he wants to bring reconciliation, even though it's sometimes hard to believe because people are like, 'So where is he then?'

Even though Ashley 'can't give an answer to that', she still feels 'passion to do it' which is 'directly linked to her faith'. Her ability to work towards God's justice, including gender and racial inequality, without having all the answers demonstrates her learning to live with ambiguity. Her intersectional identities contribute to her wanting to advocate for others. She is 'thankful' that she 'get[s] to live life with these lenses' because, despite bringing 'difficulties', they 'have enhanced my capacity to love and connect with other people'. She feels like she has been thrown out of her safe boat into the uncertain expanse of the ocean, where she can become, 'in life with God'.

Alexandra is involved in several projects as she interprets her faith through a hermeneutic of liberation. Her concern for justice is due to being in 'a lot of minority groups' as a queer woman of colour. She says: 'If we perceive God to just be for us, then we would have a very closed-minded approach to what life is. But if God is for everyone, then, you know, we would actually participate ... in helping others.'

This room is big, bright and airy, with large windows and skylights to see the sky and look outwards and onwards. The ceilings are high, with room for women to stand tall, both alone and reliant on others. This room is an open studio with a desk for imagining new futures.

Becoming looks a little like awakening; thus room 5 is not the end of a journey so much as the beginning of future movement, a time of hope and dawning. Pictures of previous rooms indicate some perspective on, and reconciliation with, previous selves.

Debra Phillips, emerging from an episode of depression, noticed that her paintings shifted from depicting dark spaces to including 'brighter tones ... flower and tree motifs and ceiling-less rooms'. In these spaces, 'the darkness becomes softer for God's light is erasing fear and dissolving despair.' Instead of a roof, 'the room is open to a vast sky of rich blue filled with stars', describing the space as a courtyard that 'is both the cognitive and the spiritual space in which God's light can infiltrate each aspect of our lived experience.'[33]

There are fewer women in this room, and inhabiting it still feels tentative since the processes of becoming and integrating are ongoing. Thus, it is important not to overemphasize becoming and belittle the importance of previous rooms. Students do not see becoming as scary, but experience it as another means of safety, a stabilizing force recognizing that perpetual seeking is not sustainable. Becoming enables critical reinterpretation of faith, including challenging conservative narratives through intersectional lenses; and encourages personal empowerment as the women claim agency within their religious and university spaces, integrate their sexuality, race and gender with their faith, and refuse to be marginalized. Women in this room actively reconstruct religious understanding to affirm their full, complex selves, and to advocate for others.

Discussing the model

Factors that hinder the women's homing render them unhome or only home tentatively, and those that facilitate homing enable exploration and becoming. In Chapter 3, Taylor refers to such factors as 'fuel': what fuel a woman has can determine what room she is in. Such fuel includes everything: a woman's relationships, self-esteem, sense of intersectionality, faith praxis, and accommodation. Varied qualities in fuel can result in different aspects of women's lives inhabiting different rooms: faith particularly facilitates safety and exploration, while gender is especially a factor in unhome and uncertain ambiguity. Awareness of the intersection of different identities often prompted movement towards integration, even when being marginalized was difficult and upsetting. A student might dwell in trauma and unhome due to having only recently moved to university, but her faith may find safety quickly under the right circumstances. Some women abide predominantly in one or two connected rooms, staying there for a while.

Multiple transitions take place both within and between rooms. While there is a sense of progression between the rooms and their order is not arbitrary, the model does not claim a linear progression. Resonant with feminist practical theology, the processes and transitionings involved in moving between rooms include pauses, gaps and overlappings. Feminist theory commonly views life as an ongoing process of becoming. Colley argues that 'life-as-transition' characterizes women's experiences, where time becomes fluid and unpredictable, in contrast to 'male' time which is generally linear and standardized. Women's transitions proceed through 'unending and fragmented' cycles of opening and closing, creating 'zig-zag or spiral movements within a web of contradictions' where each transition influences subsequent ones.[34] Movement between rooms is an iterative process of backwards-and-forwards between two realities until the new stage is sufficiently strong for the old one to be discarded. Within each room, the stability achieved in the previous room is undone, and must be made again. Yet returning to a previous room is always possible, especially at times of vulnerability or crisis.

Central to the women's experiences and the theory used in this book is the understanding that transitionings are rarely singular or narrow. Gale and Parker argue that transitionings permeate every aspect of students' daily lives. The process follows a 'rhizomatic' pattern, involving multiple narratives and fluid identities. This frames transitions as continuous becoming, where individuals integrate multiple identities and experiences without following any normative pattern. The focus remains on personal, subjective transformation across all aspects of life.[35] Taylor and Harris-Evans expand on Gale and Parker's theory, arguing that transition is a 'more spontaneous, connective, happenstance, affective and transversal practice than is normally thought'.[36]

University is not then merely a context in which women absorb new information, but rather a temporary base for the whole of their lives and identities, including relationships past and present, accommodation, romance, futurity, race, sexuality, gender and faith. In Harris's 'spirituality of pedagogy', she argues that 'each step is a dwelling place'. Women can 'return [to] or repeat' each step, and each one 'continually teaches us'. Moreover, women 'do not come to the next step by planning it beforehand, but by doing the bodily work from which the next step emerges.'[37] Dwelling in each room involves cultivating what Wright calls 'a settled space'[38] in active and fluid ways. Each room represents a meaningful space rather than just a temporary stage, and movement between rooms is not seamless. Sometimes, transitions between rooms are *intentionally resisted* rather than embraced.[39] The metaphor of 'rooms' captures both the individual nature of each woman's transitions, and how these spaces flow together in creating home. This model acknowledges the unique and non-uniform nature of university experiences, emphasizing the diversity and commonality in the women's journeys and reflecting each woman's lived experience. It is a fundamental human and theological strategy in feeling *homely enough*.

Homing is a unique model of emerging Christian women's transitions at university, taking seriously gender, faith and other marginalized identities, positioning them centrally in its development. The model addresses the theological questions set out in Chapter 1, offering reassurance of the 'many dwelling places' that Jesus teaches his disciples are within God's house.[40] It places God within each of the rooms, dwelling with the women and drawing them away from trauma and unhome. Thomas Aquinas, in his commentary on John's Gospel, writes that 'the house of God is where God dwells ... Yet the house of the Father is not only where he dwells, but he himself is the house, for he exists in himself. It is into this house that he gathers us.' He continues, 'the different rooms are the various participations in the knowledge and enjoyment of God.'[41] Examining John's theology of 'abiding' through a feminist lens, Lee argues that discipleship centres on witnessing and abiding. 'True disciples' mutually inhabit Jesus as 'the source of life', a dynamic spiritual state encompassing present reality and future potential. Abiding represents dwelling in light, a profound 'homecoming' that expresses the intimate, reciprocal nature underlying divine existence.[42]

Reflecting further on her artwork, Debra Phillips's paintings 'show the rooms of my own soul in which God lives' as 'God waited in each of the rooms'. As rooms grew brighter, she 'was reassuring my Self that ... God had remained within my "house" and was not going to leave'. Discussing moving from cramped empty rooms into bright open spaces, she too draws on the Gospel of John, where God was:

> going ahead to my future to: 'prepare a place for you, I will come back and take you to be with me' to be in God's house where I am. This moment is the beginning of the resolution of Spirit and Self.[43]

In the model, three important strands are apparent in the women's improvised movements. First, the model considers each room equally significant. It recognizes that initial rooms are dwelling places, holding as much value as later rooms, aligning with feminist principles by respecting women's diverse experiences and allowing them to develop their identities gradually and authentically, through experimentation and relationship, one room at a time. The home metaphor encompasses all aspects of women's lives, creating an inclusive framework where no experiences are considered peripheral or insignificant.

Second, in line with other studies of women's faith and identity development, the model makes clear the importance of relationships: with those who are like-minded or 'different'; with friends, family and mentors; with new people or those who know them deeply; and with God. In each room, these relationships resource the crafting of home. Relationships form the context in which they are known and loved, in which they test provisional identities, explore together, and integrate who they are becoming with the life of the world. Relationships enable safety, provide safe spaces for exploration, and facilitate becoming.

Lastly, the model emphasizes the theological importance of liminality and 'yet' in women's transitions and crafting of home. All rooms include a tentative 'in between', although this is especially found in early rooms, in keeping with the liminal nature of both student life and emerging adulthood. The women are neither children nor adults, neither childish nor mature. They are no longer in the parental home, but, as Kenyon writes, not yet in the '"real" adult … imagined home … which would signify that the leaving home process was at or near completion.'[44] Nancy Worth proposes that futurity is an important consideration in young people's transitions since they are continually open to the future, with fluid understandings of both identity and time. She describes their transitional identity: 'the entire process of youth transition [is] a process of becoming.' This becoming continues, with individuals experiencing 'multiple becomings'.[45] The women find themselves at many different thresholds, each both an ending and a beginning, and while movement is evident, fluidity and uncertainty remain.

Within this model, the women reflect on these patterns and processes to some extent. They discuss faith as both influencing and being influenced by their transitions, or at least the hope that this *will* happen. Many struggle to articulate the significance of their gender identities, except to reflect on female friendships or describe difficult gendered encounters. Traumatic experiences are reflected upon only to a certain point. Intentionality and reflection are especially witnessed in safety, in the intentional building of friendships and commitment to Christian community; and in becoming, through their deliberate decisions to broaden their awareness about their intersectional selves and the world. Rather than intentionality, the model describes women's patterns of gender and religion as, using Bourdieu's phrase, 'regulated improvisation'. This describes social practices as both structured by underlying rules and habitus, yet spontaneous, allowing creative adaptation within established social frameworks; suggesting that people do not simply follow rigid scripts, but are creatively improvising within socially learned boundaries.[46] As emerging adults, the students improvise the tentative and provisional processes that begin to establish them as mature Christian women. These improvisations are regulated within the post-feminist, university and Christian cultures and subcultures in which they live and study. The model offers a hermeneutic whereby women faithfully if tentatively inhabit each room. Each woman crafts for herself, with God and other people, *rooms of her own*.

Conclusion

This chapter has presented a model of Homing for Christian women students. When the women first arrive at university, they feel orphaned, traumatized, bewildered and overwhelmed. They long for safety, and temporarily and tentatively create this while remaining 'in between'. In their search for familiarity and comfort, they begin to invest in new relationships, deepening friendships and (wherever possible) creating chosen-families. In beginning to feel more settled, they grow in inner-dependence, resisting negative narratives that confine or define them. Some integrate their different identities, bringing together the whole of their life, in a process of becoming.

Homing emerges through relationships: with fellow Christians, with other women with shared marginalized identities, through deepening spiritual connection with God, and via encounters with those of different perspectives. This relational foundation then resources the women in negotiating their traumatic transitions and navigating their explorations and becomings. This is an intense journey of dwelling, forced in part by the transition to university and moving away from home for the first time. It is also the beginning of a new cycle of belonging and becoming as the women go on to leave university.

The next chapter offers some final conclusions on homing, and looks onwards to the next steps for this research.

Notes

1 Teresa of Ávila, *Interior Castle: The Mansions* (London: Sheed and Ward, 1944); Virginia Woolf, *A Room of One's Own* (London: Hogarth Press, 1935).
2 Paul Ricoeur, *The Rule of Metaphor: The Creation of Meaning in Language*, Routledge Classics (London: Routledge, 2006), p. 303.
3 Sallie McFague, *Metaphorical Theology: Models of God in Religious Lan-*

guage (London: SCM Press, 1983), pp. 23, 28, 133–4; Sallie McFague, *Models of God: Theology for an Ecological, Nuclear Age* (Minneapolis, MN: Fortress Press, 1987), p. 34.

4 McFague, *Metaphorical Theology*, p. 196.

5 Carol A. Taylor and Jean Harris-Evans, 'Reconceptualising Transition to Higher Education with Deleuze and Guattari', *Studies in Higher Education* 43, no. 7 (2018), pp. 1254–67.

6 See Jennifer L. Crissman-Ishler and Staci Schreiber, 'First-Year Female Students: Perceptions of Friendship', *Journal of Higher Education* 63 (2002), pp. 441–62.

7 David E. Balk, 'Grieving: 22 to 30 Percent of All College Students', *New Directions for Student Services* 121 (2008), p. 6.

8 Walter Brueggemann, *The Practice of Homefulness* (Eugene, OR: Wipf and Stock, 2014), p. 3.

9 Laura Smit, 'The Image of Home', *Theology Today* 45, no. 3 (1988), p. 312.

10 Clare Holdsworth, 'Don't You Think You're Missing Out, Living at Home? Student Experiences and Residential Transitions', *Sociological Review* 54, no. 3 (2006), p. 510.

11 Debra Phillips, 'In God's House There Are Many Rooms (Jn 14.2–27)', *Feminist Theology* 25, no. 1 (September 2016), pp. 96, 98–9.

12 William Bridges, *Managing Transitions: Making the Most of Change*, 3rd ed. (London: Nicholas Brealey Publishing, 2009), p. 23.

13 Tim Clydesdale, *The First Year Out: Understanding American Teens after High School* (Chicago, IL: University of Chicago Press, 2007), p. 27.

14 Holdsworth, 'Don't You Think You're Missing Out', p. 510.

15 Sharon Parks, *Big Questions, Worthy Dreams: Mentoring Young Adults in Their Search for Meaning, Purpose, and Faith* (San Francisco, CA: Jossey-Bass, 2000), pp. 147–8.

16 Christian Smith and Patricia Snell, *Souls in Transition: The Religious and Spiritual Lives of Emerging Adults* (Oxford: Oxford University Press, 2009), p. 236.

17 James W. Fowler, *Stages of Faith: The Psychology of Human Development and the Quest for Meaning* (New York: Harper Collins, 1981), p. 178.

18 Parks, *Big Questions, Worthy Dreams*, p. 34.

19 Alison Webster, *You Are Mine: Reflections on Who We Are* (London: SPCK, 2009), pp. 21–2.

20 Christine D. Pohl, *Living into Community: Cultivating Practices that Sustain Us* (Grand Rapids, MI: W.B. Eerdmans, 2012), p. 4; Wendy M. Wright, *Sacred Dwelling: A Spirituality of Family Life* (London: Darton, Longman and Todd, 2007), p. 86.

21 Sharon Parks, *The Critical Years: The Young Adult Search for a Faith to Live By* (New York: Harper & Row, 1986), pp. 57–8.

22 Sonya Sharma and Mathew Guest, 'Navigating Religion Between University and Home: Christian Students' Experiences in English Universities', *Social and Cultural Geography* 14, no. 1 (2013), p. 71.

23 Christian Smith, 'On "Moralistic Therapeutic Deism" as US Teenagers' Actual, Tacit, De Facto Religious Faith' in *Religion and Youth*, ed. Sylvia Collins-Mayo and Pink Dandelion (Farnham: Ashgate, 2010).

24 Liz Carmichael, *Friendship: Interpreting Christian Love* (London: T. & T. Clark, 2007), pp. 198, 200.

25 Mary F. Belenky et al., *Women's Ways of Knowing: The Development of Self, Voice and Mind*, 10th Anniversary ed. (New York: Basic Books, 1986), pp. 114-15.

26 Michael D. Berzonsky and Linda S. Kuk, 'Identity Status, Identity Processing Style, and the Transition to University', *Journal of Adolescent Research* 15, no. 1 (2000), p. 83.

27 Courtney T. Goto, *The Grace of Playing: Pedagogies for Leaning into God's New Creation* (Boston, MA: Wipf and Stock, 2016), pp. 80, 86-7, 131.

28 Alexander W. Astin, Helen S. Astin and Jennifer A. Lindholm, *Cultivating the Spirit: How College Can Enhance Students' Inner Lives* (San Francisco, CA: Jossey-Bass, 2011), p. 10.

29 Maria Harris, *Dance of the Spirit: The Seven Steps of Women's Spirituality* (New York: Bantam, 1989), pp. 2-3.

30 Taylor and Harris-Evans, 'Reconceptualising Transition', p. 1262.

31 Nicola Slee, *Women's Faith Development: Patterns and Processes* (Aldershot: Ashgate, 2004), p. 140.

32 Astin, Astin and Lindholm, *Cultivating the Spirit*, p. 147.

33 Phillips, 'In God's House', pp. 101, 106-7.

34 Helen Colley, 'Understanding Time in Learning Transitions Through the Lifecourse', *International Studies in Sociology of Education* 17, no. 4 (2007), pp. 430, 434, 438.

35 Trevor Gale and Stephen Parker, 'Navigating Change: A Typology of Student Transition in Higher Education', *Studies in Higher Education* 39, no. 5 (2014), pp. 734-53.

36 Taylor and Harris-Evans, 'Reconceptualising Transition', pp. 1255-6.

37 Maria Harris, *Women and Teaching: Themes for a Spirituality of Pedagogy* (Mahwah, NJ: Paulist, 1988), pp. 14-15.

38 Wright, *Sacred Dwelling*, p. 14.

39 For more on this concept, see James E. Côté, 'Emerging Adulthood as an Institutionalized Moratorium: Risks and Benefits to Identity Formation' in *Emerging Adults in America*, ed. Jeffrey Jensen Arnett and Jennifer L. Tanner (Washington, DC: American Psychological Association, 2006), pp. 85-116.

40 John 14.2 NRSV.

41 Thomas Aquinas, *Commentary on the Gospel of John: Chapters 13-21*, trans. Fabian Larcher and James A. Weisheipl (Washington, DC: Catholic University of America Press, 2012), p. 49.

42 Dorothy Lee, 'Abiding in the Fourth Gospel: A Case Study in Feminist Biblical Theology' in *Feminist Companion to John*, ed. Amy-Jill Levine, vol. 2 (London: Bloomsbury Publishing/Sheffield Academic Press, 2003), pp. 70-1.

43 Phillips, 'In God's House', pp. 100-1, 105-6, quoting John 14.3 NIV.

44 Liz Kenyon, 'A Home from Home: Students' Transitional Experience of Home' in *Ideal Homes? Social Change and the Experience of Home*, ed. Tony Chapman and Jenny Hockey (London: Routledge, 1999), pp. 85, 94.

45 Nancy Worth, 'Understanding Youth Transition as "Becoming:" Identity, Time and Futurity', *Geoform* 40 (2009), pp. 1050, 1058.

46 Pierre Bourdieu, *The Logic of Practice* (London: Polity Press, 1992), p. 57.

9

Conclusion

This book has used the lens of feminist practical theology to examine the characteristics of, and challenges facing, emerging Christian women in the multiple transitions of moving away from home to study at university. Part I began to identify the women's transitionings *from home to home*, describing their traumatic transitions, identity work, and attempts to craft home at university. Part II explored how Christian faith influenced these transitions, identifying elements that supported and impeded their sense of home, examining their participation in various Christian spaces and activities, and following how faith evolved while at university. Part III examined how the students navigated their multiple minority identities and experiences, including their gender, sexuality, social class, ethnicity and faith, exploring how they each crafted distinct independent identities. Part IV began with a model of Homing, theorizing the women's crafting of home at university using a metaphor of five rooms. This final chapter begins with offering some conclusions about the women's faith, feminism and feeling at home at university. Looking onwards, I then offer some recommendations for pastoral practice for both higher education and the Church, before suggesting areas for future research. Finally, I will offer some closing words.

Practical theology is sometimes critiqued, first, for discovering what is obvious common sense, and second, for misrepresenting narrative as 'uncomplicated, truthful and authentic'.[1] Yet these critiques point towards the unique place of practical theology in the theological milieu. In this book, so-called *common sense* – for example, that students experience university as traumatic, that peer and mentor support is invaluable, or that being safe is a fundamental requirement – is made even more visible and authoritative when told through 'thick' descriptions drawn from personal experience. Such narratives form the core of this book, and from them I have identified and illuminated significant trends in the enacting of women's gender and faith, in dialogue with relevant literature. Thus, practical theology deepens, theorizes and problematizes common sense, uncovering the subtleties and connections that can otherwise be easily missed, and demanding change where needed. Moreover, feminist practical theology accesses women's voices and engages in discovery through dedicated listening, in turn demonstrating women's internal realities that speak deeper truths than common sense. Such realities, when spoken out loud, change women's lives and seek to alter the confining structures that govern them. For instance, many of the women ascribed to the post-feminist belief in an already achieved equality, rendering feminism irrelevant. Yet, in inviting and analysing their narratives, experiences disproving such equality were overwhelming, demonstrating the pervasiveness of what is in fact a myth, and the necessity for a transformed culture that enables their flourishing. The two critiques then negate one another; what is common sense often makes no sense at all when seen through the lens of women's experiences.

Practical theological research, write Bennett and colleagues, must be inspired by 'a yearning for change' and make conclusions intent on 'moving and making, not mirroring'.[2] This book places emerging Christian women's experiences centrally, with the aim of influencing praxis in: transitions; Christian ministry; faith and identity development; higher education and the student experience; and intersectionality. It is also an invitation to others to carry out further research with emerging Christian adults, foregrounding questions of gender.

Faith, feminism and feeling at home

First, the university transition can unsettle students' religious identities, yet, for Christian students at English universities, actively practising their faith helps facilitate smoother transitions.[3] The women experienced their faith in overtly relational and safe terms, which enabled their crafting of home. Their closest friends were other Christian women, and in these spaces they felt comfortable revealing and exploring their authentic selves. Christianity and university were experienced as completely compatible, and faith was a vehicle for navigating and interpreting university life. The safety provided in the women's churches and Christian student societies enabled growth in confidence and inner-dependence, resourcing the women's *becoming*. Their relationships with God were adaptable according to their needs, from being a safe God who had a clear plan for their lives, to a God with whom they could explore, to the God of liberation and advocacy. A Christian identity enabled them to consider themselves distinct from other students, particularly through their rejection of the 'drinking culture' and 'lad culture'. Yet this identity also gave them the means to step out of their comfort zones, volunteer or campaign, and navigate a spiritual journey. For Perrin, 'faith has to become more complex as life does',[4] and many women saw their faith as a framework within which to engage with their subjective experiences, including through advocacy for others.

Perrin also concludes that emerging adults seek guidance on integrating their religious beliefs with the complexities of modern life. The emerging adults in Perrin's study faced some different challenges compared to those in this book – including the pressures of online personas and pornography – perhaps due to her participants being older and at different life stages. However, in keeping with this book, she also finds that they seek spiritual resourcing with their mental health, time-management and finding proper rest. She writes, 'They wanted to be holistic disciples of Jesus and felt that the church too often avoided those topics or provided little honesty or wisdom around them.'[5]

The women placed surprising importance on sermons. There was little difference between the women's different worship traditions or denominations in this regard. In fact, the women rarely mentioned the Eucharist, prayer, singing or other elements of worship services. This was the case for Taylor in her first interview, so in our follow-up conversation seven years later, I asked her to reflect on why this might have been true for her. She thought that sermons were 'easiest' to engage with, and were opportunities to learn from an expert 'worth listening to'. She saw sermons rather than 'Communion' as 'the main body of the church experience', despite being an Anglican attending weekly Eucharists. When the women heard sermons that related specifically to their lives or experiences as women or as students, they felt seen, and were resourced in their work of integration.

Second, the students considered their gender in significantly more vague and covert terms than their faith. Many struggled to articulate how they felt about being women, and when asked directly about gender they stated its unimportance in their lives. However, the students' narratives were saturated in experiences whereby being women was challenging, including through feeling vulnerable when out at night, being excluded in their studies, or the post-feminist pressure of bodily femininity. Rather than a place of safety, gender identity was a site for deferring responsibility, feeling 'in between' and rejecting maturity. Relationships with other women were the only gender-safe spaces: with peers, family members, mentors and 'intentional friends'. Women's relationality was considered the best thing about their gender, and relationships with other women enabled them to discuss difficult experiences or ask for support.

The women embodied their gender and faith in intersecting ways, enabling them to create safe chosen-families with other Christian women, to critique and resist the double-bind of faith and femininity, and to claim feminism as a Christian imperative. In these ways, faith was considered a resource in interpreting and even resisting their negative gendered experiences. However, some women considered their gender and faith distinct from and unrelated to one another and distinct from the rest of their lives, expressing bewilderment that their gender might influence their Christian belief or praxis, or vice versa. This separation was presented either as an expression of being unhome or as a means of delaying change from happening 'yet'.

Some women embraced feminism without caveat. These women had often experienced a past rupture in their gendered identity, contributing to their becoming and feminist awakening. Women who embraced feminism did so through intersectional lenses, reflecting the relationships between their marginalized identities. As Bowleg writes, these women saw that their 'social identities and inequality are interdependent ... not mutually exclusive'.[6] University, as a transformative rite of passage, holds special significance for women exploring their diverse and intersecting identities, playing a vital role in exploring religious, gendered, queer, racial and class identities.

Page and Shipley argue that, rather than religious spaces, 'the secular is perceived as the best place from which to protect and extend sexuality rights'. However, they continue, 'while "religion" is frequently blamed for anti-queer attitudes, non-religious and "secular" spaces continue to restrict, harm, and disavow non-heterosexuality.'[7] Many of the queer women found their university hostile to their sexuality, yet experienced their faith as safe spaces for family-like community, theological exploration, and relationship with a loving God. Althaus-Reid argues for the importance of such religious spaces, finding that the church restricts social care 'according to the limitations of its own heterosexual fixed theological landscape'. She finds this unacceptable, and detrimental to the Church and to the lives of women and minorities globally. Instead, the Church must begin to see that 'women's bodies are prophetic'.[8] University can be a time of traumatic transition for all women. For women to embrace an intersectional Christian feminism, churches and universities need to work alongside one another to resource women in exploring their different identities, in their relational and inner-dependent journeys, and in holistically integrating their Christian and student lives.

Finally, in feeling at home, the women longed to be 'settled' somewhere that was 'comfortable' and 'homely', resisting anything 'uncomfortable' or unfamiliar. In searching for a new church, the women used these same words, reflecting the importance of church communities as student subcultures. Faith greatly impacted upon the women's transitions, offering continuity between their previous and current selves. However, these words of comfort were never used by the women as they discussed their gendered experiences, other than when discussing safe, family-like relationships with other women. The transitions that the women experienced were mainly enhanced by the women's faith yet hindered by their gender. Faith gave the women a confidence by which to negotiate their university experience, while their gender was either dismissed as irrelevant or considered detrimental in their transitions due to the pressures and expectations of their post-feminist culture.

Moving away to university is a traumatic transition for emerging women within a neoliberal academic environment. Complex challenges include identity development, post-feminism, technology advancement, global crises, social hierarchies and mental illness, to name a few, all while accumulating an average £50,000 of debt. Nevertheless, the women were finding strategies to navigate these transitions and to craft a home for themselves. Patterns of becoming and feeling at home involved identity growth, increasing confidence, a developing maturity, and interdependence. There was some intentionality as the women were deliberate or reflective in their beliefs or praxis, especially in their second year and beyond. No single woman embraced becoming in every aspect of university life; however, every woman embraced some aspect of becoming, whether small or significant.

Parks argues that some emerging adults take 'self-conscious responsibility for one's own knowing [and] becoming'. She continues that students 'recompose' their world with 'a new awareness that more depends upon [them than] previously supposed'.[9] For the women in this book, this was done in relationship. Safe communities and encounters with those that were different, including with God, facilitated women's homing without confining them to narrow ideas or forced agreement. Lorde writes that 'without community, there is no liberation ... But community must not mean a shedding of our differences, nor the pathetic pretence that these differences do not exist.'[10] For Gen Z, Katz and her colleagues note, this looks like 'finding my fam', including 'forging new modes of community that lessen the contradiction between being a *me* and a *we*'.[11]

Recommendations for pastoral practice

The conclusions in this book have wide-reaching pastoral implications. First, I provide some recommendations for churches and chaplaincies, and those who engage with Christian students. Next, I offer suggestions for the management of higher education institutions. Lastly, I present gendered implications based on my conclusions, for all who work alongside emerging women.

Recent academic interest in higher education chaplaincy is important in seeking greater recognition of chaplaincy's valuable place both within the institutions that it serves and in the wider Church. I suggest that such Christian spaces must recognize and respond to the complex unhoming that female students experience, and the debilitating post-feminism with which Christian student subcultures interact. Katz and her colleagues argue that the best way to support Generation Z is to:

> appreciate the lessons they have to teach us: be real, know who you are, be responsible for your own well-being, support your friends, open up institutions to the talents of the many not the few, embrace diversity, make the world kinder, live by your values.[12]

These are all characteristics embedded in the theology and praxis of good university chaplaincies, and churches have much to learn from these essential values.

From 2028, emerging adults from Generation Alpha will begin university. I will be keen to see what is important for their faith and intersectional feminism at university, and I encourage all who work with Christian emerging adults to be sentinels prepared for change. Other specific recommendations for Christian leaders include:

- Create opportunities for students to encounter a range of perspectives on relevant theological issues and provide safe spaces for discussion. Such topics could include views on sex, mission and evangelism, doctrinal issues such as salvation, and mental health, together with feminist, queer and Black theologies.
- Offer resources for women's faith, including sermons, that prompt integration between Christianity and the rest of their lives and identities. Such resources must discuss gender, facilitate engagement with biblical texts and offer a space for women to doubt and wrestle with their own interwoven stories of faith.
- Facilitate safe, intergenerational, diverse and intentional spaces supportive of women.

- Re-consider how God is addressed and spoken of, and include expansive and relevant metaphors of God in conversation, prayer and worship.
- Explore avenues for improved online expressions of church and chaplaincy, in which, Guest and his colleagues argue, 'a questioning faith can be more at home'.[13]

For higher education, the importance that the women placed on their academic study is noteworthy, demonstrated through their engagement with its content, the integration of their study with their faith and other identities, their appreciation of university mentors, and their growing inner-dependence through learning. However, this book also describes how the women's study hindered them in integrating their intersectional identities with their learning. Misogyny and racism were significant factors preventing the women from fully flourishing in their studies and claiming their education for themselves.

Neoliberalism contributed to prevalent post-feminist attitudes, including the normalizing of lad culture and sexist behaviours, the rejuvenating of male entitlement and the emphasis on individualistic choice. This book demonstrates how these cultural effects narrowed the women's options and determined many of their daily experiences on account of their gender. This is a significant conclusion, challenging post-feminism's claim that equality has been achieved, and revealing such a claim to be harmful and illusory.

Interestingly, the women did not have much difficulty practising their faith at university or bringing their faith into their subject of study. This was in part due to their large number of Christian friends at university. Engagement with chaplaincies and student Christian societies enabled them to feel at home on campus as Christians. While several women did not consider their faith and studies connected, they did not see this as problematic. These women saw their faith as private, personal and separate. However, it is important that universities heed their responsibility, as Guest and colleagues argue, to 'learn to negotiate a student environment that encompasses both a confident secularity, religious resilience and a benign tolerance that sits as a majority disposition between the two'.[14]

These conclusions have significant implications for higher education institutions. While it has been beyond the scope of this book to pay more than brief attention to the nature of higher education in the UK, I suggest ways to change discourse and practice concerning emerging women, students and faith at university. With hooks, I argue that 'overall education for critical consciousness of collective political resistance'[15] is needed to transform personal, painful stories into structural change. This book demonstrates some of the harm that women experience in a neoliberal university, but also the creative strategies that they employ to counteract the lack of welcome afforded them. I recommend that, to enable their students' becoming and feeling at home, universities do more to recognize the importance of the whole of students' lives in their transitions at university, supporting well-being and flourishing in all areas of life. Specific recommendations include:

- Assign shared accommodation to like-minded first-year students, particularly according to attitudes towards alcohol consumption and sleep patterns, to avoid them feeling isolated and unhome.
- Increase specialized support for students attending their second choice of university due to missed grades, or entering university through the 'clearing' process.
- Bring students' intersectional identities into both teaching and broader structures: including critiquing patriarchal language, colonialism, racism and heterosexism.
- Offer connected teaching that encourages communal learning, sharing and asking relevant questions.
- Take seriously both lad culture and rape culture and the impact that they have on women students' experiences and norms.
- Recognize and appreciate the influence and importance of religious activity in public spaces, and improve religious literacy for all staff and students.

In relation to the students' gendered experiences, feminists do not necessarily consider the faith lives of women as worthy of consideration.[16] Yet faith cannot be seen in narrowly sexist terms, nor can it be understood simply as women's choice for their own discrimination, as secular discourse sometimes suggests. Rather, faith influences women's lives in multifaceted ways, and I encourage feminist researchers to appreciate and pay attention to women's intersectional faith lives. For anyone working with emerging women, my recommendations include:

- Name and counteract post-feminism, for example by discrediting essential assumptions of gender, recognizing 'girling' and narrow definitions of femininity.
- Take seriously faith and religion as markers of identity and praxis in women's lives.
- Encourage women to discuss together their gendered experiences in safe spaces, and to develop strategies collectively and independently to counteract challenges.

- Draw attention to the limits of 'choice feminism' and encourage women to critique the political and cultural structures that limit their lives.
- Critique gendered stereotypes, including how women are encouraged to judge or compete with one another. Encourage the celebration of honesty and commitment in women's relationships.

Questions for further research

This book has, in part, responded to the recommendations for further research made in my PhD thesis. I saw expanding upon my initial interviews as necessary, hence this research has included: a wider range of students, including international students and a doctoral student; two more higher education institutions as well as the original redbrick university; and greater numbers of working-class, queer and BAME students. I also interviewed students studying during the Covid-19 pandemic. Moreover, I reinterviewed two students from the initial research to explore their accounts of university in retrospect.

However, additional studies incorporating a broader range of perspectives would be welcome, perhaps including: mature students or students that continue to live at home; higher numbers of postgraduate students; students of other faiths and spiritualities, or no faith at all; male, transgender or non-binary students; 'hidden Christians' who do not attend any public Christian activities;[17] or emerging adults who do not attend university at all. Greater attention could also be given to students at their second choice of university, or having come to university through the 'clearing' process. The impact of Covid-19 is still being realized, and research with those learning and working at universities during the pandemic and in its aftermath must continue. Since the women included here were amid multiple transitions, this book offers a different perspective from studies with people looking back upon transitions with hindsight.[18] Additional longitudinal research would bring further insight to these transitions.

Since the first interviews were conducted, neurodiversity has emerged as a critical area requiring further research. I did not ask students about their disabilities, including neurodivergence, perhaps reflecting my own ablism. This is an omission in this work, especially since in 2023 14 per cent of university applicants reported having Attention Deficit Hyperactivity Disorder (ADHD) and/or autism. Being neurodivergent is shown to make transition more difficult, and increases the chance of experiencing other challenges including learning disabilities, depression, anxiety and eating disorders. It also makes belonging in Christian spaces more challenging.[19]

Bowleg argues that retrospective analysis of completed research allows for newer insights, and invites consideration of alternative approaches were there the opportunity to conduct the research again. This book is richer for incorporating so many different levels of data, and of my own reflection and analysis. Bowleg continues that, while much research includes questions about minority identity markers, there is a paucity of genuinely intersectional research that 'asks more and better questions that can be used to analyse intersectionality' and includes the 'ordinary people who live at the crux of structural inequality'.[20] Anyone researching with the aim of understanding intersecting marginalizations is encouraged to engage with Bowleg's work.

Further research projects could explore these and other issues only touched upon in this book, both for Generation Z and, soon, for Generation Alpha.

Closing words

Jenny: If you could sum up your first year at uni in one word or phrase, what would it be?
Alexis: Um ... kind of, 'all over the place' [laughs].
Melissa: It just becomes life ... it's just what you do.
Stephanie: Yeah, cos when I'm at uni, I stop noticing, like, I don't miss home ... when I'm at uni, I'm very much here, and then when I'm at home, I'm very much at home.

What does home feel like? 'Home' is an enfolding place of connection and nourishment, where one is understood and known. The Homing model demonstrates that while the whole of life is included in 'home', to feel at home, one must be safe, comfortable and settled. Yet home must also feel challenging or unsettling. Home is, after all, traditionally a place to leave, to set out from and begin again elsewhere. For home not to become stifling, it needs to be a place of encounter, so to feel at home is also to be free to explore new things, and to become.

The above conversation between Alexis, Melissa and Stephanie as they reflected on their first year at university offers a glimpse into their multiple transitions in crafting home. Alexis remembered the early chaotic and unsettled nature of navigating herself and her life in her new environment. Describing room 1 of the model, she had no sense of *place* but was rather in many places, feeling unhomed and 'all over the

CONCLUSION

place'. Melissa narrated how, in time, university became her new normal, the safe context for her life, releasing her to explore her faith and gender as it 'just becomes life'. Describing rooms 3 and 4, she became more inner-dependent and relaxed into 'just what you do'. Stephanie expanded upon Melissa's sense of normality by comparing it with the familiarity of her family home. Both places were home now, she no longer missed her family home and 'stop[ped] noticing' the dissonance of living at university. In this gradual move to room 5, Stephanie was learning to both separate and integrate her different selves, becoming at home.

This book has placed 26 women's processes of crafting home, including their faith, friendship and intersectional feminism, under the scrutiny of feminist practical theology, resulting in important conclusions and a sustained model of Homing. It has been a privilege and a joy to be entrusted with these inspirational women's stories and experiences. Heidi Safia Mirza claims that academic research often serves as therapy and a form of self-discovery for researchers whose studies relate to their personal experiences. Mirza claims, 'We all have stories to tell. We must tell them ... our voices must be heard.'[21] The experience of writing is inevitably a journey of exploring one's own story and seeking deeper meaning, and many times I have been taken back to my own university experiences or feminist conscientization in the process, uncovering further questions as well as some answers. Reflecting the 'circling, iterative nature of the research journey'[22] described by Bennett and her colleagues, I have been deeply engaged in this work for the best part of 15 years and have been profoundly changed by the experience. It is now time for these women's important, necessary, troubling and inspiring words to be shared with anyone who can learn from them. With all who are interested in this book, I hope to encourage and resource women's intersectional gendered and faith transitions into the future. May they feel at home.

Notes

1 Zoë Bennett et al., *Invitation to Research in Practical Theology* (London: Routledge, 2018), p. 13.

2 Bennett et al., *Invitation to Research*, pp. 8, 30.

3 Sonya Sharma and Mathew Guest, 'Navigating Religion Between University and Home: Christian Students' Experiences in English Universities', *Social and Cultural Geography* 14, no. 1 (2013), pp. 59–79.

4 Ruth H. Perrin, *Changing Shape: The Faith Lives of Millennials* (London: SCM Press, 2020), p. 238.

5 Perrin, *Changing Shape*, p. 235.

6 Lisa Bowleg, 'When Black + Lesbian + Woman ≠ Black Lesbian Woman: The Methodological Challenges of Qualitative and Quantitative Intersectionality Research', *Sex Roles* 59 (2008), p. 312.

7 Sarah-Jane Page and Heather Shipley, *Religion and Sexualities: Theories, Themes and Methodologies* (London, New York: Routledge/Taylor & Francis Group, 2020), pp. 15, 4.

8 Marcella Althaus-Reid, *From Feminist Theology to Indecent Theology: Readings on Poverty, Sexual Identity and God* (London: SCM Press, 2004), p. 100.

9 Sharon Parks, *The Critical Years: The Young Adult Search for a Faith to Live By* (New York: Harper & Row, 1986), pp. 50, 53.

10 Audre Lorde, *Sister Outsider: Essays and Speeches* (Freedom, CA: Crossing Press, 1984), p. 12.

11 Roberta Katz et al., *Gen Z, Explained: The Art of Living in a Digital Age* (Chicago, IL: University of Chicago Press, 2022), p. 122.

12 Katz et al., *Gen Z Explained*, pp. 3, 5.

13 Mathew Guest et al., *Christianity and the University Experience: Understanding Student Faith* (London: Bloomsbury, 2013), p. 207.

14 Guest et al., *Christianity and the University Experience*, p. 208.

15 bell hooks, *Talking Back: Thinking Feminist, Thinking Black* (Toronto: Between the Lines, 1989), p. 32.

16 See Dawn Llewellyn and Marta Trzebiatowska, 'Secular and Religious Feminisms: A Future of Disconnection?', *Feminist Theology* 21, no. 3 (2013), pp. 244–58; Kristin Aune, 'Much Less Religious, a Little More Spiritual: The Religious and Spiritual Views of Third-Wave Feminists in the UK', *Feminist Review* 97 (2011), pp. 32–55.

17 Mathew Guest, 'The "Hidden Christians" of the UK University Campus' in *Young People and the Diversity of (Non)Religious Identities in International Perspective*, ed. Elisabeth Arweck and Heather Shipley (Cham, Switzerland: Springer, 2019), pp. 51–67.

18 Such as, for example, in Nicola Slee, *Women's Faith Development: Patterns and Processes* (Aldershot: Ashgate, 2004); Perrin, *Changing Shape*.

19 Unite Students, 'An Asset Not a Problem: Meeting the Needs of Neurodivergent Students', 2023; Krysia Emily Waldock, 'The Impossible Subject: Belonging as a Neurodivergent in Congregations', *Journal of Disability & Religion* 27, no. 4 (2 October 2023), pp. 568–83.

20 Bowleg, 'When Black + Lesbian + Woman', pp. 322–3.

21 Emily Falconer and Yvette Taylor, 'Negotiating Queer and Religious Identities in Higher Education: Queering "Progression" in the "University Experience"', *British Journal of Sociology of Education* 38, no. 6 (2017), p. 792, quoting Heidi Safia Mirza.

22 Bennett et al., *Invitation to Research*, p. 5.

Bibliography

Abes, Elisa S., 'Constructivist and Intersectional Interpretations of a Lesbian College Student's Multiple Social Identities', *Journal of Higher Education* 83, no. 2 (2012), pp. 186–216.
Ahmed, Sara, 'A Phenomenology of Whiteness', *Feminist Theory* 8, no. 2 (August 2007), pp. 149–68.
———, *Complaint!* Durham, NC: Duke University Press, 2021.
Althaus-Reid, Marcella, *From Feminist Theology to Indecent Theology: Readings on Poverty, Sexual Identity and God*, London: SCM Press, 2004.
Althaus-Reid, Marcella, and Lisa Isherwood, 'Thinking Theology and Queer Theory', *Feminist Theology* 15, no. 3 (May 2007), pp. 302–14.
Andersson, Johan, Joanna Sadgrove and Gill Valentine, 'Consuming Campus: Geographies of Encounter at a British University', *Social and Cultural Geography* 13, no. 5 (2012), pp. 501–15.
Appleby, Jennifer A., Nathan King, Kate E. Saunders, Anne Bast, Daniel Rivera, Jin Byun, Simone Cunningham, Charandeep Khera and Anne C. Duffy, 'Impact of the COVID-19 Pandemic on the Experience and Mental Health of University Students Studying in Canada and the UK: A Cross-Sectional Study', *BMJ Open* (January 2022).
Aquinas, Thomas, *Commentary on the Gospel of John: Chapters 13–21*, translated by Fabian Larcher and James A. Weisheipl, Washington, DC: Catholic University of America Press, 2012.
Arnett, Jeffrey Jensen, *Emerging Adulthood: The Winding Road from the Late Teens Through the Twenties*, Oxford: Oxford University Press, 2004.
Astin, Alexander W., Helen S. Astin and Jennifer A. Lindholm, *Cultivating the Spirit: How College Can Enhance Students' Inner Lives*, San Francisco, CA: Jossey-Bass, 2011.
Aune, Kristin, 'Much Less Religious, A Little More Spiritual: The Religious and Spiritual Views of Third-Wave Feminists in the UK', *Feminist Review* 97 (2011), pp. 32–55.
Aune, Kristin, and Mathew Guest, 'Christian University Students' Attitudes to Gender: Constructing Everyday Theologies in a Post-Feminist Climate', *Religions* 10, no. 2 (23 February 2019), pp. 1–22.
Aune, Kristin, Mathew Guest, and Jeremy Law, 'Chaplains on Campus: Understanding Chaplaincy in UK Universities', Coventry University, Durham University, Canterbury Christ Church University, 2019.
Aune, Kristin, Simon Perfect and Ben Ryan, 'Building Bridges or Holy Huddles? Student Religious Organizations in British Universities', *Journal of Diversity in Higher Education* (27 June 2024).

Bacon, Hannah, 'Embodying a Different Word about Fat: The Need for Critical Feminist Theologies of Fat Liberation', *Religions* 14, no. 696 (25 May 2023), pp. 1–14.
Balk, David E., 'Grieving: 22 to 30 Percent of All College Students', *New Directions for Student Services* 121 (2008), pp. 5–14.
Ballard, Paul, 'Locating Chaplaincy: A Theological Note', *Crucible* (July–September 2009), pp. 18–24.
Bates, Laura, *Everyday Sexism*, London: Simon & Schuster, 2014.
Battle, Cynthia L., Joseph A. Greer, Samia Ortiz-Hernández and David M. Todd, 'Developing and Implementing a Bereavement Support Program for College Students', *Death Studies* 37, no. 4 (2013), pp. 362–82.
Bauman, Zygmunt, *The Individualized Society*, Cambridge: Polity Press, 2001.
Baumgardner, Jennifer, and Amy Richards, 'Feminism and Femininity: Or How We Learned to Stop Worrying and Love the Thong', in *All About the Girl: Culture, Power and Identity*, edited by Anita Harris, New York: Routledge, 2004.
Bebbington, David W., *Evangelicalism in Modern Britain: A History from the 1730s to the 1980s*, London: Unwin Hyman, 1989.
Beck, Ulrich, and Elisabeth Beck-Gernsheim, *Individualization: Institutionalized Individualism and Its Social and Political Consequences*, London: Sage, 2001.
Belenky, Mary F., Blythe M. Clinchy, Nancy R. Goldberger and Jill M. Tarule, *Women's Ways of Knowing: The Development of Self, Voice and Mind*, 10th Anniversary ed., New York: Basic Books, 1986.
Bennett Moore, Zoë, *Introducing Feminist Perspectives on Pastoral Theology*, London: Sheffield University Press, 2002.
Bennett, Zoë, Elaine Graham, Stephen Pattison and Heather Walton, *Invitation to Research in Practical Theology*, London: Routledge, 2018.
Berger, Teresa, *Women's Ways of Worship: Gender Analysis and Liturgical History*, Collegeville, MN: Liturgical Press, 1999.
Berzonsky, Michael D., and Linda S. Kuk, 'Identity Status, Identity Processing Style, and the Transition to University', *Journal of Adolescent Research* 15, no. 1 (2000), pp. 81–98.
Boellstorff, Tom, 'When Marriage Fails: Queer Coincidences in Straight Time', *A Journal of Lesbian and Gay Studies* 13, no. 2–3 (2007), pp. 227–48.
Bons-Storm, Riet, *The Incredible Woman: Listening to Women's Silences in Pastoral Care and Counselling*, Nashville, TN: Abingdon Press, 1996.
Booker, Mike, and Mark Ireland, *Evangelism: Which Way Now? An Evaluation of Alpha, Emmaus, Cell Church and Other Contemporary Strategies for Evangelism*, 2nd ed., London: Church House Publishing, 2005.
Bourdieu, Pierre, *Distinction: A Social Critique of the Judgement of Taste*, Cambridge, MA: Harvard University Press, 1984.
———, *The Logic of Practice*, London: Polity Press, 1992.
Bowleg, Lisa, 'When Black + Lesbian + Woman ≠ Black Lesbian Woman: The Methodological Challenges of Qualitative and Quantitative Intersectionality Research', *Sex Roles* 59 (2008), pp. 312–25.
Bridges, William, *Managing Transitions: Making the Most of Change*, 3rd ed., London: Nicholas Brealey Publishing, 2009.
———, *Transitions: Making Sense of Life's Changes*, Reading, MA: Perseus Books, 1980.
Brierley, Peter, *Pulling Out of the Nose Dive*, London: Christian Research, 2006.
Brock, Rita Nakashima, and Rebecca Ann Parker, *Proverbs of Ashes: Violence,*

Redemptive Suffering and the Search for What Saves Us, Boston, MA: Beacon Press, 2001.
Bröer, Christian, and Broos Besseling, 'Sadness or Depression: Making Sense of Low Mood and the Medicalization of Everyday Life', *Social Science and Medicine* 183 (2017), pp. 28–36.
Brookfield, Stephen, *The Skillful Teacher: On Technique, Trust, and Responsiveness in the Classroom*, 2nd ed., San Francisco, CA: Jossey-Bass, 2006.
Brown, Lyn Mikel, and Carol Gilligan, *Meeting at the Crossroads: Women's Psychology and Girls' Development*, Cambridge, MA: Harvard University Press, 1992.
Brueggemann, Walter, *The Practice of Homefulness*, Eugene, OR: Wipf and Stock, 2014.
Bryant, Alyssa N., 'Assessing the Gender Climate of an Evangelical Student Subculture in the United States', *Gender and Education* 18, no. 6 (2006), pp. 613–34.
———, 'Negotiating the Complementarian Gender Ideology of an Evangelical Student Subculture: Further Evidence from Women's Narratives', *Gender and Education* 21, no. 5 (September 2009), pp. 549–65.
Butler, Judith, 'Performative Acts and Gender Constitution: An Essay in Phenomenology and Feminist Theory', *Theatre Journal* 4, no. 40 (1988), pp. 519–31.
Calhoun, Lawrence G., and Richard G. Tedeschi, *Posttraumatic Growth in Clinical Practice*, New York: Routledge, 2013.
Campbell, Fiona, Lindsay Blank, Anna Cantrell, Susan Baxter, Christopher Blackmore, Jan Dixon and Elizabeth Goyder, 'Factors that Influence Mental Health of University and College Students in the UK: A Systematic Review', *BMC Public Health* 22, no. 1 (20 September 2022), art. 1778.
Campbell, Joseph, *The Hero With a Thousand Faces*, 1st ed., New York: Pantheon Books, 1949.
Caperon, John, Andrew Todd and James Walters, eds, *A Christian Theology of Chaplaincy*, London: Jessica Kingsley, 2018.
Carmichael, Liz, *Friendship: Interpreting Christian Love*, London: T. & T. Clark, 2007.
Cartledge, Mark J., 'God, Gender and Social Roles: A Study in Relation to Empirical-Theological Models of the Trinity', *Journal of Empirical Theology* 22 (2009), pp. 117–41.
Castillo-Montoya, Milagros, Joshua Abreu and Abdul Abad, 'Racially Liberatory Pedagogy: A Black Lives Matter Approach to Education', *International Journal of Qualitative Studies in Education* 32, no. 9 (21 October 2019), pp. 1125–45.
Claassens, Juliana, *Mourner, Mother, Midwife: Reimagining God's Delivering Presence in the Old Testament*, Louisville, KY: Westminster John Knox Press, 2012.
Clines, Jeremy M.S., 'Faiths in Higher Education Chaplaincy', Church of England Board of Education, 2008.
Clines, Jeremy M.S., and Sophie Gilliat-Ray, 'Religious Literacy and Chaplaincy' in *Religious Literacy in Policy and Practice*, edited by Adam Dinham and Matthew Francis, Bristol: Policy Press, 2015, pp. 235–54.
Clydesdale, Tim, *The First Year Out: Understanding American Teens after High School*, Chicago, IL: University of Chicago Press, 2007.
Colley, Helen, 'Understanding Time in Learning Transitions Through the Lifecourse', *International Studies in Sociology of Education* 17, no. 4 (2007), pp. 427–43.
Collins-Mayo, Sylvia, 'Choosing My Religion: Young People's Personal Christian

Knowledge' in *Religion and Knowledge: Sociological Perspectives*, edited by Mathew Guest and Elisabeth Arweck, Aldershot: Ashgate, 2012, pp. 149-63.

Cooke, Richard, Bridgette M. Bewick, Michael Barkham, Margaret Bradley and Kerry Audin, 'Measuring, Monitoring and Managing the Psychological Well-Being of First Year University Students', *British Journal of Guidance and Counselling* 34, no. 4 (2006), pp. 505-17.

Cornwall, Susannah, *Controversies in Queer Theology*, Controversies in Contextual Theology Series, London: SCM Press, 2011.

——, 'Home and Hiddenness: Queer Theology, Domestication and Institutions', *Theology & Sexuality* 23, no. 1-2 (4 May 2017), pp. 31-47.

Côté, James E., 'Emerging Adulthood as an Institutionalized Moratorium: Risks and Benefits to Identity Formation' in *Emerging Adults in America*, edited by Jeffrey Jensen Arnett and Jennifer L. Tanner, Washington, DC: American Psychological Association, 2006, pp. 85-116.

Craddock, Nadia, Aisha Phoenix, Paul White, Caterina Gentili, Phillippa C. Diedrichs and Fiona Barlow, 'Understanding Colourism in the UK: Development and Assessment of the Everyday Colourism Scale', *Ethnic and Racial Studies* 46, no. 10 (27 July 2023), pp. 2242-77.

Crenshaw, Kimberlé, 'Demarginalizing the Intersection of Race and Sex: A Black Feminist Critique of Antidiscrimination Doctrine, Feminist Theory, and Antiracist Politics', *University of Chicago Legal Forum* 139 (1989), pp. 139-67.

Crissman-Ishler, Jennifer L., and Staci Schreiber, 'First-Year Female Students: Perceptions of Friendship', *Journal of Higher Education* 63 (2002), pp. 441-62.

Daly, Mary, *Beyond God the Father: Toward a Philosophy of Women's Liberation*, Boston, MA: Beacon Press, 1985.

Dean, Jonathan, 'Feminism in the Papers: Contested Feminisms in the British Quality Press', *Feminist Media Studies* 10, no. 4 (2010), pp. 391-407.

Dutton, Edward Croft, *Meeting Jesus at University: Rites of Passage and Student Evangelicals*, Aldershot: Ashgate, 2008.

Edelman, Joshua, Alana Vincent, Paulina Kolata and Eleanor O'Keeffe, 'British Ritual Innovation under COVID-19', Manchester Metropolitan University; University of Chester; Arts and Humanities Research Council, 2021.

Elias, Norbert, *The Civilising Process*, edited by Edmund Jephcott, Oxford: Blackwell, 1994.

Erikson, Erik H., *Identity: Youth and Crisis*, London: Faber, 1968.

Escobar, Kathy, *Faith Shift: Finding Your Way Forward when Everything You Believe Is Coming Apart*, New York: Convergent Books, 2014.

Falconer, Emily, and Yvette Taylor, 'Negotiating Queer and Religious Identities in Higher Education: Queering "Progression" in the "University Experience"', *British Journal of Sociology of Education* 38, no. 6 (2017), pp. 782-97.

Ferguson, Michaele L., 'Choice Feminism and the Fear of Politics', *Perspectives on Politics* 8, no. 1 (2010), pp. 247-53.

Fletcher, Sheila, *Maude Royden: A Life*, Oxford: Blackwell, 1989.

Ford, David F., *Christian Wisdom: Desiring God and Learning in Love*, Cambridge: Cambridge University Press, 2007.

Ford, David G., Joshua L. Mann and Peter M. Phillips, *The Bible and Digital Millennials*, London: Routledge, 2019.

Fowler, James W., *Stages of Faith: The Psychology of Human Development and the Quest for Meaning*, New York: Harper Collins, 1981.

France-Williams, Azariah D.A., *Ghost Ship: Institutional Racism and the Church of England*, London: SCM Press, 2020.

Frankenberg, Ruth, *White Women, Race Matters: The Social Construction of Whiteness*, Minneapolis, MN: University of Minnesota Press, 2005.

Fredrickson, George M., *Racism: A Short History*, Princeton Classics, Princeton, NJ: Princeton University Press, 2015.

Freitas, Donna, *The End of Sex: How Hookup Culture Is Leaving a Generation Unhappy, Sexually Unfulfilled, and Confused about Intimacy*, Philadelphia, PA: Basic Books, 2013.

Froud, Helen, 'Returning from Exile? Reconciliation Within the Church after COVID-19', *Practical Theology* 14, no. 1–2 (4 March 2021), pp. 123–31.

Gale, Trevor, and Stephen Parker, 'Navigating Change: A Typology of Student Transition in Higher Education', *Studies in Higher Education* 39, no. 5 (2014), pp. 734–53.

Garcia, Claudia, Eddy Grant, Gareth J. Treharne, Hitaua Arahanga-Doyle, Mathijs F.G. Lucassen, Damian Scarf, Mele Taumoepeau, Jaimie Veale and Charlene Rapsey, '"We'll Be Okay Together": Navigating Challenges as Queer University Students in Aotearoa New Zealand', *KĐtuitui: New Zealand Journal of Social Sciences Online* 19, no. 2 (2 April 2024), pp. 190–206.

Genz, Stéphanie, 'Third Way/ve: The Politics of Postfeminism', *Feminist Theory* 7, no. 3 (2006), pp. 333–53.

Gill, Rosalind, 'Postfeminism Media Culture: Elements of a Sensibility', *European Journal of Cultural Studies* 10, no. 2 (2007), pp. 147–66.

———, 'Post-Postfeminism? New Feminist Visibilities in Postfeminist Times', *Feminist Media Studies* 16, no. 4 (2016), pp. 610–30.

Gilliat-Ray, Sophie, *Higher Education and Student Religious Identity*, Exeter: University of Exeter, 1999.

Gilliat-Ray, Sophie, Muhammad Mansur Ali and Stephen Pattison, *Understanding Muslim Chaplaincy*, Farnham: Ashgate, 2013.

Gilligan, Carol, *In a Different Voice: Psychological Theory and Women's Development*, Cambridge, MA: Harvard University Press, 1982.

———, 'Preface: Teaching Shakespeare's Sister' in *Making Connections: The Relational Worlds of Adolescent Girls at Emma Willard School*, edited by Carol Gilligan, Nona P. Lyons and Trudy J. Hanmer, Cambridge, MA: Harvard University Press, 1990, pp. 6–29.

Girlguiding, 'Girls' Attitudes Survey', 2015, https://www.girlguiding.org.uk/globalassets/docs-and-resources/research-and-campaigns/girls-attitudes-survey-2015.pdf, accessed 8.10.2019.

Giroux, Henry A., 'Neoliberalism, Corporate Culture, and the Promise of Higher Education: The University as a Democratic Public Sphere', *Harvard Educational Review* 72, no. 4 (2002), pp. 425–63.

Goto, Courtney T., *The Grace of Playing: Pedagogies for Leaning into God's New Creation*, Boston, MA: Wipf and Stock, 2016.

Graybill, Rhiannon, Meredith Minister and Beatrice Lawrence, 'Introduction: Engaging Rape Culture, Reimagining Religious Studies' in *Rape Culture and Religious Studies: Critical and Pedagogical Engagements*, edited by Rhiannon Graybill, Meredith Minister and Beatrice Lawrence, London: Lexington Books, 2019, pp. 1–20.

———, 'Sexual Violence in and around the Classroom', *Teaching Theology & Religion* 20, no. 1 (2017), pp. 70–88.

Greider, Kathleen J., *Much Madness Is Divinest Sense: Wisdom in Memoirs of Soul-Suffering*, Cleveland, OH: Pilgrim Press, 2007.

Guest, Mathew, *Evangelical Identity and Contemporary Culture: A Congregational Study in Innovation*, Milton Keynes: Paternoster, 2007.

———, 'The "Hidden Christians" of the UK University Campus' in *Young People and the Diversity of (Non)Religious Identities in International Perspective*, edited by Elisabeth Arweck and Heather Shipley, Cham, Switzerland: Springer, 2019, pp. 51–67.

Guest, Mathew, and Kristin Aune, 'Students' Constructions of a Christian Future: Faith, Class and Aspiration in University Contexts', *Sociological Research Online* 22, no. 1 (February 2017), pp. 200–12.

Guest, Mathew, Kristin Aune, Sonya Sharma and Rob Warner, *Christianity and the University Experience: Understanding Student Faith*, London: Bloomsbury, 2013.

Harris, Maria, *Dance of the Spirit: The Seven Steps of Women's Spirituality*, New York: Bantam, 1989.

———, *Women and Teaching: Themes for a Spirituality of Pedagogy*, Mahwah, NJ: Paulist Press, 1988.

Hays, Sharon, *The Cultural Contradictions of Motherhood*, New Haven, CT: Yale University Press, 1996.

Hegymegi, Eszter, Victoria Haines, Rebecca Cain and Antonia Liguori, 'Developing a Tool to Empower the Disempowered: The Components of the Feeling of Home', 2024.

Heilbrun, Carolyn, *Writing a Woman's Life*, New York: Ballantine Books, 1988.

Herbert, Clare, 'Who Is God for You?', *Feminist Theology* 23, no. 1 (2000), pp. 26–30.

Heyes, Cressida J., 'AntiÐEssentialism in Practice: Carol Gilligan and Feminist Philosophy', *Hypatia* 12, no. 3 (1997), pp. 142–63.

Hill, Jonathan P., 'Faith and Understanding: Specifying the Impact of Higher Education on Religious Belief', *Journal for the Scientific Study of Religion* 50, no. 3 (2011), pp. 533–51.

Hirshman, Linda R., *Get to Work: A Manifesto for Women of the World*, New York: Viking, 2006.

Holdsworth, Clare, 'Don't You Think You're Missing Out, Living at Home? Student Experiences and Residential Transitions', *Sociological Review* 54, no. 3 (2006), pp. 495–519.

Holloway, Richard, *Leaving Alexandria: A Memoir of Faith and Doubt*, Edinburgh: Canongate Books, 2012.

hooks, bell, *Ain't I a Woman: Black Women and Feminism*, London: Pluto, 1982.

———, 'Choosing the Margin as a Space of Radical Openness', *Framework: The Journal of Cinema and Media* 36 (1989), pp. 15–23.

———, *Talking Back: Thinking Feminist, Thinking Black*, Toronto: Between the Lines, 1989.

Hull, John, *What Prevents Christian Adults from Learning?* London: SCM Press, 1985.

Ibarra, Herminia, 'Provisional Selves: Experimenting with Image and Identity in Professional Adaptation', *Administrative Science Quarterly* 44, no. 4 (1999), pp. 764–91.

Idehen, Nosayaba, 'Racial Inclusion: Guidelines to Being a More Racially Inclusive Church' in *Young, Woke and Christian: Words from a Missing Generation*, edited by Victoria Turner, London: SCM Press, 2022, pp. 27–38.

Isasi-Díaz, Ada Maria, 'Solidarity: Love of Neighbour in the 1980s' in *Lift Every*

BIBLIOGRAPHY

Voice: Constructing Christian Theologies from the Underside, edited by Susan Brooks Thistlethwaite and Mary Potter Engel, San Francisco, CA: Harper, 1990, pp. 31–40.

Isherwood, Lisa, *The Fat Jesus: Feminist Explorations in Boundaries and Transgressions*, London: Darton, Longman and Todd, 2007.

Jackson, Carolyn, and Vanita Sundaram, *Lad Culture in Higher Education: Sexism, Sexual Harassment and Violence*, Abingdon: Routledge, 2020.

Jackson, Olivia, *(Un)Certain: A Collective Memoir of Deconstructing Faith*, London: SCM Press, 2023.

Jennings, Willie James, *After Whiteness: An Education in Belonging*, Theological Education between the Times, Grand Rapids, MI: W.B. Eerdmans, 2020.

Johnson, Richard, Deborah Chambers, Parvati Raghuram and Estella Tincknell, *The Practice of Cultural Studies*, London: Sage, 2004.

Jones, Deborah, 'Gossip: Notes on Women's Oral Culture' in *The Feminist Critique of Language: A Reader*, edited by Deborah Cameron, London: Routledge, 1990, pp. 242–50.

Julian of Norwich, *Revelations of Divine Love Recorded by Julian, Anchoress at Norwich*, translated by Grace Warrack, London: Methuen and Company, 1901.

Jung, Patricia Beattie, ed., *Good Sex: Feminist Perspectives from the World's Religions*, New Brunswick, NJ: Rutgers University Press, 2005.

Katz, Roberta, Sarah Ogilvie, Jane Shaw and Linda Woodhead, *Gen Z, Explained: The Art of Living in a Digital Age*, Chicago, IL: University of Chicago Press, 2022.

Kenyon, Liz, 'A Home from Home: Students' Transitional Experience of Home' in *Ideal Homes? Social Change and the Experience of Home*, edited by Tony Chapman and Jenny Hockey, London: Routledge, 1999, pp. 84–95.

Kershaw, Alison, 'More than Half of Young People Now Going to University, Figures Show', *Independent*, 27 September 2019. https://www.independent.co.uk/news/education/education-news/university-students-young-people-over-half-first-time-a9122321.html, accessed 18.10.2024.

Kolk, Bessel van der, *The Body Keeps the Score: Mind, Brain and Body in the Transformation of Trauma*, London: Penguin Books, 2014.

Kurland, Robert M., and Harold I. Siegel, 'Attachment and Student Success During the Transition to College', *NACADA Journal* 33, no. 2 (2013), pp. 16–28.

Lee, Dorothy, 'Abiding in the Fourth Gospel: A Case Study in Feminist Biblical Theology' in *Feminist Companion to John*, edited by Amy-Jill Levine, London: Bloomsbury Publishing/Sheffield Academic Press, 2003, vol. 2, pp. 64–78.

Legood, Giles, *Chaplaincy: The Church's Sector Ministries*, London: Cassell, 1999.

Lentin, Alana, *Racism: A Beginner's Guide*, New York: Oneworld Publications, 2012.

Lewis, Patricia, Yvonne Benschop and Ruth Simpson, 'Postfeminism, Gender and Organisation', *Gender, Work and Organisation* 24, no. 3 (2017), pp. 213–25.

Llewellyn, Dawn, 'Voluntary Childlessness and Christianity: Rejecting the Selfish Other', *Modern Believing* 6, no. 2 (2019), pp. 147–56.

Llewellyn, Dawn, and Marta Trzebiatowska, 'Secular and Religious Feminisms: A Future of Disconnection?', *Feminist Theology* 21, no. 3 (2013), pp. 244–58.

Lorde, Audre, *Sister Outsider: Essays and Speeches*, Freedom, CA: Crossing Press, 1984.

MacIntyre, Alasdair, 'The Very Idea of a University: Aristotle, Newman and Us', *British Journal of Educational Studies* 57, no. 4 (2009), pp. 347–62.

Maddox, Marion, '"Rise Up Warrior Princess Daughters": Is Evangelical Women's Submission a Mere Fairy Tale?', *Journal of Feminist Studies in Religion* 29, no. 1 (2013), pp. 9–26.

Madriaga, Manuel, and Colin McCaig, 'How International Students of Colour Become Black: A Story of Whiteness in English Higher Education', *Teaching in Higher Education* 27, no. 1 (2 January 2022), pp. 84–98.

Marler, Penny Long, 'Religious Change in the West: Watch the Women' in *Women and Religion in the West: Challenging Secularisation*, edited by Kristin Aune, Sonya Sharma and Giselle Vincett, Aldershot: Ashgate, 2008, pp. 23–56.

Massey, Kate, 'Listening for the "I": Adapting a Voice-Centred, Relational Method of Data Analysis in a Group Interview to Examine Women's Faith Lives' in *Researching Female Faith: Qualitative Research Methods*, edited by Nicola Slee, Fran Porter and Anne Phillips, Abingdon: Routledge, 2018, pp. 141–54.

Mayrl, Damon, and Jeremy E. Uecker, 'Higher Education and Religious Liberalisation Among Young Adults', *Social Forces* 90, no. 1 (2011), pp. 181–208.

McDermott, Elizabeth, '"I Wanted to Be Totally True to Myself": Class and the Making of the Sexual Self' in *Classed Intersections: Spaces, Selves, Knowledges*, edited by Yvette Taylor, Farnham: Ashgate, 2010, pp. 199–214.

McFague, Sallie, *Metaphorical Theology: Models of God in Religious Language*, London: SCM Press, 1983.

——, *Models of God: Theology for an Ecological, Nuclear Age*, Minneapolis, MN: Fortress Press, 1987.

McGrail, Peter, and John Sullivan, *Dancing on the Edge: Chaplaincy, Church and Higher Education*, Chelmsford: Matthew James Publishing, 2007.

McRobbie, Angela, *The Aftermath of Feminism: Gender, Culture and Social Change*, London: Sage, 2009.

Mead, George H., *Mind, Self and Society*, Chicago, IL: University of Chicago Press, 1934.

Miller, Philip H., and Ellin Kofsky Scholnick, eds, *Toward a Feminist Developmental Psychology*, London: Routledge, 2000.

Moody, Christopher, 'Spirituality and Sector Ministry' in *Chaplaincy: The Church's Sector Ministries*, edited by Giles Legood, London: Cassell, 1999, pp. 15–24.

——, 'Students, Chaplaincy and Pilgrimage', *Theology* 89, no. 732 (1986), pp. 440–7.

Morgans, Jenny, 'Emerging Christian Women at Uni: Intersection of Gender and Faith Identities on Campus', *Research in the Social Scientific Study of Religion* 32, Lesser Heard Voices in Studies of Religion (2022), pp. 147–63.

——, 'Faithing, Friendship and Feeling at Home: Three Women Encounter University Chaplaincy' in *From the Shores of Silence: Conversations in Feminist Practical Theology*, edited by Ashley Cocksworth, Rachel Starr and Stephen Burns, London: SCM Press, 2023, pp. 95–111.

——, 'Reflexivity, Identity, and the Role of the Researcher' in *Researching Female Faith: Qualitative Research Methods*, edited by Nicola Slee, Fran Porter and Anne Phillips, Abingdon: Routledge, 2018, pp. 189–202.

Morton, Nelle, *The Journey Is Home*, Boston, MA: Beacon Press, 1985.

National Union of Students, 'Hidden Marks: A Study of Women Students' Experiences of Harassment, Stalking, Violence and Sexual Assault', 2010. https://www.nus.org.uk/mental_health#2021, accessed 5.07.2024.

——, 'Mental Health Policy', 2021.

Newman, John Henry, *The Idea of a University*, London: Baronius Press, 2006.

BIBLIOGRAPHY

Nouwen, Henri, *Lifesigns: Intimacy, Fecundity, and Ecstasy in Christian Perspective*, Garden City, NY: Doubleday, 1986.

Nye, Caroline, and Matt Lobley, 'COVID-19, Christian Faith and Wellbeing', University of Exeter, 2020.

Oakley, Lisa, and Kathryn Kinmond, *Breaking the Silence of Spiritual Abuse*, Basingstoke: Palgrave Macmillan, 2013.

O'Donnell, Karen, *The Dark Womb: Re-Conceiving Theology Through Reproductive Loss*, London: SCM Press, 2022.

O'Donnell, Karen, and Katie Cross, eds, *Bearing Witness: Intersectional Approaches to Trauma Theology*, London: SCM Press, 2022.

O'Donohue, John, *Anam Cara*, London: Bantam Books, 1999.

Office for National Statistics, 'Coronavirus and the Impact on Students in Higher Education in England: September to December 2020: A Summary of Research into How the Coronavirus (COVID-19) Pandemic Has Affected Students in Higher Education in England During the Autumn Term of 2020', December 2020.

Page, Sarah-Jane, and Heather Shipley, *Religion and Sexualities: Theories, Themes and Methodologies*, London, New York: Routledge/Taylor & Francis Group, 2020.

Page, Sarah-Jane, Andrew Kam-Tuck Yip and Michael Keenan, 'Risk and the Imagined Future: Young Adults Negotiating Religious and Sexual Identities' in *The Ashgate Research Companion to Contemporary Religion and Sexuality*, edited by Stephen J. Hunt and Andrew Kam-Tuck Yip, Farnham: Ashgate, 2012, pp. 255–74.

Parks, Sharon, *Big Questions, Worthy Dreams: Mentoring Young Adults in Their Search for Meaning, Purpose, and Faith*, San Francisco, CA: Jossey-Bass, 2000.

———, *The Critical Years: The Young Adult Search for a Faith to Live By*, New York: Harper & Row, 1986.

Pearce, Sacha, and Jan Collis, *Creating Space: Story, Reflection and Practice in Healthcare Chaplaincy*, Durham: Sacristy Press, 2022.

Perfect, Simon, 'Relationships, Presence and Hope: University Chaplaincy during the COVID-19 Pandemic', Theos Think Tank, 2021.

Perrin, Ruth H., *Changing Shape: The Faith Lives of Millennials*, London: SCM Press, 2020.

———, 'Searching for Sisters: The Influence of Biblical Role Models on Young Women from Mainstream and Charismatic Evangelical Traditions' in *The Faith Lives of Women and Girls*, edited by Nicola Slee, Fran Porter and Anne Phillips, Farnham: Ashgate, 2013, pp. 111–19.

———, *The Bible Reading of Young Evangelicals: An Exploration of the Ordinary Hermeneutics and Faith of Generation Y*, Eugene, OR: Pickwick Publications, 2016.

Persha, Jerry, 'Toward Developing an Adequate and Comprehensive Understanding of Evangelization' in *The Study of Evangelism: Exploring a Missional Practice of the Church*, edited by Paul W. Chilcote and Laceye C. Warner, Cambridge: W.B. Eerdmans, 2008, pp. 313–28.

Phillips, Anne, *The Faith of Girls: Children's Spirituality and Transition to Adulthood*, Farnham: Ashgate, 2011.

Phillips, Debra, 'In God's House There Are Many Rooms (Jn 14.2–27)', *Feminist Theology* 25, no. 1 (September 2016), pp. 96–110.

Phipps, Alison, and Geraldine Smith, 'Violence Against Women Students in the UK: Time to Take Action', *Gender and Education* 24, no. 4 (2012), pp. 357–73.

Phipps, Alison, and Isabel Young, 'Neoliberalisation and "Lad Cultures" in Higher Education', *Sociology* 49, no. 2 (2015), pp. 305–22.
Plakhotnik, Maria S., Natalia V. Volkova, Cuiling Jiang, Dorra Yahiaoui, Gary Pheiffer, Kerry McKay, Sonja Newman and Solveig Reißig-Thust, 'The Perceived Impact of COVID-19 on Student Well-Being and the Mediating Role of the University Support: Evidence from France, Germany, Russia, and the UK', *Frontiers in Psychology* 12, no. 642689 (July 2021), pp. 1–13.
Pohl, Christine D., *Living into Community: Cultivating Practices that Sustain Us*, Grand Rapids, MI: W.B. Eerdmans, 2012.
Poots, Amy, and Tony Cassidy, 'Academic Expectation, Self-Compassion, Psychological Capital, Social Support and Student Wellbeing', *International Journal of Educational Research* 99, no. 101506 (2020), pp. 1–9.
Porter, Fran, *It Will Not Be Taken Away from Her: A Feminist Engagement with Women's Christian Experience*, London: Darton, Longman and Todd, 2004.
Puwar, Nirmal, *Space Invaders: Race, Gender and Bodies Out of Place*, Oxford, New York: Berg, 2004.
Rambo, Shelly, 'Making a Case for College and University Chaplaincy: Howard Thurman as Guide', *Journal of Pastoral Theology* 34, no. 1 (2 January 2024), pp. 35–52.
Ransford, H. Edward, 'The Prediction of Social Behavior and Attitudes' in *Social Stratification: A Multiple Hierarchy Approach*, edited by Vincent Jeffries and H. Edward Ransford, Boston, MA: Allyn & Bacon, 1980, pp. 265–95.
Raymond, Janice G., *A Passion for Friends: Toward a Philosophy of Female Affection*, London: The Women's Press, 1986.
Reddie, Anthony, *Is God Colour-Blind? Insights from Black Theology for Christian Faith and Ministry*, 2nd ed., London: SPCK, 2020.
——, 'Prologue' in *Young, Woke and Christian: Words from a Missing Generation*, edited by Victoria Turner, London: SCM Press, 2022, pp. ix–xii.
Redfern, Catherine, and Kristin Aune, *Reclaiming the F Word: Feminism Today*, London: Zed Books, 2013.
Rich, Adrienne, 'Claiming an Education: Speech Delivered at the Convocation of Douglass College', 1977.
——, 'Taking Women Students Seriously', *The Radical Teacher* 11 (1979), pp. 40–3.
Richter, Phillip, 'Denominational Cultures: The Cinderella of Congregational Studies?' in *Congregational Studies in the UK: Christianity in a Post-Christian Context*, edited by Mathew Guest, Karin Tusting and Linda Woodhead, Aldershot: Ashgate, 2004, pp. 169–84.
Ricoeur, Paul, *The Rule of Metaphor: The Creation of Meaning in Language*, Routledge Classics, London: Routledge, 2006.
Robinson, Marilynne, *Home*, London: Virago Press, 2009.
Robinson, Simon, and Mike Benwell, 'Christian Chaplaincy in the Post-Modern University', *Modern Believing* 41, no. 1 (1999), pp. 31–43.
Rohr, Richard, *Everything Belongs: The Gift of Contemplative Prayer*, New York: Crossroad Publishing Company, 2003.
Ryan, Ben, 'A Very Modern Ministry: Chaplaincy in the UK', Theos Think Tank, 2015.
——, 'Theology and Models of Chaplaincy' in *A Christian Theology of Chaplaincy*, edited by John Caperon, Andrew Todd and James Walters, London: Jessica Kingsley, 2018, pp. 79–99.

BIBLIOGRAPHY

Saiving, Valerie, 'The Human Situation: A Feminine View', *Journal of Religion* 40 (1960), pp. 100–12.
Savage, Sara, Sylvia Collins-Mayo, Bob Mayo and Graham Cray, *Making Sense of Generation Y: The Worldview of 15- to 25-Year-Olds*, London: Church House Publishing, 2006.
Scarbrough, Alexandrina, and Carolyn Hicks, 'Student Gender and the Probability of Referral for Counselling in a College of Further Education', *British Journal of Guidance and Counselling* 26, no. 2 (2007), pp. 275–36.
Scharff, Christina, *Repudiating Feminism*, Farnham: Ashgate, 2012.
Schlossberg, Nancy K., 'The Challenge of Change: The Transition Model and Its Implications', *Journal of Employment Counseling* 48 (2011), pp. 159–62.
Schlossberg, Nancy K., Elinor B. Waters and Jane Goodman, *Counselling Adults in Transition: Linking Practice with Theory*, 2nd ed., New York: Springer, 1995.
Schneider, Floyd, *Friendship Evangelism*, Eastbourne: Monarch, 1989.
Schüssler Fiorenza, Elisabeth, *But She Said: Feminist Practices of Biblical Interpretation*, Boston, MA: Beacon Press, 1992.
Schweisfurth, Michele, and Qing Gu, 'Exploring the Experiences of International Students in UK Higher Education: Possibilities and Limits of Interculturality in University Life', *Intercultural Education* 20, no. 5 (October 2009), pp. 463–73.
Sharma, Sonya, 'When Young Women Say "Yes": Exploring the Sexual Selves of Young Canadian Women in Protestant Churches' in *Women and Religion in the West: Challenging Secularisation*, edited by Kristin Aune, Sonya Sharma and Giselle Vincett, Aldershot: Ashgate, 2008, pp. 71–82.
Sharma, Sonya, and Mathew Guest, 'Navigating Religion Between University and Home: Christian Students' Experiences in English Universities', *Social and Cultural Geography* 14, no. 1 (2013), pp. 59–79.
Sharma, Sonya, and Sheryl Reimer-Kirkham, 'In Plain View: Gender in the Work of Women Healthcare Chaplains', *Social Compass* (2022), pp. 1–17.
Shepherd, Nick M., *Faith Generation: Retaining Young People and Growing the Church*, London: SPCK, 2016.
———, 'Religious Socialisation and a Reflexive Habitus: Christian Youth Groups as Sites for Identity Work' in *Religion and Youth*, edited by Sylvia Collins-Mayo and Pink Dandelion, Farnham: Ashgate, 2010, pp. 149–55.
Slater, Victoria, *Chaplaincy Ministry and the Mission of the Church*, London: SCM Press, 2015.
Slee, Nicola, *Seeking the Risen Christa*, London: SPCK, 2011.
———, *Women's Faith Development: Patterns and Processes*, Aldershot: Ashgate, 2004.
Slee, Nicola, and Helen D. Cameron, 'Peering into the Shadows or Foregrounding the Feminine? Feminist Rewritings of the Parable of the Prodigal', *Practical Theology* 7, no. 1 (2014), pp. 50–62.
Smit, Laura, 'The Image of Home', *Theology Today* 45, no. 3 (1988), pp. 305–14.
Smith, Christian, 'On "Moralistic Therapeutic Deism" as US Teenagers' Actual, Tacit, De Facto Religious Faith' in *Religion and Youth*, edited by Sylvia Collins-Mayo and Pink Dandelion, Farnham: Ashgate, 2010, pp. 41–6.
Smith, Christian, and Patricia Snell, *Souls in Transition: The Religious and Spiritual Lives of Emerging Adults*, Oxford: Oxford University Press, 2009.
Speck, Jane, 'King's College London' in *Being a Chaplain*, edited by Miranda Threlfall-Holmes and Mark Newitt, London: SPCK, 2011, pp. 34–6.
Stanton, Elizabeth Cady, *The Woman's Bible*, Boston, MA: Northeastern University Press, 1993.

Tasker, Yvonne, and Diane Negra, 'Introduction' in *Interrogating Postfeminism: Gender and the Politics of Popular Culture*, edited by Yvonne Tasker and Diane Negra, Durham, NC: Duke University Press, 2007, pp. 1-26.

Taylor, Carol A., and Jean Harris-Evans, 'Reconceptualising Transition to Higher Education with Deleuze and Guattari', *Studies in Higher Education* 43, no. 7 (2018), pp. 1254-67.

Tedeschi, Richard G., and Lawrence G. Calhoun, *Trauma and Transformation: Growing in the Aftermath of Suffering*, London: Sage, 1995.

Teresa of Ávila, *Interior Castle: The Mansions*, London: Sheed and Ward, 1944.

The Archbishops' Council, *Common Worship: Ordination Services*, London: Church House Publishing, 2007.

The Methodist Church, 'Chaplaincy Essentials: A Resource for Nurturing Chaplains in the Essential Skills for Their Work', Trustees for Methodist Church Purposes, 2015.

Thomas, Dave S.P., and Kathleen M. Quinlan, 'Why We Need to Reimagine the Curricula in Higher Education to Make It More Culturally Sensitive', *Widening Participation and Lifelong Learning* 23, no. 3 (9 December 2021), pp. 37-47.

Threlfall-Holmes, Miranda, and Mark Newitt, eds, *Being a Chaplain*, London: SPCK, 2011.

Todd, Andrew, 'Responding to Diversity: Chaplaincy in a Multi-Faith Context' in *Being a Chaplain*, edited by Miranda Threlfall-Holmes and Mark Newitt, London: SPCK, 2011, pp. 89-102.

Todd, Nathan R., Elizabeth A. McConnell, Charlynn A. Odahl-Ruan and Jaclyn D. Houston-Kolnik, 'Christian Campus-Ministry Groups at Public Universities and Opposition to Same-Sex Marriage', *Psychology of Religion and Spirituality* 9, no. 4 (November 2017), pp. 412-22.

Turner, Victor, *The Ritual Process*, New York: Aldine Publishers, 1969.

Turner, Victoria, 'Introduction' in *Young, Woke and Christian: Words from a Missing Generation*, edited by Victoria Turner, London: SCM Press, 2022, pp. 1-16.

Unite Students, 'An Asset Not a Problem: Meeting the Needs of Neurodivergent Students', 2023.

Vaccaro, Annemarie, 'Third Wave Feminist Undergraduates: Transforming Identities and Redirecting Activism in Response to Institutional Sexism', *NASPA Journal About Women in Higher Education* 2, no. 1 (30 January 2009), pp. 1-25.

Valentine, Gill, 'Negotiating and Managing Multiple Sexual Identities: Lesbian Time-Space Strategies', *Institute of British Geographers* 18 (1993), pp. 237-48.

———, 'The Ties that Bind: Towards Geographies of Intimacy', *Geography Compass* 26 (2008), pp. 2097-110.

Valentine, Gill, Sarah L. Holloway and Mark Jayne, 'Contemporary Cultures of Abstinence and the Night-Time Economy: Muslim Attitudes Towards Alcohol and the Implications for Social Cohesion', *Environment and Planning A* 42, no. 1 (2010), pp. 8-22.

Village, Andrew, and Leslie J. Francis, 'Lockdown Worship in the Church of England: Predicting Affect Responses to Leading or Accessing Online and In-Church Services', *Journal of Beliefs & Values* 44, no. 2 (3 April 2023), pp. 280-96.

Vincent, Ben, Sonja Erikainen and Ruth Pearce, eds, 'TERF Wars: Feminism and the Fight for Transgender Futures', *Sociological Review* 68, no. 4 (2020).

Waldock, Krysia Emily, 'The Impossible Subject: Belonging as a Neurodivergent in Congregations', *Journal of Disability & Religion* 27, no. 4 (2 October 2023), pp. 568-83.

Walters, James, and Margaret Bradley, 'Chaplaincy and Evangelism' in *A Christian Theology of Chaplaincy*, edited by John Caperon, Andrew Todd and James Walters, London: Jessica Kingsley, 2018, pp. 143–58.

Ward, Frances, *Lifelong Learning: Theological Education and Supervision*, London: SCM Press, 2009.

Webber, Michelle, 'Transgressive Pedagogies? Exploring the Difficult Realities of Enacting Feminist Pedagogies in Undergraduate Classrooms in a Canadian University', *Studies in Higher Education* 31, no. 4 (August 2006), pp. 453–67.

Webster, Alison, *You Are Mine: Reflections on Who We Are*, London: SPCK, 2009.

Welcher, Rachel Joy, *Talking Back to Purity Culture: Rediscovering Faithful Christian Sexuality*, Westmont, IL: InterVarsity Press, 2020.

Wilcox, Paula, Sandra Winn and Marylynn Fyvie-Gauld, 'It Was Nothing to Do with the University, It Was Just the People: The Role of Social Support in the First-Year Experience of Higher Education', *Studies in Higher Education* 30, no. 6 (2005), pp. 707–22.

Williams, Rowan Clare, *A Theology for Chaplaincy: Singing Songs in a Strange Land*, Cambridge: Grove Books, 2018.

Willoughby, Brian, and James L. Spencer, *The Marriage Paradox: Why Emerging Adults Love Marriage yet Push It Aside*, Oxford: Oxford University Press, 2017.

Wintre, Maxine Gallander, and Mordechai Yaffe, 'First Year Students' Adjustment to University Life as a Function of Relationships with Parents', *Journal of Adolescent Research* 15, no. 1 (2000), pp. 9–37.

Woodhead, Linda, 'Foreword: Chaplaincy and the Future of Religion' in *A Handbook of Chaplaincy Studies: Understanding Spiritual Care in Public Places*, edited by Christopher Swift, Mark Cobb and Andrew Todd, Farnham: Ashgate, 2015, pp. xvii–xxii.

———, 'Gendering Secularisation Theory', *Women, Gender and Research (Kvinder, Køn Og Forskning)* 1–2 (2005), pp. 24–35.

Woolf, Virginia, *A Room of One's Own*, London: Hogarth Press, 1935.

World Health Organization, *Growing Up Unequal: Gender and Socioeconomic Differences in Young People's Health and Well-Being*, Copenhagen: World Health Organization, 2016.

Worth, Nancy, 'Understanding Youth Transition as "Becoming:" Identity, Time and Futurity', *Geoform* 40 (2009), pp. 1050–60.

Wright, Wendy M., *Sacred Dwelling: A Spirituality of Family Life*, London: Darton, Longman and Todd, 2007.

Yip, Andrew Kam-Tuck, and Sarah-Jane Page, *Religious and Sexual Identities: A Multi-Faith Exploration of Young Adults*, Farnham: Ashgate, 2013.

Zewolde, Solomon, '"Race" and Academic Performance in International Higher Education: Black Africans in the UK', *Journal of Comparative & International Higher Education* 14, no. 3a (11 July 2022).

Index of Names and Subjects

Abes, Elisa S. 138, 181, 198
academic study 26, 28–30, 39–43, 57, 60, 75, 79–80, 83, 137, 140, 194–201, 214, 220, 221, 222, 237
  exams, essays 26, 29, 57, 60, 79
  lectures, seminars 32–3, 40–1, 60, 198–9, 221
  study of STEM subjects 30, 80, 83, 137, 140, 157, 199–200
  study of theology *see* theology
Ahmed, Sara 167, 188, 196, 202
alcohol 17, 23, 31–4, 49, 91, 118, 142, 156, 214–15, 238
Althaus-Reid, Marcella 86, 96, 133, 157, 174, 181
Anglicanism 72, 90–1, 92, 98, 102, 103, 105, 106, 108, 109, 110, 112, 119, 121, 159, 163, 164, 218–19, 233 *see also* student societies
Anglican Society *see* student societies
appearance 7, 133–4, 137–8, 151, 162, 173, 175, 176
  and sexuality 138, 175, 176
  clothing 20, 137–8, 139, 149, 171, 172, 173, 175
Arnett, Jeffrey Jensen 2, 3, 53, 199, 200
Astin, Alexander and Helen Astin 74–5, 83, 88, 122, 220, 222
Aune, Kristin 7, 13n31, 105, 109, 119, 132, 138, 167, 171, 175, 183

bereavement 18, 26–7, 28, 40, 82, 116, 214

Bible/Scripture 8, 77, 81–3, 84, 90, 99, 102, 104, 115, 120, 121, 122, 123, 124, 131, 152n1, 156, 162, 164, 166, 171, 172, 173, 174, 178, 193, 218, 226, 230n40
Black Lives Matter *see* race
Bourdieu, Pierre 18, 183, 227
Bowleg, Lisa 155, 170, 203n3, 234, 240
boyfriends *see* romantic partners
Bridges, William 47, 215
Bryant, Alyssa N. 105, 144, 165

Catholicism 92, 98, 103, 163, 171, 106, 110 *see also* student societies
Catholic Society *see* student societies
celibacy *see* sexuality
chaplaincy/chaplains 1, 4, 10, 72, 76, 78, 83, 89, 92, 98, 105, 107, 108–13, 116, 126n31, 163, 183, 192, 218, 236–7
Christian Union *see* student societies
churches 1, 5, 8, 10, 35, 50, 55, 71, 87, 88, 89, 90, 98–103, 105, 109, 112, 113–17, 120–1, 122, 123, 124, 157–61, 163, 167, 168, 169, 170–2, 173, 174, 175, 177–9, 181–2, 183, 191–2, 212, 215, 216, 218, 222, 231, 232, 233, 234, 236, 237
  and Covid-19 41, 113–17
  and gender 157–75
  attendance 4–5, 24, 31, 41, 78, 82, 83, 91, 93–4, 98–103, 104, 107, 110, 118, 158, 160, 163, 164, 165, 166, 167, 180, 219

257

finding a church 74, 100–103, 120, 149, 166, 180, 217
class 1, 2, 3, 4, 10, 11, 18, 19, 29, 57, 152, 155, 156, 157, 178, 181, 183–7, 189, 190, 197, 201, 202, 223, 231, 234, 239
clothing *see* appearance
Clydesdale, Tim 25, 52, 54, 72, 155, 169, 200, 215
cognitive dissonance 35, 52, 55, 91, 134, 135
Colley, Helen 6, 61, 225
communion/Eucharist 114, 124, 233
confidence 9, 10, 28, 36, 38, 41, 42, 47, 49–52, 56–9, 60, 62–4, 65–6, 74, 76, 87, 88, 94, 102, 107, 118, 124, 134, 138, 148, 151, 168, 171, 174, 199, 201, 202, 217, 218, 219, 220, 221, 232, 235, 237
Cornwall, Susannah 3, 182
Covid-19 1, 3, 10, 17, 27, 39–42, 46, 64, 81, 98, 110, 113–17, 120, 124, 160, 189, 214, 239, *see also* churches

daily life management 25, 56, 73, 215, 221
deconstruction *see* evangelicalism
Dutton, Edward Croft 88, 96n33, 104, 112, 117

employment/career 2, 57, 134, 135, 161–2, 167, 185
Eucharist *see* communion
evangelicalism 4, 38, 71, 78, 82, 89–94, 98, 102–3, 104, 105, 106, 111, 118–19, 121, 158, 159, 161, 164, 165, 166, 167, 173, 178, 179, 191 *see also* theology
  deconstruction 82, 89–94, 159
evangelism/conversionism 4, 10, 33, 78, 90, 91, 92, 98, 102, 104, 107, 109, 112, 117–20, 121, 122, 123, 124, 216, 220, 236

families 20, 22, 23, 26, 27, 32, 35–6, 37, 40, 42, 47, 56, 61–4, 65, 73, 74, 82, 98, 99, 102, 115, 150, 151, 163, 165, 166, 169, 176, 177, 178, 179, 180, 185, 189, 190, 192, 213, 214, 217, 227, 233
family home 2, 10, 19, 20, 26, 39–40, 54, 57, 61, 74, 177, 227, 241
family support 5, 18, 20–2, 25
  mothers 20, 21, 64, 98, 150–1, 163, 165–6, 180
  parents 20–2, 30, 40, 56, 61–3, 65, 74, 165, 177, 185, 190, 192, 214
  siblings/only children 19, 40, 151, 177
femininity *see* gender
feminism 6–7, 9, 11, 50, 53, 84, 122, 131–2, 135, 136, 139, 140, 141, 145–8, 152, 155–6, 157, 167, 170–5, 178, 182, 198, 199, 212, 219, 222, 225, 231, 232, 234, 238–9, 241, *see also* post-feminism
  and faith 155, 167, 170–5, 178, 182, 219, 222, 226, 234, 236, 238, 241
  intersectional feminism 155–6, 178, 222, 234, 241
Freshers' Week 17, 23, 31–2
friends 1, 9, 10, 18, 19, 23–6, 29, 32, 33, 37, 40, 41, 43, 48–52, 55, 57, 59, 60, 61–5, 73, 76, 79, 82, 87–9, 90, 91, 92, 93, 99, 100, 101, 102, 104, 105, 106, 107, 110, 114, 115, 117, 118, 119, 133, 134, 138, 140, 142, 143, 144, 148–51, 152, 156, 158, 159, 162, 167–70, 176, 177, 178, 180, 181, 185, 186, 187, 189, 190, 196, 199, 201, 212, 214, 216, 217, 218, 219, 220, 227, 228, 232, 233, 236, 237, 241
  chosen families 49–52, 62, 64–5, 101, 106, 107, 124, 149, 152, 168, 170, 190, 217, 218, 219, 228, 234–5

INDEX OF NAMES AND SUBJECTS

Christian friends 40, 64, 76, 87–9, 90, 91, 92, 93, 99, 100, 101, 102, 104, 105–7, 115, 159, 167–70, 178, 180, 219, 232, 237
female friends 29, 64, 133, 138, 140, 142, 148–51, 152, 167–70, 190, 218, 227, 232
new friends 10, 19, 24–5, 37, 40, 41, 48–52, 57, 60, 61–5, 88, 90, 91, 100, 102, 107, 148–51, 152, 187, 190, 214, 216, 217, 218, 219, 228
old friends 23–4, 26, 37, 43, 61–5, 100, 214
see also housemates
Fowler, James W. 49, 51, 56, 62, 76, 78, 101, 102, 167, 217

Gale, Trevor and Stephen Parker 6, 26, 225
gap year/gap experience 25, 48, 57, 122, 147
gender
  and faith 9, 52, 55, 83–7, 103, 105, 107, 142–5, 155–75, 178, 182, 194–201, 220, 224, 227, 233–4, 241
  and studying 29–30, 137, 194–201
  essentialism 9, 104–5, 131, 132–4, 148, 157, 158, 163, 171, 198, 215, 216, 238
  femininity/masculinity 6–7, 84, 85, 105, 131, 136–8, 139, 140, 146, 147, 155, 156–7, 158, 161, 162, 171, 173, 174, 177, 215, 233–4, 238
  women's Christian leadership 55, 84, 90, 102–4, 107, 121
  see also feminism, lad culture
Generation Alpha 1, 2, 236, 240
Generation Y/Millennials 1, 2, 3, 10, 35, 73, 84, 94, 98
Generation Z 1, 2, 3, 4, 10, 31, 35, 50, 84, 98, 124, 166, 235, 236, 240
Gill, Rosalind 7, 136, 138, 139, 146

Gilliat-Ray, Sophie 107, 126n36
Gilligan, Carol 133, 148, 150, 169, 197
girlfriends *see* romantic partners
Girlguiding 35, 137, 153n14, 175
girls, girling, girly 51, 53–4, 84, 88, 133, 136, 137, 139–41, 147, 148, 150, 156, 169, 186, 216, 222, 238
God 1, 7–9, 10, 13n37, 35, 53, 63, 64, 71, 72, 73, 74, 75, 76, 79, 80–7, 91, 92, 93, 105, 106, 107, 109, 113, 115, 116, 120, 121, 122, 123, 124, 158, 159, 161, 164, 165, 168, 169, 170, 171, 174, 177, 178, 179, 180, 181, 182, 188, 191, 192, 193, 199, 200, 202, 211, 212, 214, 216, 218, 220, 221, 222, 223, 224, 226, 227, 228, 232, 234, 235, 237
  gender of God 83–7
Holy Spirit 73, 85, 171, 218
Jesus Christ 8, 80, 85, 88, 90, 91, 104, 109, 119, 123, 170, 171, 174, 175, 192, 193, 222, 226, 233
Guest, Mathew 4, 10, 21, 31, 34, 37, 39, 42, 74, 98, 99, 103, 104, 105, 106, 107–8, 109, 110, 119, 156, 179, 183, 186, 187, 192, 202, 218, 237

Harris, Maria 77, 147, 220
Holdsworth, Clare 19, 20, 33, 49, 111, 184, 214, 215
home
  homesickness 19, 30, 100, 212, 214
  leaving home 19–23
  unhome 9, 19, 30, 157, 201, 211, 212–15, 217, 224, 226, 234, 238, 240
  see also family home
housemates/flatmates 18, 23, 24, 40, 41, 51, 57, 61, 64, 65, 92, 118, 164, 184, 186, 214, 217, 218, 220

259

Hull, John 53, 55, 61, 73, 121, 135, 147

identity 4, 5, 18, 19, 20, 25, 32, 33–4, 34–8, 42, 47, 49, 51, 52, 55, 62, 65, 71–3, 77, 78, 79, 87–8, 89, 90, 94, 98, 99, 101, 102, 104, 105–6, 124, 131, 136–7, 138, 139, 148, 155–6, 157, 160, 169, 170, 174, 176, 177, 178, 179, 180, 181, 183, 184, 189, 190, 191–2, 201, 202, 215, 216–17, 219, 227, 231, 232, 233, 234, 235, 238, 240

independence, freedom 21, 25, 53, 56–8, 61, 62, 63–4, 74, 77, 87, 93–4, 102, 115, 139, 181, 219, 220, 221, 238

inner-dependence 55–7, 61, 63, 65, 74–7, 101, 148, 199, 202, 218, 228, 232, 237, 241

interdependence 10, 61–5, 123, 168, 221, 234, 235

interfaith *see* multifaith

international students 10, 40, 64, 111, 185, 188, 192, 194–6, 239

Internet 50, 131, 170, 233, 237
and Covid-19 39–42, 113–17, 165–6
social media 3, 50, 137 *see also* media

Jesus Christ *see* God

journey, spiritual 7–9, 71, 74–6, 82, 109, 124, 147, 159, 166, 167, 169, 177, 220, 233

Katz, Roberta 4, 50, 124, 202, 235, 236

lad culture 131, 141–5, 151, 215, 232, 237, 238 *see also* sexual harassment

Lewis, Patricia 6, 132, 135, 145

loneliness 1, 9, 10, 17, 19, 22–7, 32, 40, 42, 49, 52, 62, 81, 117, 213–15

marriage 2, 92, 123, 139, 158–62, 166–7, 171, 179, 181, 182

masculinity *see* gender

McFague, Sallie 85, 96n27, 211, 212

media 7, 131, 132, 136–9, 145, 146, 171, 175, 185

mental health 1, 10, 17, 24, 27–30, 39–41, 42, 175, 179, 215, 224, 233, 236, 239–40
anxiety 17, 26, 27–30, 40, 51, 60, 136, 196
therapy/counselling 27, 29, 151, 178, 220, 241

mentors 18, 87, 88, 89, 151, 165, 167–70, 217, 227, 231, 233, 237

Methodism 98–9, 103, 106, 108, 110, 173, 182 *see also* student societies

Methodist Society *see* student societies

methodology 9–10, 149, 170, 211, 212

middle class *see* class

Millennials *see* Generation Y

modesty 137–8, 158, 171–4, 220

motherhood 2, 54, 134, 136, 158, 159, 161–2, 167

multifaith, interfaith, other faiths 50, 75, 78, 91, 105, 108, 109, 112, 116, 119, 120, 124, 200, 222, 239

music, choirs 8, 32, 77, 90, 113, 115, 124, 139, 169, 199, 233 *see also* worship

neoliberalism 1, 5, 6, 145, 173, 235, 237, 238

neurodivergence 10, 239–40

Page, Sarah-Jane 156, 158, 159, 160, 161, 176, 177, 179, 180

parents *see* families

Parks, Sharon 8, 21, 25, 48, 52, 56, 58, 60, 62, 63, 72, 74, 88, 150, 154, 169, 199, 215, 217, 218, 235

patriarchy 7, 84, 86, 132, 133, 135, 143, 157, 159, 170, 173, 175, 178, 191, 197, 198, 222, 238
Perrin, Ruth H. 1, 3, 6, 78, 81, 90, 94, 103, 124, 158, 161, 163, 169, 233
Phillips, Anne 51, 89, 140, 169, 204, 250
Phillips, Debra 215, 224, 226
Phipps, Alison 7, 141
post-1992 universities 10, 13n46, 29, 112
post-feminism 2, 6–7, 11, 131, 132–41, 143, 144, 145, 146, 148, 152, 155, 163, 167, 171, 174, 215, 228, 232, 233, 235, 236, 237
postgraduate/doctoral students 39, 40, 51, 239
prayer 77, 79, 81, 82, 83, 84, 87, 88, 89, 91, 99, 104, 113, 115, 124, 164, 168, 233, 237

queer *see* sexuality

race 1, 10, 11, 22, 152, 155, 156, 157, 165–6, 170, 172, 176–7, 178, 184–6, 187–201, 202, 215, 219, 220, 223, 224, 225, 236
  Black Lives Matter 3, 189, 193, 197
  see also theology, Black
redbrick universities 10, 13n46, 112, 185, 186, 194, 239
Reddie, Anthony 1, 187, 188, 192, 193
romantic relationships 2, 40, 41, 61, 63, 65, 91, 144, 158–62, 173, 177, 180, 182, 221
Russell Group 10, 13n46, 29

Scharff, Christina 135, 145
Schlossberg, Nancy K. 5, 17, 18
school 22, 24, 27, 29, 58, 185, 186, 190, 199, 216, 223
science *see* academic study
Scripture *see* Bible

sermons 10, 55, 98, 102, 114, 120–2, 124, 165–6, 233, 236
sexuality 1, 2, 10, 11, 38, 64, 87, 91, 103, 105, 123, 137, 138, 152, 155, 158, 159, 175–83, 202, 222, 224, 225, 231, 234
  celibacy 17, 132, 136, 138, 139, 141–5, 157, 158–62, 171, 172, 174, 179, 236
  homosexuality, queer 3, 10, 32, 38, 50, 83, 84, 86, 87, 88, 90, 91, 92, 102, 111, 116, 121, 123, 125, 156, 158, 159, 160, 161, 175–83, 202, 215, 222, 223, 234, 236, 239
  transgender 3, 84, 131, 171, 239
sexual harassment 138, 142, 189, 198, 238 *see also* lad culture
Sharma, Sonya 49, 106, 111, 156, 161, 202, 218
singing *see* music
Slee, Nicola ii, 51, 74, 77, 79, 80, 87, 131, 147, 167, 168, 169, 206n73, 221
Smith, Christian 21, 34, 73, 77, 216, 218
social justice 63, 122–4, 222, 223
  see also volunteering
Student Christian Movement *see* student societies
student societies 103–8
  Anglican Society (AngSoc) 92, 103, 105, 106, 108, 110, 119, 121, 218–19 *see also* Anglicanism
  Catholic Society (CathSoc) 103, 106, 110 *see also* Catholicism
  Christian Union, UCCF 32, 75, 78, 90, 91, 92, 103–8, 110, 111, 112, 116, 117–19, 164, 165, 168, 180, 220
  Methodist Society (MethSoc) 103, 106, 108, 110 *see also* Methodism
  Navigators 103, 106, 118
  Student Christian Movement 103, 105, 108
study *see* academic study

Taylor, Carol A. and Jean Harris-Evans 6, 36, 212, 221, 225
theology 1, 4, 9, 75, 78, 83–7, 89, 90–2, 102, 121, 155, 159, 160, 163, 164, 170, 174, 177, 178, 179, 181, 182, 193, 212, 219, 225, 226, 231–2, 236, 241
  Black theology 155, 193, 219
  conservative evangelical theology 90–2, 121, 159, 160, 163, 164, 177
  feminist theology 9, 84–5, 170, 174, 178, 212, 225, 226, 231–2, 241
  liberation theology 1, 83, 87
  queer theology 86, 87, 182
  study of theology 75, 83
transgender *see* sexuality

Valentine, Gill 49
van der Kolk, Bessel 18, 43n4, 62, 65
vocation, calling 83, 113, 161, 163, 164, 165, 166, 180, 182, 199–200
  to ordained ministry 113, 163, 164, 165, 166, 180, 182
volunteering 10, 33, 41, 57, 58, 98, 104, 105, 117, 122, 123, 137, 157, 216, 221, 222, 232 *see also* social justice

Webster, Alison 35, 37, 217
women's leadership *see* gender
Woodhead, Linda 108
working class *see* class
worship 5, 74, 84, 91, 100, 102, 109, 110, 113, 114, 116, 120, 163, 220, 233, 237
Wright, Wendy M. 87, 217, 225

www.ingramcontent.com/pod-product-compliance
Lightning Source LLC
Chambersburg PA
CBHW022044290426
44109CB00014B/971